The Language of Dissent

The
LANGUAGE
of
DISSENT

Edward Schillebeeckx on the Crisis of Authority in the Catholic Church

DANIEL SPEED THOMPSON

UNIVERSITY OF NOTRE DAME PRESS

Notre Dame, Indiana

Manufactured in the United States of America

Material in this book has appeared previously under the following titles:
"Epistemological Frameworks in Schillebeeckx's Fundamental Theology,"
Philosophy and Theology 15, 1 (2003); "Schillebeeckx on the Development of
Doctrine," *Theological Studies* 62 (June 2001); and "The Church as Sacrament:
Schillebeeckx's Contribution to the Construction of a Critical Ecclesiology,"
Religious Studies and Theology 17, 1 (June 1998).

Library of Congress Cataloging-in-Publication Data
Thompson, Daniel Speed, 1964–
The language of dissent : Edward Schillebeeckx on the crisis of
authority in the Catholic Church / Daniel Speed Thompson.
p.   cm.
Includes bibliographical references (p.   ) and index.
ISBN 0-268-03358-7 (cloth)—ISBN 0-268-03359-5 (paper)
1. Catholic Church—Teaching office.   2. Catholic
Church—Infallibility.   3. Church—Authority.   4. Schillebeeckx, Edward,
1914–   I. Title.
BX1746.T475   2003
262'.02'092—dc21

2003004347

To

My wife, Jennifer,

Who is always a sign of hope

Contents

Foreword

Edward Schillebeeckx, O.P.

The reality of suffering and threatened humanity is, in my view, the central problem for us as we enter the third millennium. People suffer from disease, from social injustice, from the evil that they do to one another, and especially in massive numbers from the incomprehensible evils of the Holocaust and numerous forms of genocide.

This grave reality makes me question the nature of the link between suffering humanity and the church. In the Roman Catholic Church, the church, the "community of God," is called the "sacramentum mundi" (*Lumen Gentium*, par. 1), which means that it is a religious community oriented toward a finite and autonomous world which serves this threatened world by being a religious signpost within it.

However, although I am a member of the Roman Catholic Church, I mean by "church" all the members of the Christian community. As part of the great "community of humanity," they are spread in multicultural and multireligious communities over our entire (now threatened) planet; and they have the very human task of living with one another (and with their ecological environment) in mutual solidarity, in peace and goodwill, despite their differing views of human nature and society.

Few will dispute that this world, seen empirically and historically, is generally experienced as a mixture of sense and nonsense, of happiness and sorrow, of many smaller and greater joys or pains. But over and beyond this view, we also see the indisputably great, immeasurably deep, senseless, unjust, and unbearable suffering undergone by countless people. Systematic terrorism, finally, intensifies the fear, which leaves many people with the impression that we live in a disrupted and chaotic world.

Compelled by these facts, we are ultimately forced to speak of a "history of suffering" affecting most of the world's population. In a world subject to the unavoidable forces of globalization—where the suffering of many lonely people, even in Western countries, is often concealed or silenced—this history raises a central and difficult question for us.

When it follows the path of Jesus Christ, the church, by the force of its own nature, is oriented, as "sacrament of the world," toward the problems of our world. Since I am, culturally speaking, a Western thinker and believer, I consider the nature of the church's service to the late modern world (with its secular and autonomous sectors, values, and norms) a focus of theological concern. Out of regard for people who suffer, the nature of this connection cries out for a representation of the church and its rendering of the evangelical message which is credible to men and women in our threatened world. Ethical coherence and credibility are, therefore, the most important presuppositions of the church's service to the world and at the same time are the consequences of its message that God's kingdom is among human beings. In addition to the ethical and sociopolitical dimensions, the Christian life of faith also has a "mystical" dimension, that is, the constitutive, emotional, and at the same time cognitive aspect of personal union with God within God's *ecclesia*. In other words, the "theologal" dimension of faith. I call this God-centered character of Christian faith "mystical," although it can have many levels of intensity from the daily life of faith to deeply experienced mysticism, which, nevertheless, never surpasses the limits of our act of believing.

The cognitive or epistemological aspect of the mystical or theologal dimension of faith has at least two sides. The first is a cognitive contact with the reality of a creative, liberating, redeeming, and sanctifying transcendent Mystery, which is closer to us than we are to ourselves. The other side is the confessing, conceptual, and imaginative representations of faith, which by their nature are embedded in the diverse sociocultural contexts of human society. These two aspects can never be cleanly separated from one another, but they can be distinguished: whoever has a different understanding of humanity also has a different concept of God. The truly theologal or "mystical" dimension of faith in God refers to the nonconceptual dimension of what is, nevertheless, our "cognitive" faith-filled contact with the invisible God. Faith in God without a representation of that faith is meaningless, if not impossible, and moreover is historically ineffective. At the same time, the absolute and grace-filled presence of the divine Mystery repeatedly shatters all our images and representations of God.

In our late modern time, believers often misunderstand or distort this tension between the Christian faith's orientation toward the world and its theologal orientation. In our society's secularized environment, this creates polarization and even crises in some Christian communities. People seem to forget the consequences of our belief in what we clumsily call an inaccessible Mystery. It is indeed this, yet this mystery has also been given rough contours and intense "content"—at least in the great tradition of Christian religious experience. In this tradition the mystery becomes very specifically focused on humanity, on God, and God's whole world of creation. This Christian tradition of experience has long said, and still says today, that the God of Abraham, Isaac, and Jacob, the Father of Jesus the Christ, is a God of human beings ("*theos pros hémas*"): a God who envelops people in care and sympathy. This Greek-patristic view is anything but Hellenistic. This is not a God who manipulates the work of his hands like puppets kept dancing on invisible divine strings. In the Christian faith, God posits the universe, including our earth, with its own laws and real but finite, authentic autonomy (with its own laws of evolution, for example). God creates people with their own human autonomy, with real—albeit finite and thus situation-bound and conditioned—authentic human freedom, which the divine Mystery respects. We thus have to do with a living, transcendent God with a human and so a worldly face. He or She is no "thing" or empty void but for us an unnamable but name-eliciting, spiritual (and thus suprapersonal) source of inspiration, orientation, and energy.

If this human face of God becomes obscured, distorted, and disfigured by our behavior and by our (poor) conveyance of the Gospel, it becomes impossible for people in our world, who are aware of their own (finite) autonomy, responsibility, and discretion, to see the message of God's kingdom as liberating. Despite a lack of appreciation for this fact, for the sake of credibility, all religions regardless of their transcendent message—and thus the Christian Church also—are immediately subject to the critical standard of "humanity," which demands respect for human dignity and thus for human rights.

With regard to the human face of the world and of the church, I see many serious dangers facing humanity and thus all forms of religion in these early days of the third millennium, the future which has already begun. Besides the existing traditional forms of social injustice in our world and churches, if we analyze the impulses in the last decades of the second millennium, I see (without having to gaze in a crystal ball), among many other dangers, two profound threats. First, the many types of fundamentalism which—whether in God's name, in the name of a political ideology, or in the name of an absolutely free market economy which tolerates no impartial supervision—do injustice to people, affront human authenticity, and thus cut off every uncritically participating religion from its own authentic sources of inspiration. Second, the ethnic nationalism which is spreading ever more violently around the world and which is probably a variety of fundamentalism (namely, because it is a negation of the historical, temporal, and spatial situatedness of our imaginative and conceptual articulations of what we proclaim as truth). Those familiar with history know that some churches, which are often eager to condemn certain sociopolitical views, often stand hesitant or silent before the violent and subtle ethnic nationalism responsible for ethnic cleansing and the brutal rejection of "the stranger": there is now a clearly real danger of self-satisfied complacency in one's own views, along with a growing failure to appreciate the "otherness" of others.

Doubtless the specific situations throughout our world are extremely complex. Structures and locations of power, in particular, are a massive, tenacious reality that are difficult to change. However, in such situations the zeal for more human dignity, with its call for justly consequent convictions and insights, dare not become naïve, let alone fanatical—although, unfortunately, this admonition is often used as a convenient alibi for ignoring the situation.

That the problem of the third millennium will lie, for religious people, chiefly in the nature of the relationship between the church and the suffering world, raises new questions. In the twentieth century a divide that had been in preparation from the start of modern times arose between the way the Gospel is presented and the experience of believers. Many Catholics in the Western world feel that they stand marginalized on the outer edges of their church, either because they find no answers to the questions raised by their deepest human experiences or because they are given answers or instructions for questions they have not put. This situation makes it impossible to discuss problems and doubts in the church just at the time when they are increasing. This in turn erodes the church's credibility. There is a worsening "short-circuit" between believers' questions and the actual representations of the faith (with the practices that they imply, which are then connected to an antiquated view of humanity, society, and concomitant views of God).

On the one hand, the church's "human face" is a precondition for a coherent and credible presentation of the evangelical message; on the other hand, the church must repair the "short-circuit" that has arisen between believers' questions and representations of the Christian message that have become incredible in a postmodern period. Only then will the church, as "sacramentum mundi," effectively serve suffering and threatened humanity with its religious message and create the conditions in which it is possible for interested believers to listen to a presentation of the Gospel message which is "to the point." A hermeneutical method of theology which brings about a reciprocal and critical confrontation between our existential and sociocultural questions and doubts and the Christian tradition of experience (with Scripture as its constitutive starting point) is therefore very urgently needed. Luckily, we are witnessing the start of such a theological project that keeps in focus the theocentric, yet person- and world-directed inspiration and orientation of the Christian message, which comes from a God who is concerned with humanity. In this way theology can continue to serve humanity.

That is why I end with a note of hope. For it is exactly the negative or contrast experiences in the world and church in the twentieth century, with its Holocaust and ethnic genocides, with its experiences of ecclesial "short-circuits" between religious authorities and Christian believers, that arouse an indignation that is the converse of a latent expectation. It is a hope—relying on the "good news of Jesus" confessed as the Christ, Son of God, our Lord and Brother—that things can and must be done differently in the world and in the churches. In the third millennium there is hope for a church which will have both a more humane Christianity and a more Christian and God-directed humanity.

That is the "spirit" in the "letter" of this book by Daniel Speed Thompson. I am grateful to him that I was allowed to write a preface for his book. All authentic criticism in this book arises from the author's two-fold, church-oriented, and deeply religious convictions. First, that humanity and a religious (even "mystical") orientation toward God strengthen one another like two inseparable magnetic poles which need one another. And, second, that the conceptual, imaginative, and even dogmatic enunciations of the Christian tradition of religious experience bring religious truth to expression but always in a historical, limiting, and halting perspectival articulation. This places "religious truth" within a horizon that is ever open to shifting and often new cultural environments and ways of thinking. Without this, religion cannot really take root, it cannot function and, for the loyal believer, it becomes inaccessible, because it is alienated from life and incomprehensible.

Theology, in all its unavoidable diversity of approaches, in its role as a servant of the church's pastoral magisterium, and as a participant in interreligious dialogue, must continually listen meticulously and attentively to the religious truth that has already come to expression, while at the same time (and with unceasing self-criticism) seeking cautiously and critically for new articulations. Sometimes, thanks to their evangelical "new look," these new articulations will only be able to keep alive practical Christian identity—living and practicing the kingdom of God—through a cultural break with obsolete views of humanity and God.

Translated by Catherine Romanik, edited by Daniel Speed Thompson

Introduction

In the last fifteen years tensions have increased in the Roman Catholic Church between progressive theologians and the current magisterium, under the conservative leadership of Pope John Paul II and the Congregation for the Doctrine of the Faith. Already strained by more than two decades of controversy after the Second Vatican Council (1962–65), including the disciplining of well-known theologians like Hans Küng, Jacques Pohier, Leonardo Boff, and Charles Curran, relations between theologians and the magisterium have been further polarized by events of the last few years.[1]

In 1989 the Congregation for the Doctrine of the Faith issued a statement which required that all "teachers in any universities whatsoever who teach disciplines which deal with faith and morals" make an expanded profession of faith and take an oath of fidelity. The profession of faith, besides the traditional Niceno-Constantinopolitan Creed, required firm belief in teachings declared definitively by the magisterium and additionally mandated "the religious submission of will and intellect to the teachings which either the Roman pontiff or the college of bishops enunciate when they exercise the authentic magisterium, even if they proclaim these teachings in an act that is not definitive."[2] The oath of fidelity had a similar requirement.[3] Seemingly intended to quash progressive dissent in Catholic colleges, universities, and seminaries, where theologians used the noninfallible character of some church teachings as grounds for dissent, the statement mostly fell on deaf ears, with only a few schools actually instituting the practice.

Perhaps because of this resistance, in 1990 the Congregation issued "The Ecclesial Vocation of the Theologian" (*Donum Veritatis*). Although conceding that theologians played an essential role in deepening the understanding of the faith and hence enjoyed a freedom of research within the boundaries of their discipline, the document also stated that the very act of faith which made

1

theologians Catholic also bound them to various levels of adherence to the authoritative declarations of the church's magisterium. Theological dissent from these declarations was possible privately and in very restricted circumstances, but it could not be publicly expressed without both causing a scandal to the faithful and distorting the theologian's function in the church.[4] According to this document, theologians should explicate and defend the teaching of the magisterium but not create public debate about their positions or rely on any "political" methods to further discussion. The magisterium's voice, or echoes of it, was to be the only one heard publicly in the church.

In August of that same year Pope John Paul II issued the apostolic constitution *Ex Corde Ecclesiae* on the identity and mission of Catholic universities and colleges. Following in the wake of the constitution *Sapientia Christiana* (1979), which concerned specifically ecclesiastical and pontifical universities, *Ex Corde Ecclesiae* affirmed the special mission of all Catholic universities and colleges within both church and world, and the need for academic freedom in order to carry out that mission properly. However, the constitution also affirmed that the particularly Catholic nature of these universities and colleges needed to be protected by having a sufficient number of "faithful Catholics" among the faculty, boards of trustees, and presidents, and that the university needed to recognize its connection to the wider church and the church's magisterium. More specifically, any teacher in the theological disciplines needed to receive a mandate from the competent ecclesiastical authority in order to be able to teach, a requirement which followed from canon 812 of the revised Code of Canon Law (1983).[5]

Ex Corde Ecclesiae was greeted with a mixture of approbation and caution by Catholic academics around the world. The task of implementing the constitution fell to the national episcopal conferences, in conversation with academics and university administrators in their respective countries. In the United States, with its unique history of Catholic higher education, the implementation process involved extensive consultation among bishops, university presidents, and faculty, which resulted in the 1996 draft implementation decree. Although the bishops of the United States approved this document by an overwhelming majority (224–6), Rome rejected it, saying that it did not put enough emphasis on a clear juridical relationship between the magisterium and theologians. After further consultation, the bishops in 1999 approved a far more restrictive draft, which spelled out in more detail the nature of the *mandatum* that theologians were to seek from their local ordinary. As of this writing, the process of implementation has been completed.[6]

These conflicts over the role of theologians are symptomatic of a series of debates on doctrine and ethics in the Catholic Church since Vatican II which have made dissent not only a question for theologians but for the whole Catholic community as well. The signature controversy in the decade after the council concerned the permissibility of using artificial birth control within marriage. With the publication of *Humanae Vitae* in 1968 and the resulting worldwide re-action of laity and theologians, public theological dissent from church teachings became a new feature in the post–Vatican II Catholic landscape. With this dis-sent came the first attempts by the magisterium in the postconciliar period to si-lence or control theologians.[7] However, within a few years the great majority of the laity had tacitly, if not publicly, dissented from this encyclical by their own practice. For better or worse, an automatic reception of church teaching by the Catholic population worldwide became a thing of the past. Their silent *non placet* was an indicator of the emergence of new forms of the Catholic commu-nity in the postconciliar church, which either implicitly or intentionally were re-shaping the relationships between church and world, and among laity, clergy, and magisterium within the church.

One significant example of the emergence of new ideas of community within Catholicism was the development of feminist theology in the late 1960s and early 1970s and the concurrent consciousness-raising among many Catholic women. Their calls for increased participation in the church's min-istry brought the question of women's ordination to the forefront. Despite the Congregation for the Doctrine of the Faith's 1975 decree, *Inter Insigniores,* which stated that the church had no power to ordain women because of the abiding example of Jesus and the apostles (among other reasons), more and more Catholic theologians and believers accepted the possibility of women's ordination. A brief but sharp reaffirmation of the traditional teaching by John Paul II in 1994, *Ordinatio Sacerdotalis,* prepared the way for the Congregation's 1995 "Reply to the 'Dubium.'" Approved by the pope, it stated that the posi-tion on the ordination of women enunciated in *Ordinatio Sacerdotalis* was an infallible teaching insofar as the pope was confirming the constant teaching of the "ordinary and universal magisterium" of all the bishops.[8] The theological stakes had been raised higher. Previously, some theologians had argued that public dissent from noninfallible teachings of the magisterium was permis-sible, however not from infallible ones.[9] Now, alongside some technical ques-tions as to whether the Congregation itself can propose that a doctrine be recognized as infallible (even with papal approval), the larger question now looms about the possibility of dissent from an infallibly proposed doctrine of the magisterium. Granting this possibility automatically calls into question the infallibility both of the pope and the extraordinary and ordinary magisterium of the church, a question muffled at least in Catholic circles since the 1979 censure of Hans Küng, who had explicitly denied the doctrine.[10]

Beyond these specific doctrinal and ethical issues and beyond questions about papal and magisterial infallibility, public theological dissent in the postconciliar period marks the emergence of different fundamental understandings of the nature and mission of the church. These sometimes competing ecclesiologies predate the council, are contained in the tensions within the council documents themselves, and come fully to expression only because of the galvanizing effect of controversies over teachings like *Humanae Vitae* and women's ordination. One example is the biblical metaphor of the church as people of God, which Yves Congar and other preconciliar ecclesiologists attempted to recover as the essential complement to the hierarchy and which *Lumen Gentium* affirmed as the common identity of all Christians before hierarchical distinction. After the council, for many it becomes a separate ecclesiology, used in the service of an egalitarian model of the church and often placed in antithesis to a *communio* ecclesiology of the Body of Christ, an equally biblical metaphor, but one used to justify essential distinctions between members of the church and a more traditional view of authority. Questions about church authority or the role of theologians in the church are ultimately questions about the nature of the church itself. Yet differences in ecclesiology have their roots in even more fundamental differences.

This work will argue that questions about the nature of the church are at heart questions about how God is revealed to human beings, how human beings experience that revelation and obtain knowledge of God, and how human beings attempt to express that revelation, especially in language. For the church, in its simplest definition, is the community of people called together in response to their experience of God in Jesus. The church continues to thrive after its originating event only insofar as this community mediates a real experience of that event across the generations. Everything else that the church does or has, one might argue, must serve this end or be part of an ossifying inertia or an ephemeral accommodation. The church community has the role, even in the midst of its errors and limitations, of mediating the tradition of the experience of revelation and of providing a context for appropriating this experience anew. But the church is not merely the passive conduit for the transmission of revelation; the actual functioning church concretely represents and shapes the way in which this revelation is presented. Thus differently structured churches mediate different concepts and experiences of revelation to their respective communities.

To test this hypothesis with a somewhat extreme example, let us look very briefly at the Society of Friends, or Quakers, for whom church polity is at its simplest. The believers gather and worship in a circle of silence, waiting for the Spirit of God to speak directly to each participant. No believer is raised above the others; no church structure exists beyond the gathering of the circle. In this sense, the Society of Friends' fundamental belief in the immediate and direct accessibility of God's presence to all believers shapes the polity of the church community.[11] A conception of the "location" of revelation underlies this radically simplified ecclesiology. Yet in practice this ecclesiology also first shapes the conception and experience of revelation for the generations that follow. Quaker ecclesial polity depends on, represents, and reinforces an underlying understanding of revelation. If this hypothesis proves true more generally, then theologies of revelation and theologies of the church exist in a mutually determinative relationship made concrete by the actual praxis within Christian communities.

In the particular case at hand, Catholic ecclesiology, as put into practice by actual Catholic communities, both depends on and concretely represents a theology of revelation. The so-called classic picture of the Catholic community, drawn on biblical roots, developed in the Middle Ages, reaffirmed by the Council of Trent (1545–62), and accentuated by Vatican I (1869–70), depicts the church as a pyramidal hierarchy with the highest spiritual authority possessed by the pope as the Vicar of Christ. The pope delegates authority to the archbishops and bishops, who in turn have power over the pastors of local churches, the pastors then over other priests and women religious, and all clergy over the laity.[12] In a parallel and correlative way, Catholic theologians developed a fundamental theology that stated that God's revelation in Jesus was contained in two sources, Scripture and tradition, both of which were necessary for possessing the fullness of the deposit of faith. This deposit of faith was passed on from the apostles to the later church communities under the guardianship of the bishops, the successors to the apostles. These bishops, under the leadership of the successor of Peter, the Bishop of Rome, the pope, performed the magisterial function of watching over the deposit of faith, teaching from it and declaring which doctrines accurately expressed its content and which did not. Hence the magisterium of the church had the indispensable function of judging which doctrines and practices could mediate the original revelatory event of Jesus. In practice, since the magisterium, particularly the papal magisterium, was seen as the final and infallible authority in such matters, its decisions were seen as revelatory in some sense themselves. Coupled with the pyramidal structure just described, Catholic ecclesiology concretely illustrated a theology of revelation wherein the church mediated God's originating revelation through the spiritual power and authority of the pope. All other mediations—doctrinal, ethical, liturgical—depended on this ultimate authenticating mediation.[13]

At least that was the dominant view from Rome. One could argue on historical grounds that although many clergy and laity lived out of this mutually reinforcing understanding of ecclesiology and revelation, countercurrents have always existed. Patristic traditions of episcopal elections by the local community and the conciliarism of the Council of Constance offered hints of an alternative ecclesiology;[14] the family ritual and personal devotion of popular Catholicism gave mediated access to God outside of the formal structures of parish and public liturgy.[15] Catholics have seen the function of the church community and the "locus" of revelatory experiences in many different ways over the centuries. Nevertheless, it remains true that the dominant picture of the church in the last century before the Second Vatican Council was the "monarchical" model just outlined and that these countercurrents had been forced to the fringes of theology or did not come to any recognized theological expression at all. *Lumen Gentium, Gaudium et Spes,* and the other documents of Vatican II both opened the doors for the development of these latent theological currents and provided a seedbed for competing fundamental and ecclesiological claims which have broken the hold of the pyramidal view of the church and offered a more decentralized, egalitarian, participatory, and experiential ecclesiology.

In the wake of the last thirty turbulent years after the Second Vatican Council, these different currents, both old and new, have not only emerged and developed, they have frozen into polarized positions which leave little room for dialogue and little possibility for real church unity. The issue of theological dissent is a bellwether for this deeper polarization. If progressive theologians and the conservative magisterium have reached such an impasse about theological method and church authority, their respective ecclesiological and fundamental presuppositions must also be at an impasse. Given both John Paul II's willingness to use censure and coercion to restore elements of the preconciliar pyramidal ecclesiology, and given the resultant dismissal of the magisterium's claims by many theologians, this situation poses grave dangers for church unity, church credibility, and theological and academic integrity. In this atmosphere of renewed absolutist claims and attempts to impose uniformity on the whole church, is there any possibility of legitimate theological dissent and the formation of alternative, critical communities within the Catholic Church? What are the roles and boundaries, if any, of such dissent and such communities within the church? How are these phenomena related to each other? How does the church judge concerning the validity of these phenomena? How does the church preserve an authentic unity within plurality, without lapsing either into a suffocating uniformity or a dissipating pluralism? These are the questions that have prompted my inquiry.

This book does not directly address the latest and perhaps most profound crisis of confidence in the Catholic Church since the council: the twofold scandal of clerical sexual abuse of children and the apparent willingness of some bishops to conceal this abuse from the laity and the civil authorities by reassigning priests known as sexual offenders to other parishes or dioceses. Profoundly shaken by these revelations, many Catholics now are asking themselves: Whom can we trust? What should the church do for victims of abuse? What steps should be taken to protect children from clerical sexual predators? How can accused clerics receive due process from the church and civil law? How and to what extent can the bishops be held accountable to the church and before civil law for these crimes?

The detailed study to follow (researched and written well before the scandal broke) cannot respond to all of these complex legal, theological, psychological, and personal questions. However, it can offer some resources for Catholics interested in thinking about the nature of the church, the authority of the magisterium, and the role of the laity in church leadership. Like all Catholic matters postconciliar, the clerical sex abuse scandal has already become ammunition for the polarized parties in the Catholic Church. Liberals see it as clear testimony to the corruption of the celibate and hierarchical model of church governance; both the crimes and their concealment are horrifying products of a culture of sexual repression and clerical privilege. Conservatives, no less horrified by the scandal, see its roots in the insidious infiltration of a culture of sexual permissiveness—taught by dissenting theologians in Catholic colleges and seminaries—into the ranks of the clergy, and in an episcopate unwilling to teach and enforce traditional standards of Catholic morality. In this atmosphere, when Catholics ask about whom they can trust now and why such a disaster could have occurred, they are also implicitly asking about the holiness and sinfulness of the church, the grounding of the authority of bishops and priests, the role of theologians and teachers, the ways in which the laity can speak, and indeed the meaning of Catholic identity itself. Although my focus will be on the specific problem of the relationship between dissent in the church and the magisterium, all of these issues will be treated in this book.

This work will argue that both theological dissent and critical communities of alternative practice are necessary within the church and that democratic forms of church governance are ultimately the best, if imperfect, means of discernment and judgment about the limits of such dissent. I will pursue this argument on the basis of a careful examination of the thought of Edward Schillebeeckx (1914–). His theology, when constructively examined and extended, offers a way of seeing the role of theological dissent and critical communities in the church that succumbs to neither authoritarianism nor schismatic pluralism. Yet, although Schillebeeckx's theology avoids these twin dangers, it also passionately and persuasively argues for a radically altered church structure that should be built up from the ground level in the Catholic Church.

However, it is not simply because Schillebeeckx's ecclesiology supports such a conclusion that he is the subject here. Nor is it because he himself has been investigated by the Congregation for the Doctrine of the Faith several times for allegedly heterodox or dissenting positions. Schillebeeckx's theology is worthy of study because it offers an illustration of the mutual relationship between theologies of revelation and theologies of the church, and hence it is a way for constructively thinking about issues of theological dissent and the formation of critical communities in the church.

Much of Schillebeeckx's theological work, especially after 1966, has been engaged in seeking an "understanding of faith" which can bridge the distance between present-day human experience and the experiences of the first disciples of Jesus. To this end, Schillebeeckx has devoted himself to an exhaustive study of contemporary philosophy and other disciplines within the humanities, with a particular emphasis on epistemology and the philosophy of language. From this broad and eclectic reading Schillebeeckx has fashioned a complex structure for understanding human experience and knowledge and their relationship to the salvific and revelatory experiences claimed by believers in the Christian church. Only such a fundamental discussion of human experience and knowledge, he argues, can provide an adequate context for plausibly discussing Christian revelation.[16] If the hypothesis I suggested above is correct—that theologies of revelation inform theologies of the church and ultimately shape the concrete praxis of Christian communities (and vice versa)—then one should be able to trace back conflicts over the nature of the church to different theoretical and practical understandings of the continuing mediation of revelation. In the current impasse over theological dissent and alternative community structures, differing conceptions of the nature of the church are contesting. Underneath these, differing conceptions of revelation and its mediation are in conflict. Therefore it seems logical to approach these two ecclesiological problems from what seems like a remote point: a discussion of human experience and knowledge and how humans receive, interpret, and express revelation. Schillebeeckx's epistemology and theology of revelation provide a needed base for a further discussion of ecclesiology. His fundamental theology, applied consistently to his ecclesiology, will support the thesis that the church is a community where theological dissent and the formation of alternative community structures must exist, although within the correlational and practical mediation of Christian faith, and where democratic forms of church governance are the imperfect but best means of discernment and judgment.

There is no way clear of the current impasse without some conflict. If Schillebeeckx's theology is a persuasive picture of the relationship between human knowledge of revelation and the concrete structures of the church, then he also offers a vision of the church which both differs quite radically from the current "official" church structures within the Catholic Church and criticizes those critical communities which have detached themselves utterly from the tradition and the wider ecumene of other Christian communities. Although his theology does not offer a bland compromise of some "middle way" between the polarized camps, it does offer the hope for a radically altered Catholic Church which nevertheless remains faithful to the broad intention of the New Testament and the Christian tradition; indeed, it remains faithful insofar as it is radically altered. For, as Schillebeeckx says, "Continuity can therefore also be only apparent-continuity. A certain *break*, such as that of Vatican II, can really mean a rediscovery of the deepest tendencies of the Gospel."[17] In the hope of illustrating how this seeming paradox can be true within the Catholic Church, I will turn first to Schillebeeckx's discussion of human experience and knowledge as the formal structure in which all experiences of salvation and revelation must take place.

one | Human Experience, Knowledge, and Action

Schillebeeckx's Epistemological Framework

On December 13–15, 1979, Edward Schillebeeckx took part in a "conversation" in the chambers of the Congregation for the Doctrine of the Faith in Rome. It was the culmination of a series of questionnaires posed by the Congregation since 1976 to Schillebeeckx and his replies.[1] According to the Congregation's secretary, Monsignor Jerome Hamer, the "conversation" was "meant to be a stage in a process of clarification" of questions which the Congregation had about Schillebeeckx's massive works, *Jesus: An Experiment in Christology* and *Christ: The Experience of Jesus as Lord*.[2] For these three days Schillebeeckx faced a panel of three exegetes and theologians, led by the undersecretary of the Congregation, Monsignor Alberto Bovone, and fielded their prepared questions, which the panel did not provide him beforehand.[3] The questions covered a range of issues about Jesus, including his divinity, resurrection, and virgin birth as well as more general questions about magisterial and conciliar authority and theological methodology.

More than a decade later, Schillebeeckx recalled in an interview with an Italian journalist that one of his interlocutors, a moderate Thomist theologian named Albert Patfoort, O.P., questioned Schillebeeckx's use of hermeneutics in theology.

> Each of the three theologians had half an hour to talk. Patfoort caused me trouble. He asked me questions which were out of place and ingenuous. He asked me to explain hermeneutics to him. I replied with a slogan from St. Thomas (he was an observant Thomist): *Quidquid recipitur, ad modum recipientis, recipitur* (whatever is received is received in a way

suited to the recipient). "Ah, now I understand," he said. "Fine, fine." That was that.[4]

Schillebeeckx's response to Patfoort will be the starting point for my exploration of his epistemology. That Schillebeeckx thought it possible to explain hermeneutics in Thomist language indicates a continuity at a fundamental level in the structure of his thought, especially about the motivation for his research into epistemology. Although after 1966 Schillebeeckx abandons a strictly Thomistic framework for understanding theology in favor of an eclectic mix drawn from a broad variety of contemporary schools of philosophy, his later explorations into hermeneutics and critical theory can be seen as attempts to follow that slogan from St. Thomas in the light of a different situation. For from the beginning of his career as a theologian, Schillebeeckx has been concerned with understanding "concrete, contemporary Christian experience," as Robert Schreiter puts it.[5] In order to do this, Schillebeeckx has sought both to understand the Christian tradition, especially the scriptural sources, in all its breadth and diversity, and to understand how the contemporary believer can appropriate and live from this tradition in the often radically changed circumstances of the current day. Both tasks, but especially the latter, require a thorough grasp of the *modum recipientis*, that is, an understanding of the human subject and how he or she both knows the world and can come to know God through revelation. As Schillebeeckx has found earlier theological and philosophical frameworks insufficient for fully meeting this task, he has discarded them, or, rather, he has amended them to fit into his revised framework. Thus elements of his earliest epistemological theory persist in his later theology and have a significant effect in these later frameworks.[6]

The constructive interpretation of Schillebeeckx's epistemology offered here will also illuminate the fundamental pattern of his thinking in general. Throughout this work I will use the phrase "nonantithetical and dialectical relationship" to describe that fundamental pattern.[7] "Dialectical relationship" refers to the nondualistic nature of his thought. All objects, subjects, events, ideas—all experiences, in short—exist only within a network of irreducible, continually dynamic, and mutually informing relationships. Schillebeeckx consistently gives these relationships a certain ontological priority, which subordinates analytical separation to a more encompassing process of synthesis and unity. "Nonantithetical" further specifies the nature of these dialectical relationships by distinguishing them from a Hegelian or Marxist dialectic of historical opposition and overcoming, and a Barthian dialectic of transcendent Otherness opposed by human self-delusion and disobedience. In Schillebeeckx's dialectical thinking, unity is not created by the overcoming of some fundamental opposition but by the reestablishment of the irreducible and cooperative relationships which make up all of reality, including the very nature of God.

This nonantithetical and dialectical pattern of thinking can be clearly seen in Schillebeeckx's epistemology. Using the metaphor of a circle to describe this pattern, I will distinguish three circles in his epistemology: the ontological circle of subject and object, where knowledge is mediated in a limited fashion by concepts; the hermeneutical circle of context, new experiences, and reformed context, where knowledge is mediated by historical tradition, present encounter, and future anticipation; and the critical circle of theory and praxis, where knowledge is mediated by negative contrast experiences, ideology critique, and action on the behalf of suffering humanity. My description of these circles will be both diachronic and synchronic; Schillebeeckx moves from the first to the third of these circles over the course of his career, but the first two circles underlie his most fully developed theory of epistemology. The last circle is the most complex form of his epistemological understanding, but it depends on the first for its fundamental nonantithetical and dialectical nature and on the second for its turn toward history and narrative as categories of knowledge.

Although Schillebeeckx certainly is concerned with understanding the *modum recipientis* of the contemporary person, his theological approach, especially in his later career, has become less formal and systematic. He does not lay out a formal epistemology, so his epistemological discussions must be extracted from his other writings on (theological) anthropology, experience, revelation, and salvation. For this reason his discussions of knowledge are often allusive and emphasize, even in his later works, one circle more than another. Because of this, the schema which I have just introduced must be seen only as a rough formalization of his thought—a formalization, however, which I hope will clarify his understanding of human knowledge, offer a tentative explanation for some of its inconsistencies, and provide a solid base for a discussion of salvation and revelation.

The First Epistemological Circle:
Perspectivalism and Phenomenological Thomism

Pope Leo XIII's *Aeterni Patris* (1879) established Thomism as the official theology and philosophy of the Catholic Church. Condemnations of the theological innovations of Modernism occurred under Pius X (in the syllabus of Modernist errors in the decree *Lamentabili* and the encyclical *Pascendi Dominici Gregis*). In the wake of these declarations Catholic dogmatic theologians, both restricted in their choices of theological methods and cowed with regard to public expressions of divergent views, adopted a highly conceptualist, logical, and abstract style of Thomism which would provide a powerful intellectual framework to combat the errors of the day: subjectivist Modernism as well as such old foes as Protestantism and modern Enlightenment thought.[8]

Yet as the dust settled after the Modernism controversy, some Catholic theologians and philosophers again turned to modern philosophy in an attempt both to free dogmatics from an excessively narrow conception of revelation and to continue, however cautiously, some dialogue with contemporary thought. When Schillebeeckx entered the Dominican novitiate in 1934 and began studying philosophy a year later at Louvain, he encountered Dominicus De Petter, a philosopher who was attempting just such a rethinking of Thomas in relation to contemporary philosophy.[9] Drawing on the phenomenological tradition of Edmund Husserl and Maurice Merleau-Ponty, De Petter argued for an "implicit intuition" of reality that lay under the strictly conceptual form of knowledge. Prior to their knowledge and use of concepts, human beings have an epistemological link with the world around them. As Philip Kennedy summarizes it:

His theory asserted that human knowledge involves more than concepts. He explained a non-conceptual element in knowledge by claiming that intuition forms an intrinsic part of the human intellect. Intuition is here conceived as a contemplative or spiritual link between an individual subject and the reality which is external to the subject. Intuition is thought to be a direct experience of objective reality as well as a participation in the absolute meaning of reality.[10]

Yet because such an intuition is implicit, its expression must rely on concepts which mediate it. Like Joseph Maréchal, his contemporary at Louvain, De Petter bases his epistemology on a dialectical relationship of the unthematized (the implicit intuition of reality) and the thematized (the expression and explanation of this in concepts). Knowledge of God, therefore, has both a positive aspect—the direct grasp on God's reality provided by implicit intuition—and a negative aspect—the recognition that all human concepts used to express this intuition themselves do not directly apply to God and fall well short of capturing the divine reality.[11]

Kennedy argues that De Petter's epistemology is a "post-Kantian theory of knowledge where knowledge is seen as a synthesis involving contributions from a knowing subject and an object known."[12] Avoiding both a naïvely realist epistemology where the mind is the passive recipient of knowledge and a purely subjectivist or idealist view which sees the mind as the creator of knowledge, De Petter formulates in Thomistic language "the central insight of the phenomenological analysis of consciousness, namely, the principle of the intentionality of consciousness."[13] This dialectic of the objective and subjective elements of knowledge will be inherited and developed by Schillebeeckx in the early years of his career.

At Louvain, De Petter set the young Schillebeeckx to work on developing aspects of his thought. Schillebeeckx recalls, "He gave me the task, in my third year of philosophy, that is, between 1937 and 1938, of finding out the best ways of overcoming conceptuality. I remember that I made an analysis of the relationship between question and answer in my essay and looked in that direction for the non-conceptual element in reason."[14]

From this early beginning and for nearly the next thirty years, Schillebeeckx developed, refined, and theologically applied the epistemological framework initially handed on to him by De Petter.

After his education at Louvain in philosophy and theology and his ordination as a priest in 1941 (the same year, incidentally, that both De Petter and Chenu were dismissed from their teaching posts),[15] Schillebeeckx continued his theological studies there and also began teaching at the Dominican House of Studies. After the war he was sent to Paris and Le Saulchoir to pursue his doctoral work. In Paris he encountered the second great influence in his theological and philosophical formation: the Dominican theologian and historian M. Dominique Chenu. Chenu taught Schillebeeckx to read Thomas within the context of the theologians and philosophers of his day, that is, historically and not just conceptually and abstractly. Although not a systematic philosopher or theologian like De Petter, Chenu also provided Schillebeeckx with a way past the conceptualist epistemological presuppositions of the contemporary Thomist theology by arguing that human beings in particular historical situations generate doctrinal declarations and theological systems and that the modern reader must at least initially understand them in their original context. Timeless truths only come wrapped in historical garments. Again, Philip Kennedy summarizes the twin influences of De Petter and Chenu:

The two sought to lead Catholic theology away from any kind of excessive attachment to a naively mimetic view of theological language. They also emphasized contemporary experiences as a source for theology. Much of Schillebeeckx's work has been devoted to continuing their project. From De Petter, above all, he learned that every concept of God is in fact godless, that is, every concept falls short of adequately explaining who or what God is. From Chenu he learned that doctrines are the fruits of *human* creativity and reflection.[16]

As Kennedy observes, much of Schillebeeckx's later work is devoted to continuing his mentors' project. In the section to follow, I will argue that Schillebeeckx's early epistemology reflects both the teachings of De Petter and Chenu and his own abiding interest in the problem of the relationship of the universal and the concrete particular. The epistemological structures that he developed and called "perspectivalism" or "perspectivism" are the specific source and exemplification of the nonantithetical and dialectical form of thinking which shapes all his works.

This "perspectivalism" is an attempt to develop an epistemology which will avoid the twin errors of abstract conceptualism and purely subjectivist Modernism but will nevertheless preserve human knowledge of God and the truth of dogmatic statements. In order to do this, in this first circle of epistemology, Schillebeeckx describes knowledge as a noetic connection between the active, intending subject and the known object.[17] This connection is mediated but not contained by concepts created by the human mind. At a deeper level than concepts, this noetic connection depends on the ontological connection of all being with its source, the creating and transcendent God.[18]

As did De Petter and Maréchal before him, Schillebeeckx presents his epistemology by way of an exegesis of Thomas Aquinas, although he will later express this perspectivalism using less explicitly Thomist language.[19] In an early article, "The Non-Conceptual Intellectual Dimension of Our Knowledge of God According to St. Thomas," Schillebeeckx sets out to analyze Thomas in order to "find out to what extent Aquinas himself accepted an aspect in our knowledge of God that transcends our concepts, and whether he looked for this non-conceptual dimension in the dynamism of the spirit or in a certain objective dynamism of the content of being which is not open to concepts as such."[20]

What follows is an analysis of the conceptual dimension of human knowledge of God and the relationship between the *ratio concepta* and the *actus significandi* in Aquinas. Schillebeeckx recognizes that Aquinas did teach that a conceptual element was a necessary part of our knowledge of God, but he also emphasizes that for Aquinas such concepts, even when taken through the *via negationis* and the *via eminentiae,* still have a creaturely origin and are not in themselves directly applicable to God.[21] Furthermore, as Schillebeeckx goes on to argue, human beings do possess a real noetic grasp of God's reality, but this can only be discovered by an analysis of the *actus significandi* which transcends the *ratio concepta,* that is, the concepts created by the human mind.

Using less technical language, Schillebeeckx will say in the later "Concept of Truth" that, first, human beings know the truth in an imperfect, evolving, and relative way which is always capable of further amplification and refinement.[22] Second, despite this relative nature of knowledge, human beings nevertheless grasp objective truth and in fact are shaped by it.[23]

What allows Schillebeeckx to make these affirmations is an underlying ontology of relation, drawn from his Thomist understanding of creation. The subjective and relative human knower also is objectively located in a relationship with the whole of reality, including God. This fundamental relationship is conceptually inexpressible but nevertheless orients the halting concepts of human knowledge toward absolute truth.

> In the modern view, insofar as it accepts an absolute reality at all, reality (as truth) is seen as the never wholly-to-be-deciphered background of all our human interpretations. The ontological basis, as the mysterious source of a still hidden fullness of meaning, remains the same and does not change, but the human interpretation of this basis, and thus man's possession of truth, grows and evolves. This is, however, drawn in one definite direction by this implicit ontological significance, so that the truth is always apprehended more and more concretely, even though it is never completely apprehended.[24]

Schillebeeckx's earlier work makes clear the metaphysical basis for this conclusion. One of the basic tenets of Thomist metaphysics is that causes contain their effects potentially, whereas effects bear a certain *similitudo* to their causes, which varies according to the type of causation. In the special case of the relationship between God and the world, God is indeed the cause by way of creation of the world and hence creation bears a certain *similitudo* to God. Yet God's nature is so utterly transcendent to the world that Thomas cannot concede any possibility of conceptually grasping this *similitudo*. So human beings possess knowledge of God, knowledge of their creaturely *similitudo* to

God, which allows them to apply creaturely concepts to God (the *actus signifi-candi*) by way of remotion and eminence. Yet at the same time human knowers cannot form a concept of the very *similitudo* which makes such an act of attribution possible. Schillebeeckx summarizes it so:

> Aquinas therefore affirms on the one hand that we know that a likeness exists between the creature and God, and on the other hand that this creaturely likeness escapes the grasp of our specific, and even of our merely generic conceptual knowledge. It is, in his view, impossible to grasp this *similitudo* conceptually. The importance of this affirmation is that it is precisely *this* similitude (as the essential aspect of dependence on God or absolute participation) which, according to Aquinas, forms the basis of the objective value of our knowledge of God. The really existing *similitudo* of the creature to God is therefore an immanent *beyond* of our predicamental and conceptual knowledge.[25]

Human beings therefore possess knowledge of God which cannot be captured in concepts, but which is nevertheless "objective." Because of the "really existing *similitudo* of the creature to God," the human act of naming God with concepts drawn from human experience, the *actus significandi*, also aims at the objective reality of God, even if the concepts used in the *actus significandi* cannot grasp the divine reality directly. "The act of signifying goes further than the *ratio nominis*, but it exceeds this *ratio* in the direction envisaged by the content itself, in such a way that the reality is really envisaged, but not conceptually grasped."[26]

Unlike Maréchal, who according to Schillebeeckx locates the non-conceptual element of human knowledge of God in the subjective dynamism of the human spirit, Schillebeeckx locates this element in the objective dynamism of the content of human concepts of God. The reasoning is classically Thomist. Since God is the creator of all and the final cause of all, all creation tends toward God. Hence both the "objective dynamism" of the human knower and the "objective dynamism" of the world from which the knower draws concepts lead toward God. Therefore these concepts, born of the fundamental interrelationship between human knower and world, have an "objective dynamism" toward the *res significata*, God. Yet since all creation is also radically different from God, these concepts can only point in a correct, objective, but incomplete way to the divine reality. Even the *transcendentalia*, the concepts of the perfections of God, can only perform a limited function in this regard.

What we have here is a positive intellectual content that *directs* us *objectively* towards God's own mode of being. Our so-called "concepts of God" really define an intelligible content that is, however, *open* to the mystery. The typically noetic value of our knowledge of God is therefore situated in a projective act, in which we *reach out for* God, but do not grasp him in understanding, although we are well aware that he is to be found in the precise *direction* in which we are reaching.[27]

This distinction between a simple conceptual grasp of God's being and an objectively true projection toward God's being through conceptual content is the key to his "perspectivalist" epistemology. The concepts humans use for God, as described above, are "open to the mystery" and provide "in a confused but objective way" a perspective on the divine reality.[28] Because both human beings and the world *tendere in Deum* (on account of God's final causality)[29] and because human beings and the world are interrelated through creation, human concepts drawn from created realities can provide a glimpse of the fundamental orientation which underlies all their existence.

Yet the human being as knower stands in a dialectical relationship with absolute truth. For although human knowledge is more than a subjective or intersubjective apprehension of truth, it is not an absolute grasp in itself. The ever-expanding and always to be refined human apprehension of truth is shaped and regulated by the nature of absolute truth itself, which forms the other active pole in Schillebeeckx's dialectic of knowledge.[30] God, both through graced creation and created grace, gives knowledge of God's self through creation and the human concepts drawn from it. In this dialectic of knowledge, based itself on a deeper dialectic of ontological relationship, human knowledge both has a perspective on truth and yet never comes to complete unanimity. Both poles of the dialectic remain in play and so the human knower must recognize both the absolute truth grasped in limited form by his or her own knowledge and the possibility of other perspectives contributing to this refinement of knowledge.[31]

The ultimate aim of Schillebeeckx's epistemological considerations is a clearer understanding of the truth status of Christian dogmatic statements. Again attempting to avoid both Modernistic relativism and the conceptual abstractions of the current Thomist school, Schillebeeckx uses the perspectivalist epistemology to argue for a logical distinction between the "real essence of the dogmatic affirmation" and the "secondary aspects relating to the form in which the definition is couched."[32] On a broader scale, since human beings possess truth through human concepts which are true but inadequate expressions of the fundamental absolute truth and mystery of all reality, dogmas are also true but inadequate expressions of the mystery of salvation history, that is, the mystery of God acting in time for the sake of human beings.[33] Conversely, since both human apprehension of truth and human concepts reflect the objective dynamism toward ultimate reality inherent in creation, dogmas also point to and are shaped by absolute truth. I will return to these themes in the chapters on revelation and on the church.

At this stage in Schillebeeckx's career, "action" or "praxis" does not play a significant role in the formation of his epistemology. For example, when reflecting in 1961 on the "appeal to human existential experience" in current dogmatic theology, Schillebeeckx says that, although faith and reflection on faith are ultimately to be integrated into one concrete Christian life, theology as such needs a certain distance from action and praxis.

> Faith and reflection about faith are, however, two completely different orientations of the spirit. Although faith is an "existential act," theology as a science is not. As reflection, theology is an act which, *as such*, stands outside man's affective and practical attitude toward the reality of faith. Although it does come within the sphere of living faith, it nonetheless preserves a certain "distance" from life, partly so as to stress the orientation of religious practice towards reality.[34]

Schillebeeckx always recognizes that knowledge of God is not the private province of the theologian. Nevertheless, at this early stage, one's "affective and practical attitude" toward the reality of faith is clearly separated methodologically from the reflection on and formal explication of the fundamental mystery of salvation. Knowledge of God requires the graced mediation of concepts which objectively point toward God, and the theologian has the primary task in the church of analyzing and understanding these concepts (along with and under the authority of the teaching office). Despite its concern for the "concrete Christian experience" of all believers in the church, then, Schillebeeckx's epistemology at this point still has an idealistic and intellectualist bent which is separated from the praxis both of the theologian and of the "ordinary" believers in the pews.

Another category that will play an important role in Schillebeeckx's later epistemology is the historicity or temporality of the human subject. At this early stage he is already concerned with overcoming the abstract conceptualism of the dominant schools of Thomist theology, which rendered knowledge of God and the dogmatic concepts flowing from this in a distinctively ahistorical manner. In opposition to this, Schillebeeckx argues that human beings express their graced knowledge of God in the conceptual forms appropriate to a particular period. Because of the active role both of the human knower and God in the process of knowledge, these concepts are true but inadequate perspectives on the divine reality. Prior to the concepts themselves, there is the reality of relationship with God. This relationship, however, only comes in and through historical events. Hence history is a category in Schillebeeckx's early epistemology primarily as the history of the actions of God on behalf of the human race and the human response to them.[35] Because of this primacy of salvation history, the early Schillebeeckx sees human historicity in developmental terms: human beings come to greater and greater knowledge of God over the course of human history, culminating in the salvific event of Jesus of Nazareth. The church preserves, explicates, and develops this knowledge of God over the centuries through the different conceptual frameworks fitting different eras. The emphasis at this point is less on the radical historicity of the human subject than on the developmental historicity of human concepts based on God's historically mediated relationship to humanity. Schillebeeckx's concept of history at this point attempts to encompass ideas of change and refinement but does not yet deal with the problems of the inevitable breaks in history: difference, meaninglessness, and suffering.

Despite these limitations, which Schillebeeckx himself will recognize in a later stage of his thought, his perspectivalist epistemology lays both a material and formal groundwork for his further epistemological discussions and, indeed, for all of his thought. Materially speaking, although he will abandon the phenomenological Thomist framework, with its emphasis on knowledge as implicit intuition mediated by concepts, he will retain the idea that all knowledge of God is partial and that all expressions of that knowledge reflect the historical perspective of the subject. Formally speaking, although he will abandon the idea that human knowledge can simply be described by the circle of the intending subject in an irreducible, conceptually mediated relationship with the object, he will retain the idea that human knowledge can only be understood by placing it within similar irreducible, nonantithetical and dialectical relationships. Furthermore, beyond even explicit considerations of epistemology, from his use of De Petter's phenomenological reading of Thomas all the way down to his latest works on church and the sacraments, this same formal feature dominates his work: mutually informing relationship stands prior to analytic separation or opposition.[36] So, despite the fact that he drops his perspectivalist position soon after Vatican II, the legacy of this viewpoint shapes his thinking on every specific theological topic, including theological dissent, church authority, and the role of critical communities in the church.

The Second Epistemological Circle: Schillebeeckx's Hermeneutical Turn

Schillebeeckx uses his perspectivalist epistemology through the period of the Second Vatican Council (1962–65).[37] Not long after the close of the council, though, Schillebeeckx decisively abandons the phenomenological and Thomist language he had used for almost two decades to describe human knowledge of God. As he says in a later work, he made "a clear break with the 'implicit intuition' of the meaning-totality maintained by the classical philosophy like that of D. de Petter, L. Lavelle and the French *philosophes de l'Esprit.*"[38] What led Schillebeeckx to such a change?

The immediate context for the passage quoted above from *Jesus: An Experiment in Christology* gives some clues. While discussing the question on the possibility of making theological assertions about a universal meaning of history, Schillebeeckx states, "Whether some salvific activity on God's part does indeed take place in Jesus of Nazareth must up to a point be a matter of actual experience and be expressible in faith language." As a result of this, "the theologian's 'hypothesis' (the thesis of faith) must be capable in one way or another (not apodictic but very significant) way of being tested by and finding support in the reality of man, his world and society, in short in our historical experience."[39] This assertion leads Schillebeeckx to his "clear break" with the philosophy of De Petter because this "classical" picture posited a participation in the totality of meaning within the confines of a mostly Christian culture. In the contemporary context, where the old "plausibility structures" no longer obtain and "divergent ideologies" compete for the field, Christian claims of knowledge of the total meaning of history must now "be replaced by the idea of an anticipation of a total meaning amid a history still in the making."[40]

These passages indicate a greater emphasis on two things: the concrete historical experience of the human subject and the complex contemporary situation in which this experience takes place. Although present in his earlier work, these two emphases take on a new importance in Schillebeeckx's post–Vatican II work and lead him to seek a new understanding of faith that better fits the changed situation.

The council itself is the proximate catalyst for these changes in his thought. The relationship of church and world has always been a central theme for Schillebeeckx.[41] However, only in the wake of the council's acceptance of dialogue with the world and modern forms of thought, and its consequent recognition of the need for a pluralism in theological expression and method,[42] does Schillebeeckx have the mandate, impetus, and intellectual freedom to investigate more broadly the problem of the "understanding of faith" in the specific situation of modernity. As Philip Kennedy puts it, Schillebeeckx goes in search of "verification-criteria to put in the service of a reformulation of faith in terms of contemporary experience."[43] More specifically, Kennedy argues that after 1966 Schillebeeckx attempts to come to grips with the "Lessing problem," that is, "how a particular historical event can be said to mediate universal significance and truth."[44] In other words, the open windows and dialogue promoted by the council led Schillebeeckx to a serious reappraisal of the meaning of Jesus of Nazareth in the modern world.

In the explosive and optimistic years immediately following the council, Schillebeeckx embarked on a nearly decade-long exploration of contemporary theology, biblical exegesis, and philosophy in order to fulfill the aims listed above. His reading in philosophy touched on nearly every school of twentieth-century thought: semiotics, structuralism, linguistic analysis, critical theory, and the thought of Ludwig Wittgenstein and Emanuel Levinas as well as other philosophical approaches.[45] However, immediately after his 1966 "clear break" with phenomenological and personalist Thomism, Schillebeeckx turned first to the hermeneutics of the humanities, as represented in the thought of Martin Heidegger, Hans-Georg Gadamer, and Paul Ricoeur.

This turn to hermeneutics is the basis for what I call the second circle of Schillebeeckx's epistemology. About this turn, Kennedy asserts that Schillebeeckx's "philosophical groundwork has changed its outer vocabulary while retaining its inner syntax."[46] This second circle is indeed a translation of his perspectivalist epistemology and nonantithetical, dialectical framework into a new philosophical language. Yet this translation is also a transformation as well; Schillebeeckx does not simply cover the inner syntax of thought with new philosophical terminology, but he also makes substantial shifts in content. One should also note that Schillebeeckx will only use this second hermeneutical circle by itself for a short time, before he rethinks it in the light of critical theory and its emphasis on praxis. However, given the frequency with which he still uses the ideas, it is clear that he never abandons the hermeneutical framework to the same extent that he made a "clear break" with the first circle of epistemology; he merely sets it into the context of what I am calling the third and final epistemological circle of theory and praxis, where it is usually couched in discussions of revelation and the authority of experience.

The second epistemological circle in Schillebeeckx's thought is based on the premise that human beings understand the world through interpretative experience. This interpretative act always exists in a dynamic, historical, and hermeneutical circle of pre-understanding or horizon, new experience, and re-shaped horizon. Within this irreducible circle, human beings come to know the objective world interpretatively as this world presents itself to the human knower.

In numerous places in his work, Schillebeeckx presents the basic idea of this circle.

> On the one hand, experience presumes that "something" (an occurrence in nature and history, contact with another human being, etc.) is to be experienced; on the other hand, the experience of this occurrence presumes an interpretative framework which co-determines what we experience. Learning from experiences comes about by bringing new individual experiences into connection with knowledge we have already gained and experiences we have already had. This brings about a dialectic. The entirety of previous experience becomes a new interpretative framework or "horizon of experience," within which we interpret new experiences. At the same time, however, new individual experiences subject this interpretative framework to criticism and correct it, or allow previous experiences to be seen in a new connection. In other words, our experience always occurs within an already established interpretive framework, which in the last analysis is nothing other than the cumulative-personal and collective experience, a tradition of experience.[47]

In order to unpack this dense paragraph (and others like it throughout Schillebeeckx's work), I will focus on four aspects: concrete, interpretative experience and its elements; the pre-understanding of the human subject, expressed in "theories" or "models" and brought forward by historical tradition; the irruption of the objectively other "real" in interpreted experience; and the epochal nature of interpretative frameworks.

After the publication of the *Jesus* and *Christ* books, Schillebeeckx received many questions and criticisms regarding his discussion of human experience and interpretation and their relationship with revelation. He responded to these questions and others in the *Interim Report on the Books* Jesus *and* Christ. It is here that one finds the most complete discussion of concrete experience and the elements contained in it.

As a result of his reading of the hermeneutical philosophy of Heidegger, Gadamer, and Ricoeur, Schillebeeckx consistently argues that human beings do not experience the world in a "raw" state and then make interpretations of what they experience. Rather, in an irreducible fashion, human experience is co-constituted by interpretation; interpretation makes real experience both possible and expressible. As Schillebeeckx puts it, "we see interpretatively."[48] Yet this concrete interpretative experience of the world has different elements in it. Somewhat confusingly, Schillebeeckx begins his discussion of the relationship between experience and interpretation in the *Interim Report* by seemingly denying their mutually co-constituting nature.

> The second hinge on which my two Jesus books turn is concerned with the relationship—in human experience and therefore in the experiential aspect of revelation—between the element of experience and the element of interpretation or expression of experience. Regardless of the way in which other authors intend the term, I shall call this latter the "interpretative element."[49]

However, Schillebeeckx immediately goes on to deny that "experience" is an uninterpreted event to which elements of interpretation are then added.

> Interpretation does not begin only when questions are asked about the significance of what one has experienced. Interpretative identification is already an intrinsic element of the experience itself, first unexpressed and then deliberately reflected on.[50]

Here Schillebeeckx makes a first distinction between different *levels* of interpretative identification: human beings first make an unexpressed interpretative identification as part of the experience and then, upon further reflection, deepen and expand that interpretative identification which may bring to light further authentic dimensions of the original experience. In order to clarify this point further, Schillebeeckx employs the distinction (drawn from linguistic analysis) between first-order and second-order *affirmations* about experiences and uses the analogy (as he does elsewhere) of the experience of love.

> Real love is fed by the experience of love and its own particular ongoing self-expression (in I, 548f., I called expressions of the first, original, interpretative experience "first order" affirmations). However, this growing self-expression makes it possible to deepen the original experience; it opens up the experience and makes it more explicit (in I, 548f., I called these expressions of a further, reflective, interpretative experience "second order" affirmations, without meaning to suggest that they were therefore affirmations of secondary importance).[51]

Schillebeeckx makes one further distinction about the constituent elements in interpretative experience.

> However, there are interpretative elements in our experiences which find their foundation and source directly in what is actually experienced, as the content of a conscious and thus to some degree transparent experience, and there are also interpretative elements which come to us from elsewhere, at least from outside this experience, though it is never possible to draw a clear distinction.[52]

This passage reintroduces some confusion into his discussion, but I think that it is best understood as a distinction between the *sources* of the interpretative elements. On first glance it may seem to be a repetition of the distinction between the various *levels* of interpretative identification, but the distinctions are subtly different. Here Schillebeeckx argues that some human experiences manifest their interpretative elements because of the very nature of the experience. They, in a sense, interpret themselves in a "transparent" fashion. Human beings also draw other interpretative elements from outside the immediate self-interpreting experience in order to make the interpretative identification, but these two sources, Schillebeeckx tells us, cannot be distinguished clearly in any interpretative identification. Note that he does not say that the "extrinsic" *sources* for the interpretative identification must only come into play at the reflective *level* of interpretation of experience. One could argue that any unexpressed interpretative experience contains interpretative elements both self-manifested by the experience and drawn from outside sources. The process of reflection on experience will simply deepen the recognition of both sources in making the interpretation.[53]

Schillebeeckx's sense of the complex interplay between experience and interpretation rests on the philosophical assumptions about the fundamental historicity and linguisticality of the human subject that he has drawn from the work of Heidegger, Ricoeur, Gadamer, and others. As Schillebeeckx understands these thinkers, human beings are co-constituted by their location in time and culture; language and history are not simply expressions of human experience and knowledge, but the very framework that makes experience and knowledge possible. At an early stage in his dialogue with hermeneutics, he states:

> All understanding takes place in a circular movement—the answer is to some extent determined by the question, which is in turn confirmed, extended or corrected by the answer. A new question then grows out of this understanding so that the hermeneutical circle continues to develop in a never-ending spiral. Man can never escape from this circle, because he can never establish once and for all the truth or the content of the word of God. There is no definitive, timeless understanding which raises no more questions. The "hermeneutical circle" thus has its basis in the historicity of human existence and therefore of all human understanding. The interpreter belongs to some extent to the object itself that he is trying to understand, that is, the historical phenomenon. All understanding is therefore a form of self-understanding.[54]

In another place, using language drawn primarily from Heidegger, Schillebeeckx links this historicity of human existence with the linguistic emergence of being itself. Language, instead of simply being what we use to speak about and understand being, actually is prior to concrete speech and is the constitutive medium through which the manifestation of being comes to reality.

> Our relationship with language is therefore not speaking, but listening. The act of speaking cannot be reduced to the structure of linguistic elements or to the subjective intention of the subjects speaking. Heidegger has defined the act of speaking as a mode of being in which being is so constituted that it can be said or expressed. In Heidegger's philosophy, the "linguistic event" is identical with the "ontological difference," that is, the distinction between being and beings, in which being is not *a* being, but the ground or *logos* of beings. This ontological difference is an event of being itself, an act which allows the being to move into the foreground, which throws light on the being.[55]

Therefore language has "itself a hermeneutic function." Since language "lets beings appear in being," the human knower only knows through the medium of language; in other words, "what is manifested thus passes through the filter of human language."[56] In another nonantithetical and dialectical relationship, then, the human subject and objective world are now both responsible for the emergence of being through language. "Speech is therefore being subject to the openness of being, and at the same time the responsibility of man who is speaking and who thus protects being in its openness."[57]

The purpose of this brief excursus into these philosophical underpinnings is to show how in the second circle of his epistemology, Schillebeeckx shifts from a conceptual mediation of the relationship of subject and object (i.e., the first circle) to one rooted in the historical and linguistic nature of human existence. Only through language, which is rooted in human historical temporality, does the human knower grasp the world, even if language itself can always contain more than is specifically said. This shift explains why Schillebeeckx sees all experience as interpreted experience, because the linguistic medium of encounter with the world signifies that human beings understand themselves and the world around them by participating in the creation of *meaning*. Just as the reader participates in the creation of the meaning of a text through interpretation, the human subject creates meaning in the world by interpretative experience. (Schillebeeckx would be quick to point out, however, that human beings do not simply create meaning entirely subjectively. The objective world manifests itself in the interpretative experience of the human subject and provides, much like the concept did in his perspectivalist period, a "positive direction" for interpretation.)[58]

The human subject does not participate in the creation of meaning through language outside of time. Because human beings are inescapably historical, their language is not their own immediate creation but something given them by their historical context. Hence every human being approaches a new experience only from a tradition, that is, from the accumulated linguistic expressions of past experiences that provide a horizon of understanding. In the hermeneutical circle the new experiences can "break into" the already given horizon of experiences and reshape it, but no experience is possible without the pre-understanding provided by tradition.[59]

This pre-understanding is the source for the "external" interpretative elements that blend with the "inner" interpretative elements provided by the objective quality of the experience itself. However, as Schillebeeckx's understanding of hermeneutics deepened over the years,[60] he argued that this pre-understanding not only served as a source for interpretative elements in the concrete experience but also as a source for the "theory" or "model" which shaped individual experiences into a general framework of meaning, or, as he often puts it, served as an "experience with experiences."[61]

What more precisely does Schillebeeckx mean by "theory" or "model"? Using the terms almost interchangeably with "pre-understanding," Schillebeeckx writes:

> It is said that a theory never comes into being as a result of inference from experiences; it is an autonomous datum of the creative spirit by means of which human beings cope with new experiences while already being familiar with the long history of experience. Consequently what people call a religious experience contains not only interpretation (in the sense of particular concepts and images) but also a theoretical model on the basis of which divergent experiences are synthesized and integrated.[62]

There are two features to note here. First, as mentioned above, a "theory" or "theoretical model" integrates concrete individual experience with its interpretative elements into a synthesis of wider (or paradigmatic) meaning. It does so not only after the fact by "fitting" an experience into a wider preexisting framework, but before as well. Since all human beings stand within the hermeneutical circle and never approach an experience except through the mediation of a prior tradition, they always approach a new experience with at least an implicit theory. From this theory comes the external interpretative elements used to interpret new experience, which in turn can give rise to a new theory or a new general synthesis of previous experiences.

However, the creation of this theory is not simply a matter of induction from experiences. Schillebeeckx's second point is that theory is "an autonomous datum of the human spirit" or "the result of the creative initiative of the human spirit."[63] In the hermeneutical circle, as Schillebeeckx understands it, there continues the dynamic and dialectical relationship of subjective knower and objective reality which he described earlier in his career using phenomenological, existentialist, and Thomist terms. As we have seen, the human subject actively participates in the creation of meaning by using the *sources* for interpretative elements, both internal and external. The subject also creates meaning by reflection on and expression of experience in the various *levels* of first- and second-order affirmations. Both these sources and levels, however, are set in the broader context of the theoretical *models* which the subject creates (not alone, but in the intersubjective community of language, culture, and tradition) to integrate all past and new experiences into an overarching way of seeing the whole of the world.

Yet, just as in the first circle, the subjective and objective exist only in a nonantithetical and dialectical relationship. Although some critics have argued that Schillebeeckx's adaptation of hermeneutics should not allow him to maintain this dialectical relationship,[64] he consistently holds that human subjective creativity is met by the self-manifesting and self-directing nature of the objective world itself. Human interpretative experience is never simply the creation of the human spirit. Reality irrupts in experience, takes interpretative elements and models from the tradition's pre-understanding, and reshapes them into a new understanding and new affirmation. Schillebeeckx's maintaining of this dialectic allows him room to speak of religious experience and revelation within the context of human experience (see chapter 2).

At first Schillebeeckx talks about this objective side of the dialectic in language that is reminiscent of his earlier perspectivalist views, although this language is now placed within the discussion of the hermeneutical circle and focuses on the interpretation of texts. For example, in "Towards a Catholic Use of Hermeneutics," Schillebeeckx writes at several points about the reader's need to submit to the authority of the text, or, better, to the reality to which the text gives witness.

> Thus the meaning of a text is indeed related to the question that is asked—it is only in the context of this question that the text can be meaningfully understood. The answer (which is nevertheless given by the *text* itself) thus transcends what is literally in the text. And yet the interpreter is obedient to the authority of the text and his asking of questions and his preliminary drafting of answers are constantly corrected in a contemporary reinterpretative understanding of the text itself.[65]

Then, more specifically regarding this surplus of meaning in the text to which one is nevertheless obedient, Schillebeeckx goes on to say:

> But this "intended meaning" is included in a meaning which has not yet been consciously perceived by the author himself and has still to be unveiled—a meaning, that is, which is implicit in everything that is expressed in this "saying and intending" and which discloses itself without having been thematically intended.

Taking the texts themselves as his point of departure, the interpreter therefore goes beyond the texts and their meaning and enquires about the *reality* to which the texts intentionally or unintentionally bear witness.[66]

In the particular case of the interpretation of the Bible and the Christian tradition, Schillebeeckx argues that, although each believer interprets from her or his existential situation and pre-understanding, there is an "objective perspective of faith" which as a "dynamic self-identity" is the permanent element in faith's historical understanding. The reality behind the text in this case is the ongoing relationship of God with humanity which also stands behind the contemporary believer's reading of the text.

The objective *perspective* of faith, which is not in itself thematic and cannot be conceptualized, is thus to some extent brought to light and expressed *in* reinterpretation as it were by a circuitous route (via the interpretative aspect of the act of faith), with the consequence that it becomes a power for action which is directed towards the future.[67]

This early approach to hermeneutics was marked by its emphasis on the understanding of texts. As Schillebeeckx searches for a more solid ground on which to rest his new theological method, he shifts his usage of the hermeneutic circle from the understanding of texts to the more general concept of human experience. His reading in semiotics, structuralism, linguistic analysis, and other philosophy convinces him that a general hermeneutic theory must clearly distinguish the relationship of reader and text from the relationship of two communicating speakers, with the latter having a certain priority.[68] Nevertheless, Schillebeeckx's refined hermeneutical theory will still assume the self-manifestation of reality as an essential part of the hermeneutical circle. As we have seen in his discussion of concrete experience and interpretation, some interpretative elements have their source in the experience itself; that is, some experiences have such a quality that they "transparently" manifest their meaning, even if this meaning must also be interpreted and expressed in language and concepts drawn from "external" sources.

To jump ahead somewhat, a specific example of this hermeneutical circle in operation is Schillebeeckx's much discussed exegesis of the resurrection stories in the first book of the *Jesus* trilogy. He argues that the "Easter event" was neither purely a subjective recognition on the part of the disciples of the overall value of Jesus' life and message nor a purely objective resuscitation of

Jesus accompanied by an empty tomb and visible appearances. Instead, Schillebeeckx states, the resurrection was the disciples' experience of forgiveness after the death of Jesus, at the initiative of Jesus, who "was seen" or who was made manifest to them in the significance of his earthly life and then trans-historical reality.[69] For the immediate purpose here, one should note that the Easter experience is the paradigmatic example of the nonantithetical and dialectical relationships that structure Schillebeeckx's thinking. The Easter event is a dialectic of the subjective faith of the disciples and the objective manifestation of the living Jesus which meet in an experience that has an inner, self-interpreting power.

> First of all we must draw a distinction—even if an inadequate one— between "Easter experience" and the articulation factor in this "experiential event," the resort to language, which is at the same time an interpretation within a given horizon of understanding. The term "experiential event" is used advisedly in order to exclude a purely "subjective" experience. To put it another way: after his death Jesus himself stands at the source of what we are calling the "Easter experience" of the disciples; at all events what we meet with here is an experience of grace. But *qua* human experience it is self-cognizant and spontaneously allied with a particular expression of itself.[70]

Whether evoked by a text or present in an experiential encounter, according to Schillebeeckx the real or the objective always forms an irreducible pole in the hermeneutical circle. Yet because the subjective (and intersubjective) human knower only meets the objectively real in interpretative experience, the human grasp on the real is always partial, and conditioned by the situation of the knower. In this sense, at least, Schillebeeckx's first circle and second circle of epistemology agree with each other, despite the obvious differences in the two perspectives.

One of the greatest differences between the two circles is Schillebeeckx's more thoroughgoing embrace of the radical historicity of the human subject in the second circle. Concrete experience is always interpreted experience; interpretation relies on both internal and external elements; these external elements are often drawn from the historical traditions within which all understanding must take place; these traditions in turn form pre-understandings and theoretical models which integrate the diversity of human experience into overarching views of self, world, and God.

However, theoretical models and traditions of understanding themselves are thoroughly enmeshed in the tide of history. Beyond even models and pre-understandings handed down by tradition, according to Schillebeeckx, the hermeneutical circle at its broadest also includes what I call the "epochal" level. In order to grapple with the question of understanding the significance of Jesus in a modern world centuries removed from the forms of thought and life in the ancient world, Schillebeeckx introduces a three-fold distinction to explain the rhythms of cultural change in history.[71] First, there is " 'fact-constituted history' or 'ephemeral history,' with its brief and rapidly expiring rhythm; the events of everyday come and go." Second, there is " 'conjunctural history,' which is more expansive, has a more profound reach, and is more comprehensive, but then at a much slower tempo or rate of change; in other words a cultural conjuncture lasts a long time." (Schillebeeckx also calls this plane the "epochal" further below.) Finally, there is " 'structural history,' with a time-span of centuries, almost bordering on the central point between what moves and what does not, although not standing outside of history."[72] Schillebeeckx likens the relationship between these three planes to that of "a turning but stationary top, around which everything revolves fast or not so fast."[73] Since human thinking is as much bound to these planes as any other element of human life, Schillebeeckx uses this schema to explain how thinking from the past can both be alien to contemporary forms of thought and yet in some way understandable to them. Beyond the ephemeral level of the mundane and the "modish," the conjunctural level preserves over a longer period of time the intellectual spirit of the age.

> Now what has been called the "epochal horizon of the intellect," of thinking done within the bounds of "interpretative models" (with the mark of a particular period upon them) or a horizon of "current" experience—all this I would put in the second plane of "history"; in other words, the particular horizon of experience and intellection, conditioned by the spirit of the age, belongs to "conjunctural history": this is more firmly and deeply based than is day-to-day thinking and experience with their fleeting character; a given intellective horizon, therefore, persists through a whole period.[74]

Beneath even these slow changes in conjunctural history is the even more slowly moving structural history of humanity. Schillebeeckx argues that this structural history manifests itself in the different periods of conjunctural history and allows for human understanding across these periods. This does not mean, however, that structural history contains some timeless "essence" of human nature; Schillebeeckx consistently states that, just as a concrete experience is always a dialectic of encountered reality and interpretative elements, structural history is only manifested in the particular thought forms of a period of conjunctural history.

> We must remember that even in that sector these three planes of non-simultaneity are not parallel nor separately procurable but criss-crossing one another; together they form just a single history of thinking. We do not mean to say that in addition to changing concepts in man's thinking there are also lastingly valid concepts which can be supposed to survive intact every more or less fundamental shift in the experiential or world horizon. We do mean that the basic structure of human thinking asserts itself in the conjuncturally conditioned ideas and in the changing horizon of man's understanding and experience.[75]

Schillebeeckx places "interpretative models" within the conjunctural level of human history. Hence these models reflect a wider "spirit of the age" and also manifest the deeper structural elements of human history. However, as history proceeds and a new phase of conjunctural history arises, these interpretative models will themselves need interpretation. Because of the deep structures of human history this reinterpretation is possible; because of the shifts over time, this reinterpretation is necessary.[76] Human understanding, therefore, takes place in a hermeneutical circle that spans historical epochs where even tradition itself is subject to the slow changes of the thought forms of a particular age.

In distinction from the first circle, the relationship of praxis to knowledge becomes a topic of explicit reflection in this second circle. Since much of this material comes from a later period of Schillebeeckx's thought when he placed more explicit emphasis on the interrelationship of theory and praxis, it is difficult to distinguish what belongs to each circle. In the formative intellectual interim between 1966 and 1971, when Schillebeeckx first turned to the hermeneutics of the humanities and then started to move beyond them, he makes suggestive hints about the importance of praxis but does not develop these ideas further at the time. For example, near the end of "Towards a Catholic Use of Hermeneutics," Schillebeeckx suggests that the ultimate test of the orthodoxy of any new Christian interpretation is orthopraxis.

What Bultmann has called the "Woraufhin," what biblical interpretation "points to," cannot, in the last resort, therefore be what Bultmann meant it to be; it must be orthodoxy (the correct interpretation of the promise insofar as it has already been realized in the past) as the basis of the orthopraxis whereby the promise realizes a new future in us. It is only in the sphere of action—of doing the faith—that orthodox interpretation can be inwardly fulfilled.[77]

In an even stronger fashion, Schillebeeckx writes in another article from roughly the same time:

> The *identity* of the new concept of God with the original Christian message will have to come indirectly to light in the activity of Christians themselves. If a reinterpretation of the Christian message produces an activity in which its identity with the Gospel cannot be discovered, this interpretation cannot be a Christian interpretation. It will therefore be apparent that there is a special kind of *understanding* which is appropriate to statements about faith—such statements, after all, have nothing to do with ideology. Hermeneutics consisting of the very practice of Christian life are therefore the *basis* for the concrete exegesis of ancient, biblical or magisterial texts.[78]

In both of these examples, particularly in the first one, orthopraxis functions as a *test* for correct interpretation. At this stage Schillebeeckx does not yet consider praxis as a *source* of knowledge, or, more precisely, he does not see it as paired with theory as part of a dialectical relationship in which knowledge occurs. The second example indicates a move in this direction, but Schillebeeckx will only complete this move when he engages in a constructive dialogue with the critical theory of the Frankfurt School.

The second circle of Schillebeeckx's epistemology places the human subject thoroughly within the flow of human history. In this historical perspective, human beings know the world around them through an interpretative encounter with it. This encounter always occurs within the larger circles of language, tradition, and theoretical models and yet stands open to the objectively real which manifests itself in experience. As thoroughly enmeshed as human beings are in history and language, Schillebeeckx in this circle sees that this language and history, no matter what the spirit of the age, can express this encounter with reality and, reflecting his central concern, can express the encounter with the divine reality within the conditions of human finitude.

The Third Epistemological Circle: Critical Theory and Praxis

Schillebeeckx's optimistic embrace of the hermeneutics of the humanities mirrors the euphoria that swept the Catholic world following the Second Vatican Council. However, it did not take long for a combination of internal and external factors to force Schillebeeckx to reconsider his early and relatively simple equation of textual hermeneutics with the reinterpretation of the Christian faith for the modern world. Already a well-known figure in Dutch Catholicism, Schillebeeckx became an internationally known theologian through his work at the council, his travels, and his participation in founding the theological journal *Concilium*. At the same time that his reputation grew around the world, his involvement in the daily life of the Dutch Church and society, never far from his theological concern, took on even greater public prominence. During the course of the council and its aftermath, the Dutch Catholic Church quite unexpectedly changed from one of the more conservative churches in Europe to one of the most progressive. Taking with full seriousness the council's calls for collegiality and the active participation of the laity in all the dimensions of the life of the church, Dutch Catholics during the period of 1965–70 conducted an experiment in actual collegial structures of church governance, the Dutch Pastoral Council, which involved bishops, clergy, and laity in setting national policy for the Dutch Church.[79] At the same time "contestation groups" arose on both the right and the left, the former arguing that the changes in Dutch Catholicism had gone too far, and the latter calling for the development of "critical base communities," which would serve as a leaven for both church and society.[80] In this flurry of change, Schillebeeckx attempted, along with Cardinal Alfrink, the head of the Dutch Church, to steer a middle course that would keep all the elements in the church in communion with each other. Nevertheless, during this period Schillebeeckx also identified himself with the cause of the communities and, in the words of one commentator, became their "sympathetic theological critic and spokesman."[81] His connection with these communities also led him to make a more critical evaluation of his earlier turn to hermeneutics as a basis for theological methodology.[82]

Schillebeeckx's reputation and sympathetic identification with the critical communities in the Dutch Church did not leave him immune from criticism. In the final years of the 1960s, a group of young theologians, mostly Belgian and Dutch, formed a group often called the "theologians of contestation."[83] These thinkers challenged both of the strategies then prevalent for framing the church's theological approach to the modern world. The first approach so criticized, a "theology of the christianisation of the world," hearkened back to the old medieval synthesis and was still present as a form of "ecclesiological narcissism" in Vatican II's statements on the relationship of the church and the modern world.[84] The second option, a "theology of the secularization of the world," argued that "*modernity, in so far as it realizes the 'secularisation of the world' and the 'historization of human existence' is actually and rightly the historical result of the Christian faith.*"[85] According to the theologians of contestation, this premise leads theologians of secularization to create a dualism of church and world that accepts the secularized world as a natural result of the historical dynamics of Christian faith. On the other hand, this secularization forces the church to emigrate from society into a world of privatized and invisible spirituality. The concrete relationship between the church as a social institution and the wider society is ignored.[86] Consequently, this too easy *rapprochement* between secularized society and withdrawn church allows for no real critical praxis in relation to either institution.[87]

The theologians of contestation recognized that some theologians had attempted to overcome these deficiencies in the theology of secularization by constructing a "political theology" or a "dialectical theology of society." However, these attempts also did not sufficiently overcome the dualism of church and world that makes the theology of secularization politically ineffective. Schillebeeckx is named in this connection.

What one could call the *dialectical theology of society* and *political theology* try to "correct" the theology of secularization, but (precisely as "theology"!) seem to gloss over its fundamental structures. The "correction" aims at the personalism or the anthropocentric character of the theologians of secularization. For this reason, they let themselves be inspired by a *theory of history* which has its source within the problematic of the Enlightenment, such as it has been thematised and extended by Hegel or by the left-wing Hegelians and Ernst Bloch. It seems that E. Schillebeeckxs [*sic*] himself is drawing near to this new theological form of thought.[88]

More specifically, the authors refer to the article translated into English as "The New Image of God, Secularization and Man's Future on Earth." In this essay Schillebeeckx introduces the concept of God as the future of humanity and argues that this concept better fits the existential situation of contemporary people by bringing the biblical message of promise and fulfillment into a dialectical harmony with this situation. For the theologians of contestation, this harmonization falls prey to the same critique that they lodged against the theology of secularization: Schillebeeckx is not sufficiently critical of the phenomenon of secularization and still, despite the hints of a praxis-oriented theology in this essay, remains largely on the level of the ideal. The theologians of contestation pose the following question to any theologian who wants to talk about the political importance of the practice of the faith: "Do the actual bearers of the 'liberating critique' of society and of the 'negative mediation' have any *reason* whatsoever, theoretical or above all practical, for 'identifying' themselves with ecclesial institutions?"[89] In other words, what is the practical reality of Christian faith and ecclesial life that brings about liberation in society? What is the source for a concrete Christian critique of society and church?

These critical questions, accompanied by the explosive changes in Dutch and worldwide Catholicism, led Schillebeeckx to embark on a year-long intellectual journey for a more adequate grounding for his contemporary reinterpretation of the understanding of faith. As mentioned above, Schillebeeckx, building on his explorations into phenomenology and hermeneutic philosophy, sought insight from linguistic analysis (especially Wittgenstein and I. P. Ramsey), structuralism, semiotics, and other philosophical perspectives. Although all of these provided useful insights, which Schillebeeckx integrated eclectically into his own viewpoint, the most important conversation partner for Schillebeeckx's later theology, and the main source for what I am calling the third circle of his epistemology, is the critical theory of the Frankfurt School.[90]

Drawing on both the first (Theodor Adorno, Max Horkheimer) and second (the early Jürgen Habermas) generations of critical theory, Schillebeeckx in effect translates the second circle of hermeneutics, into the third circle of theory and praxis. His earlier concern with experience becomes a focus on negative contrast experiences; the importance of linguistic pre-understanding becomes a focus on ideology critique; the historicity of human existence becomes a focus on the narratives of human suffering.

More formally stated, the third circle of epistemology is founded on the idea that human knowledge of objective reality comes through practical mediation and the theoretical expression inseparably attached to it. Privileged moments in this circle of praxis and theory are negative contrast experiences, where knowledge of reality comes both through reality's resistance to human expectations and human, active, hopeful resistance to that which destroys human flourishing. Because of the narrative structure of human experience, the history of contrast experiences narrated in the history of human suffering is an especially privileged source of knowledge.

As with the other circles, Schillebeeckx's discussion of the relationship of theory and praxis must often be analytically separated from other contexts. This move toward praxis, already hinted at in the second circle, becomes the backbone of this new epistemological and thereafter theological understanding. Responding to the critical movements in society, church, and theology, Schillebeeckx, because of his dialogue with the Frankfurt School, rejects his earlier reliance on the hermeneutics of the humanities because it still aims at a purely theoretical grasp of the truth, even if it takes into account the conditions of history and language. Schillebeeckx now argues that these very conditions of history and language also contain the possibility of ideological distortion and that therefore ideology critique is necessary. Ideology critique, as he describes it elsewhere, means "the unmasking of the naïve idea that *being* and *language* (= thinking and speaking), in spite of all the conceptual inadequacy already recognized classically, should always correlate to each other according to their content."[91] Hermeneutic philosophy can fall into this naïve equation either by postulating a universal meaning of history or by relying on a positive pre-understanding of the human being that is too narrowly conceived. Either of these attempts can too easily cover over the possible contradictions and distortions that are part of any historical situation.[92] Hearkening back to Marx's dictum (and its retrieval by the Frankfurt School) that the purpose of philosophy is not to understand the world but to transform it, Schillebeeckx argues that praxis is a necessary element in the human grasp of the truth. This truth cannot be theoretically possessed under the conditions of human history because of human finitude and possible distortion; it can only be enacted in an anticipatory way. The practical and proleptic nature of truth becomes the new framework for epistemology.

Schillebeeckx expresses this in the context of a proper understanding of theological hermeneutics.

> In interpreting the past in the light of the present, then, it should not be forgotten that eschatological faith imposes on the present the task of

transcending itself, not only theoretically, but also as a change to be realised. Only the critical attitude towards the present, and the resulting imperative to change and improve it, really open access to the coming truth. The basic hermeneutic problem of theology, then, is not so much the question of the relationship between the past (scripture and tradition) and the present, but between theory and praxis, and this relationship can no longer be solved idealistically, by a theory of Kantian pure reason from which consequences flow for the practical reason, but it will have to be shown how the theory appears in the praxis itself.[93]

Schillebeeckx notes that the basic hermeneutic problem is indeed the relationship between theory and praxis, but his own writings often do not provide a clear picture of this relationship. On the one hand, praxis becomes an "inner element of the principle of verification" of truth.[94] When specifically discussing the relationship of orthodoxy and orthopraxis, Schillebeeckx can say "faith in action as hope for all, a faithful praxis of prayer and liberating action becomes the foundation of all further theological and interdisciplinary theory-building."[95] So with regard to epistemology, praxis is both the *disclosive source* for and *critical test* of truth and its theoretical expression. On the other hand, Schillebeeckx will also say that praxis is always accompanied by a theoretical expression,[96] and, even more important, praxis alone is not a sufficient criterion for truth. To cite just one example from another context, Schillebeeckx argues that the praxis of critical Christian communities is not justified simply because it is being done.

> Thus the practice of particular Christian, and above all critical, communities was the stimulus and challenge to this study. Does this mean that the actual alternative practices of these Christian communities and their leaders in relation to the ministry become the "norm and truth," and thus determine the reading of earlier texts? Not at all: this would be the pure empiricism of pragmatism. Even pastoral effectiveness is not decisive in matters of truth; in this sense I reject the so-called principle of "orthopraxis" as a principle of truth. (In that case the "orthopraxis" of a thorough-going Nazi would also validate the "orthodoxy" of Nazism as truth! I.e., thorough-going belief in a doctrine does not make that doctrine true or sound.) The actual practice of Christian communities, legally or illegally, depending on the norms of canonical church order, is the interpretandum, i.e., what must be justified in theory, and must per-

haps be criticized. For a theologian, what is called Christian practice is never a direct norm, but his agenda, i.e., that which he must clarify secundum scripturas, in the light of the great Christian tradition.[97]

Here in theological language Schillebeeckx argues that praxis must find its justification in the broader context of a narrative tradition. However, this narrative tradition expresses its pre-understandings in terms of theoretical models which in turn express the spirit of the age and shape these narratives themselves. Hence, in a reciprocal fashion, praxis finds its *disclosive source* and *critical test* in theory. The tension here in Schillebeeckx's work is that he wishes to place theory and praxis in this reciprocal relationship while clearly maintaining the primacy of praxis over theory.[98]

Although this presentation seems "paradoxical," as Kennedy notes, I would argue that this is another example of the nonantithetical and dialectical thinking that pervades Schillebeeckx's work. Furthermore, it is here, I think, that the first two epistemological circles meet the third in yet another dialectic. Schillebeeckx's earlier thought rests on a dialectic of the active interpreting subject and the objective determining reality. Particularly in the second circle, he describes this experience of knowledge in terms of disclosure. In the move to this third circle, he sets the disclosure experience within this circle of theory and praxis, a circle based on a transformative model of truth. Yet Schillebeeckx argues that there is a dialectical relationship between these models. Disclosure of truth at the level of meaning necessarily accompanies the perception of truth realized in praxis. Otherwise, emancipative praxis runs the risk of being without content.

> Beyond that we do not experience a liberating truth in an authentic praxis without at the same time perceiving the disclosure of what here and now is recognized as true. The meaning-revealing "disclosure" model of truth cannot be separated from the "meaninglessness-explaining" transformative model of truth. Any praxis, which really enslaves human beings, is indeed excluded a-priori as a candidate for truth; but on the other hand even "effective," that is, actually liberative praxis is therefore still not a "norm of truth." If liberative praxis discloses no meaning and no truth, the danger exists that it becomes a matter of a contentless emancipation, which, as truncated emancipation, in the long run again becomes enslaving of human beings.[99]

The ultimate standard for truth according to this passage is whether a praxis will enslave human beings and destroy them. Using a term drawn from Ernst Bloch's philosophy, Schillebeeckx will name this standard the *humanum,* which is the always hoped for fullness of human life and the criterion of authentic praxis and its accompanying theory. But this *humanum,* as Schillebeeckx describes it, is only known in anticipation and hope, never in its positive fullness. Hence he will argue that human beings come into contact with this *humanum* only through negative experiences and human resistance to this negativity. Therefore the resolution of this tension between theory and praxis, or, more specifically, the models of truth contained in this interrelationship, Schillebeeckx finds in the categories of negative contrast experiences and narratives of human suffering.

In his search for a more universal grounding for a contemporary interpretation of Christian faith, Schillebeeckx turns to the negative dialectics of Adorno, Horkheimer and, to an extent, Ricoeur.[100] Offered originally by these philosophers as a critical rethinking of the Marxist view of society, these "negative dialectics" oppose the hegemony of scientific and Enlightenment rationality in contemporary culture and instead argue for a constant critical posture against any attempt by modernity to claim an ultimate and positive definition of humanity. The basis of this critical posture is not another positive (and possibly ideological) view of humanity but an experience of the *humanum* realized through negative experiences of suffering and threat. Schillebeeckx's use of negative dialectics will focus on two dimensions of these negative contrast experiences: first, the experience of refractory reality which interrupts human hopes and plans and in extreme cases threatens human life; second, the vague knowledge of the *humanum* gained from the passive reception of suffering and the active resistance to that which threatens human life. As Schillebeeckx puts it,

> Human beings live from assumptions and hypotheses, from projects and constructs, and so from trial and error. Their plans constantly run the risk of being destroyed by the resistance and arbitrariness of a reality which does not always measure up to rational human anticipations. When reality offers resistance to human designs and thus implicitly neutralizes them, we find ourselves in living contact with a reality *independent* of us, a reality not conceived or created by human beings. One can therefore say that reality draws near to us through alienation and the disintegration of what we have already achieved and of our future plans.

Because of this, it is not the self-evident, but the scandal of an arbitrary reality which becomes the hermeneutical principle for the disclosure of reality.[101]

According to Schillebeeckx this "scandal of an arbitrary reality" is not the last word in the negative contrast experience. As I mentioned above, the inner human resistance to this scandal and the active human attempts to overcome it rest upon a basic, if diffuse, anticipatory knowledge of the *humanum*, the fullness of human life. Schillebeeckx argues that such resistance always accompanies these negative contrast experiences, no matter what the cultural setting, and therefore forms a more universal basis of knowledge.[102] So the anticipation of the *humanum*, in whatever form this takes, is also a universal aspect of knowledge. In stating this, Schillebeeckx differs from the critical theorists of the Frankfurt School insofar as he thinks that a purely negative critical theory runs the risk of becoming an ineffective ideology.[103] A positive anticipation of wholeness and actual, if fragmentary, experiences of it fill out the epistemological possibilities of the negative contrast experience. In a more succinct form, Schillebeeckx designates the type of knowledge derived from negative contrast experiences as "practical-cum-critical,"[104] or as having "cognitive, critical, and productive" force.[105] However, he argues that negative contrast experiences could only give rise to action on the basis of this anticipated *humanum*. Resistance and praxis, and therefore the knowledge derived from them, can only come from this fundamental human hope.

Schillebeeckx critiques critical theory itself for its practical ineffectiveness and ideological staleness. He attempts to ground this theory's usefulness not only in the concrete positive and anticipatory experiences of the *humanum*, as mentioned above, but also through a connection with the narratives of human suffering and their epistemological force.

Schillebeeckx's wide-ranging and eclectic reading during this period led him to embrace a narrative model for human knowledge and ultimately for theology. Influenced by Steven Crites's 1971 article "The Narrative Quality of Experience,"[106] Schillebeeckx couples this use of narrative categories with his earlier hermeneutical and later critical thinking to create the idea of the critical epistemological power of narrative traditions, particularly the narratives of the accumulated history of human suffering. Broadening the scope for the consideration of negative contrast experiences (which still could be conceivably interpreted in individualistic terms), Schillebeeckx locates these experiences in narratives of suffering, where social and political oppression, destruction, and resistance must be given their full weight in any presentation of what is known as true.

> This implicit knowing about the hidden magnets of reality which become manifest in negative experiences has something extraordinarily positive about it, even though it is a kind of knowing which is not completely objectifiable or capable of articulation. It is precisely for this reason that the negative contrast experiences can never be a goal in themselves, for then it would become unproductive. The authority of experience *culminates* therefore in human histories of suffering: the suffering of failure and renunciation, the suffering of physical pain, the suffering from evil and injustice, the suffering of love, of guilt and finitude. The great moments of the revelation of reality lie here in and through the *finite experiences* of human beings.[107]

However, this accumulated history of suffering is not a source of knowledge simply as a reminder from the past. Given the constant and necessary interplay between theory and praxis in this third epistemological circle, the narratives of human suffering, like the negative contrast experiences of which they are made, have epistemological force only as an impetus for action in the present situation. The history of human suffering must become actualized in a contemporary circle of theory and praxis to overcome suffering if that history is to carry its full weight.[108]

This third circle of epistemology contains a densely overlapping web of nonantithetical and dialectical relationships. Theory and praxis form the fundamental relationship. But this dialectical circle must itself be dialectically related to concrete negative contrast experiences and the narratives of human suffering lest it remain too abstract and without real effect on the suffering world. However, negative contrast experiences and the narrative of human suffering only have epistemological force when they give rise to authentic praxis to overcome suffering. As we have seen, at every level of Schillebeeckx's epistemology, objective reality always forms one pole of the relationship as it directs, molds, and interrupts the purely subjective dimension of the human knower. In this third circle, reality again shapes knowledge. Here real liberation from suffering is the touchstone for reality. Suffering itself is the interruptive shock which brings the knower face to face with reality; but the active overcoming of evil discloses the fullness of reality, the positive counterpoint to the stories of suffering, the *humanum* which is never fully grasped but always present in hope. At this point the purely epistemological discussion blends into the theological for Schillebeeckx, for the positive human experience of the *humanum* in turn will find its basis in the inexhaustible and pure positivity of God.

In this complex experience of suffering, hope, and resistance, Schillebeeckx discovers the surest ground for an epistemology which is critically conscious, oriented to praxis, and ultimately open to the saving presence of God.[109] I have argued that this "third circle" represents Schillebeeckx's most articulated understanding of epistemology, but it also rests on the foundation of the previous two circles (and also on certain theological presuppositions which will be made more clear in chapter 2). Yet even if this third circle is the most complete form of his thought, Schillebeeckx does not always use all of its elements in any particular discussion of epistemology or experience. For example, at times he apparently relies on the second circle and does not make clear the role of praxis in relationship to knowledge.[110] Nevertheless, on the whole, the dialectical relationships of theory and praxis, negative contrast experiences and narratives of suffering, make up the framework for his later uses of both perspectivalist and hermeneutical language, even if these earlier circles also are the presuppositions of the last.

On the basis of this epistemology, Schillebeeckx finally will draw some conclusions about human beings and human language. Eschewing any sort of "essentialist" view of humanity or any nonideological view of language, he will instead argue for certain "anthropological constants" which are "'dangerous memories' of everything which humanity has gained, in historical situations which have mostly run an unhappy course, in wisdom and painful insights into the conditions of true humanity."[111] In short form these "constants" are: human freedom must be set in the context of a relationship with the natural world; "personal identity is not possible without real human mutuality"; humans live in a dialectical and necessary relationship between personal identity and social institutions; human history is a process of learning through success and failure; human survival and flourishing depend on far more than natural instinct or the "survival of the fittest"; and human beings need "all-embracing conceptions, a 'universe of meaning' or vision, a kind of all-encompassing project which bestows meaning into which they seek to bring their individual experiences, if they do not wish to lapse into nihilism."[112] Similarly, on the basis of this understanding of epistemology, Schillebeeckx summarizes the relationship between knowledge, experience, ideology, and language. First, language is both the medium in which experience occurs and the means of its expression. Language is divorced from neither human contexts nor human cognitive ability. Therefore it is distinct from experience and can have an ideological function. Second, language can obscure or distort the experience that it originally was intended to express. Third, appeals to "direct experience" must be greeted with critical analysis, because language located in a particular context always mediates experience to the knower. Fourth, language and its speakers come from a very specific social position and therefore linguistic usage must be critically appraised with an awareness of the situation and its interests. Fifth, language uses models that are creations of the human intellect that synthesize diverse experiences. Sixth, language contains "projective elements" which arise from the relationship between the "sub-conscious (personal and collective) and reflective consciousness" and produce cultural and master symbols which create a vision of the future for human beings. Finally, religious language itself always contains nonreligious elements drawn from the experiential background of the human knower.[113]

"Whatever is received is received in a way suited to the recipient." Thomas's dictum still holds true in Schillebeeckx's thought, even as he has constructed an enormously complex understanding of human knowledge, action, and language. Humans use language, receive knowledge, and come to the truth through these three epistemological circles. And only within these circles will the experience of salvation come to expression in the language of revelation. To cite another maxim of Thomas with which Schillebeeckx would surely agree, "Grace does not destroy nature, but perfects it."

two | Salvation and Revelation in the
Context of Human Experience

I argued in the first chapter that on the basis of his early formation in the phenomenological Thomism of De Petter, Schillebeeckx expresses his thinking in
a series of often overlapping (and occasionally bewildering) nonantithetical
and dialectical relationships. Long after he had set aside his mentor's philosophical framework for the more fertile fields of hermeneutics and critical
theory, Schillebeeckx still retained as formal features of his thought the rejection of strict dualisms and the attempt to synthesize disparate elements into
dynamic and mutually determining relationships. Analysis precedes synthesis
in Schillebeeckx's thought, but the ultimate goal (and one might add, the original starting point) is the dialectical unity of synthesis.[1] Since these formal features hold for all of his thought, the analytic moments of this work are only
that, moments which must be reintegrated into a synthesis if the full complexity and depth of his thought is to become apparent.

From the previous discussion it is clear that Schillebeeckx is not interested
in laying out a purely formal epistemology. As some of the quotations illustrated, the structures of this epistemology can only be extracted from other
discussions of revelation and the specifically Christian knowledge of God.
This is not surprising, given that, being a theologian, Schillebeeckx's main
concern is to show how contemporary people can experience and speak meaningfully about God. His far-reaching epistemological forays are the necessary
first stage for any discussion of revelation, but the human situation is only
one pole of yet another nonantithetical and dialectical relationship in Schillebeeckx's thought. As his epistemology moves toward his theological presuppositions, Schillebeeckx's understanding of how human beings know the
truth ultimately comes to depend on an understanding of how God is related
to the world.

The purpose of this chapter is to explain more clearly the second pole of this nonantithetical relationship, the one between God and the world as captured by the concepts of creation, salvation, and revelation. An examination of these concepts in Schillebeeckx's thought, and of the specifically Christian event of salvation and revelation as manifested in the life, death, and resurrection of Jesus of Nazareth, will lead to a discussion of Schillebeeckx's Christology, particularly as he has presented it in his later works. It is in these concepts, especially as concentrated in the person of Jesus, that Schillebeeckx locates the positive content of truth, the most complete expression of the *humanum*.

Creation, Salvation, and Revelation: God's Concern for Humanity

In Schillebeeckx's theology, salvation and revelation are terms for God's effective favor toward human beings and the explicit naming of this action as coming from God. They logically depend on his doctrine of creation, even though this doctrine only can be discovered through the explicit language of salvation and revelation. Schillebeeckx states that "creation is the foundation of all theology,"[2] and Philip Kennedy has gone so far as to say that creation is the "one word" which "designates the nucleus of his theological thought."[3] Logically speaking, creation does provide a foundation and background for all his other theological discussions. However, with regard to his intellectual formation and style of thinking, it is his early training in the phenomenological Thomism of De Petter that shapes the formal approach he takes to that doctrine itself. Seeing the God-world relationship in terms of an "ontology of relation," as Kennedy puts it, must derive in part from the phenomenological idea of the irreducible and dialectical relationship of subject and object and in part from the Thomist ontology of the ineluctable similitude of creator and creature. Nonantithetical and dialectical thinking shapes Schillebeeckx's theology to such an extent that it perhaps has no nucleus at all, only a series of interrelationships in constant process.

Nevertheless, creation is the necessary background for discussing salvation and revelation. What does Schillebeeckx mean by the term? Briefly put, creation is the continuing act of the infinite and transcendent God who establishes and preserves creatures in their finitude and is present and immanent to creatures precisely through their finitude. As Kennedy observes, Schillebeeckx's treatment of the doctrine of creation has remained consistent from nearly the beginning of his career, in the unpublished 1956–57 lecture notes titled "Theologische Bezinning op het Scheppingsgeloof" ("The Theological Consciousness of Creation-Faith") down to *Church: The Human Story of God* (1992).[4] In all of these expositions, he first of all denies that creation is an *explanation* (in some quasi-scientific sense) for the world and for human existence. He also denies that creation should be thought of in terms of either emanationism (which would make the world simply a degraded part of God) or dualism (which would depict the world as radically evil and radically separated from the transcendent goodness of God). Drawing on the Thomistic doctrine of creation, which states in part that creation is an act of God unlike other forms of finite causation,[5] Schillebeeckx first argues that creation by God establishes creatures in their good finitude.

> In deliberate contrast to views of this kind [i.e., emanationism and dualism], Jewish belief in creation, after a long period of growing maturity, says that God is God, the sun is the sun, the moon is the moon and man is man, and moreover that God's blessing rests precisely upon that: this is how it is good.[6]

In contrast to views that see finitude as a flaw and a wound, Schillebeeckx sees the Jewish-Christian belief in creation as affirming the fundamental goodness of human life within finite boundaries. Yet finitude is marked by suffering and ultimately by death. The special nature of creation, however, means that God's transcendence can also be immanently present even within the condition of finitude.

> It [creation] means that we may therefore be men in our humanity, albeit also in mortality and suffering. However, what is itself a very oppressive burden means at the same time that God is with and in us, even *in* our failure, even *in* our suffering, even *in* our death, just as he is in and with all our positive experiences and sensations. It also means that he is present in forgiveness for the sinner. The boundary between God and us is our boundary, and not that of God.[7]

This evocative last phrase, often repeated in Schillebeeckx's works, seems to indicate that God's transcendent nature and continuing act of creation are such that God is related to us always as a saving presence, even when the sheer fact of our finitude separates us from direct experience of God and sinfulness erects a further barrier to this experience. Describing creation as God's bound-less (boundary-less?) saving presence to creatures through their finitude means that, at its heart, creation for Schillebeeckx is primarily a doctrine of salvation and for this reason is misunderstood or even distorted if understood as an explanation for the world. Schillebeeckx can even summarize his view of creation in salvation language. "God's honour lies in the happiness and the prosperity of man in the world, who seeks his honour in God: this seems to me to be the best definition of what creation means."[8]

Creation and salvation are inextricably linked,[9] and, as theological doctrines, stand in the same nonantithetical and dialectical relationship that pervades all of Schillebeeckx's thinking. What enables Schillebeeckx to move from creation language to salvation language with such ease, and what holds these two doctrines in dialectical unity, is that in his thought they pertain to the same objective reality: God's concern for humanity. This reality holds precedence over any particular theological formulation; indeed, one could state this as a general principle of Schillebeeckx's theology: reality has a certain precedence over expressions of reality. We have seen that in all three epistemological circles reality provides a directing, shaping, and interrupting element in human knowledge. Similarly, in more strictly theological language, the reality of God's concern for humanity, the reality of salvation, takes a certain primacy over religious and theological expressions of it. Thus, the mystery or experience of salvation is the ground for speech about God. Language about revelation, doctrine, and theology all derive from this more fundamental event, even if, in true dialectical fashion, the experience of salvation never occurs outside of a human context with its forms of thought and theological understandings.

In the first half of his career Schillebeeckx customarily relied on a "salvation history" approach to describe the relationship between salvation and revelation. Having learned the lesson well from his mentors Chenu and Yves Congar, Schillebeeckx opposes the ahistorical and purely conceptual model for understanding revelation that dominated the neo-Thomist theology of the day. He argues that, instead of the revealed concept, primacy must be given to what he variously calls "the reality of salvation"[10] or "revelation in reality."[11] This salvation coming from God only encounters human beings as they actually exist, that is, in their historical reality. Therefore salvation is also a historical reality, an event that God performs in and through the created realities which make up the human world. But creation itself for Schillebeeckx is nothing more than God's saving will directed toward human beings. Because all of creation resonates, as it were, with God's saving will, even at this early stage in his thought Schillebeeckx can argue that the history of salvation is coextensive with the history of human success and failure.

> Within God's universally effective will to save, the world, as creation, as human history, and as human encounter acquires a special significance which it would not otherwise have of its own accord; it appears to us at the same time as a translation, however inadequate, of God's inward appeal to us through grace, as a means in and through which man is made more explicitly aware of this inward offer of grace, and finally as a sphere within which man may respond, either positively or negatively, to this divine appeal. That is why it is possible for us to say that, at least in the perspective of the saving mystery of Christ, the history of salvation or of perdition is as extensive as the human world itself. In other words, the history of salvation is not restricted exclusively to the religion of Israel or to Christianity, but is, because of Christ, an event of universal significance.[12]

The history of salvation may be coextensive with human history, but the two cannot simply be identified. Because of the bodily and spiritual nature of human beings, revelation in reality can only occur in and through the created realities of this world. However, because this reality is finite, God's salvific action remains veiled in the ambiguity of history unless human beings, through God's additional action, bring this reality of salvation to full expression in words. Hence salvation from God always possesses an element of knowledge and an inherent drive toward self-expression, which names it as a reality that both occurs through and in history and transcends history as well.[13] The "reality of salvation" or "revelation in reality" stands in a necessary and dialectical relationship with "revelation in word."

Mary Catherine Hilkert has argued that this interrelationship remains constant through all the stages of Schillebeeckx's theology.[14] In its earliest stage he argues that revelation in word is necessary to bring to full expression the mystery of salvation that God is working in the world. This revelation occurs first through the tradition of the prophets of Israel and culminates in the person who is also Word, Jesus Christ. "As an act of God in historical form, the whole of Jesus' human life was revelation. From his dialogue with the Father, the Son entered our human history, which thereby became, because of Jesus' human freedom, definitive saving history."[15] Yet, even the saving significance of the incarnation would not have been made manifest without the words of

Christ and of Christ's followers as authoritatively recorded in the Scriptures of the New Testament. Schillebeeckx goes on to say:

> But the definitive entry of this salvation in Christ into our history can be historically recognized only in the prophetic message of the same Christ, and only by those who believe in this message. It is only through the revelation of Christ's word that the saving significance of the revelation-in-reality which has been accomplished in the life and death of Christ becomes accessible to us historically in faith. It is precisely because salvation offers itself to us as a supernatural reality in the form of an earthly, secular reality—the humanity of Christ—that this saving reality appears as given and as revealed to us in the word.[16]

The revelation in reality of Christ, brought to full expression by Christ's own revelation in word and the word of the New Testament, is the definitive event of salvation and revelation in the whole history of salvation. From this event comes the church's doctrine and practice, both of which are watched over by the church's teaching authority which, at this stage in Schillebeeckx's thought, is the "regula promixa" of the church's belief and practice and yet also stands under the authority of the original revelatory event (see chapter 3).[17]

Although revelation in word is necessary to bring God's revelation in reality to fulfillment, the reality of God's salvation still surpasses any word that attempts to express it. Revelation in reality has a certain priority over revelation in word, even if they stand in a necessary and dialectical relationship to each other. This understanding of salvation and revelation dovetails neatly with Schillebeeckx's first epistemological circle. Concepts of God held in faith do not grasp the reality of God's being directly, but, arising from the dynamism of creation toward its Creator, provide an objective perspective or direction for the intending mind of the subject. Since God's salvation and revelation only occur in and through the conditions of human life, revelation in word must adhere to the epistemological limits of human language. Therefore, even explicit language of God's revelation is "perspectivalist," that is, it expresses an objective direction through which the mind of the believer may truly approach the reality of God's salvation, although this mystery of salvation can never be fully captured in human language.[18] Even the fullness of revelation, the event of Christ, both unveils and veils God's reality.

Another way of speaking about this dialectical relationship of salvation and revelation is to say that for Schillebeeckx they have a sacramental structure.

Schillebeeckx's doctoral thesis, *De sacramentele heilseconomie* ("The Sacramental Economy of Salvation"),[19] and its "nontechnical" shortened version, *Christ the Sacrament of the Encounter with God*,[20] both seek to offset the "sacramental magic" popularly practiced by many Catholics and reinforced by the abstract and essentialist categories of neo-Thomism. In order to do this, in the former Schillebeeckx sets the Thomist doctrine of the sacraments against the wider tradition of patristic thought; in the latter he especially emphasizes how the sacraments are not objects, but ecclesial events of encounter with the glorified Christ, who himself was the primordial sacrament of the encounter with God for the whole human race.[21] By situating the seven specific sacraments within the general sacramentality of the church and the unsurpassable and concentrated sacramentality of Christ, Schillebeeckx also raises the principle of sacramentality to the level of a fundamental theology. That is, sacramentality now becomes a framework for understanding the relationship between God and the world and the consequent generation of human language about God. When Schillebeeckx outlined the course of salvation history in this early period of his thought, he described this dialectic of revelation in reality and revelation in word as a process, anticipated in a shadowy way in the world at large and then in the life of Israel, that culminates in the life of Christ. In an exactly parallel way Schillebeeckx describes how "humanity in search of the sacrament of God" anticipated the sacramentality of Christ and the church in a vague way in pagan religions and then in partial fashion in the history of Israel.[22] As the title of his dissertation states, salvation history itself is sacramental, because God relates to the human race only sacramentally. The dialectic of revelation in reality and revelation in word matches the sacramental dialectic, so to speak; the sacraments are visible and verbal signs through which the believer encounters in the present the saving reality of God. In both cases the word brings the reality of salvation to its fullest possible expression, but in both cases this word, however God-directed, authentic, and necessary, still fall short of capturing conceptually and linguistically the working of God in human history. Salvation as experienced by the believer retains a certain priority over the expression of this experience in the language of revelation.

In the later stages of his thought Schillebeeckx maintains this understanding of the relationship between salvation and revelation. His movement toward a theology informed by hermeneutics, linguistic analysis, and critical theory does not eliminate the earlier dialectic; it merely grounds this relationship in a more complex and concrete way within the actual course of human history. In fact, in his most recent works, Schillebeeckx can say that salvation must be first understood as a this-worldly reality before one can meaningfully engage in any talk about God's revelation; there is "no salvation outside the world."[23] Schillebeeckx has translated the language of "the reality of salvation" or "revelation in reality" into the critical language of historical consciousness, negative contrast experiences, expectations of the *humanum*, and the narratives of the poor and oppressed. Yet salvation is also more than the liberation of the poor or the overcoming of the forces of evil in human life. In order to explicate this understanding of salvation, I will focus on the relationship between time and the *eschaton* in Schillebeeckx's later thought.

If creation is one of the keys to Schillebeeckx's theology, then eschatology is no less so. Throughout his career, Schillebeeckx has explicitly linked these two doctrines. The language of God's salvific will is used to talk about creation and eschatological language refers to the fulfillment of the history of salvation begun in the creation.

> Protology and eschatology imply each other. The beginning of creation and the end of time include each other and the biblical view of the eschatological kingdom is therefore able to express both with the same images of cosmic peace experienced while walking with God in the garden. They imply each other, not only in the living idea of God's providence that transcends history, but also in the very historical fact of the mystery of Christ and, as a consequence and in the light of this, both in the history of the Old Testament and in the contemporary fact of our created human existence as men who make history and who are subject to God's call to salvation.[24]

This viewpoint, although remaining largely consistent across Schillebeeckx's works, nevertheless undergoes modifications both in content and emphasis with his later moves into the second and third epistemological circles. As Schillebeeckx takes with more seriousness the inescapable historicity of human beings, eschatology moves from the periphery to become a key for explaining the relationship between this historicity and the revealing and saving presence of God. As he then considers more seriously the critical force of negative contrast experiences and the narratives of human suffering, eschatology becomes the source and ground for the language about human hope.

Not long after his 1966 "clear break" with the Thomism of his mentor, De Petter, and influenced by the optimism of the council and the theologians of hope such as Wolfhart Pannenberg and Jürgen Moltmann, Schillebeeckx offered a reinterpretation of the doctrine of God which named God as the future of humanity. Arguing that contemporary people live in a culture oriented toward building a better future for all humanity, he presents this idea as a doctrine which better meets these aspirations and, in line with the biblical dynamic of promise and fulfillment, provides an even greater source of hope than can simply human projects which are always fallible and liable to failure.[25] Schillebeeckx is later less sanguine about the optimism expressed in that essay, but he retains this emphasis on the openness of the human future and the need for a reintegration of Christian eschatological language with the experiences and expectations of people living within the contingencies of history.

Living within history means that human beings live from the past in the present with the possibilities of the future open before them. Schillebeeckx persistently situates human beings within this threefold historical dynamic and refuses to separate one element from another or to undervalue the importance of any one element.[26] Nevertheless, human beings also possess a certain transcendence over time because they can consciously and critically examine the traditions of their past and their hopes for the future.[27] This transcendence gives human beings a certain natural openness toward the future, a belief that is correlated to the idea that God is humanity's future. Mirroring the irreducible temporality of human beings, God is spoken of in the Scriptures as having acted in the past in such a way that this very action, as received and handed on in the present community of faith, is also a promise for the future. "In the bible the interpretation of a past event always coincides with the announcement of a new expectation for the future. The past is 'read again' in a manner which makes it once more actual, and thus it becomes the guarantor for the hope of a new future."[28] In this sense the dynamic of promise and fulfillment is not simply about an event in the past looking forward to an unknown future while remaining untethered to the present. According to Schillebeeckx, the present, the life of the community in its contingency and finitude, is the sole mediator of the promise for the future; it does this only insofar as the community makes actual that promise in a limited way in its own time. Like the individual inseparably enmeshed in past, present, and future, God's action in history must appear in and through these elements. Just as the individual actually lives only in the present, so the community of faith only makes real its faith in God's promise by how its recollection affects its present action. God, community, and individual relate in time, but only at the always new burning edge of the present.[29]

If this is so, what then does Schillebeeckx mean by saying that God is the future of humanity? He means that human beings experience God in the

present as the promise of an as yet unfulfilled and greater future. He argues
that a true eschatological approach to Christian faith in God, as expressed in
the Bible, places the focus on human action in the present that opens out into
the always greater future which is God's. This argument differs sharply from
an apocalyptic perspective that acts from some putative view of the future
toward the present, often with disastrous results.[30] God as the future of humanity does not mean that God will act only in some Armageddon-to-come to
save human beings; it means that God's action in the present saves people by
leading them toward an always greater future of God's ultimate salvation. As
Schillebeeckx poetically puts it at the end of *Church: The Human Story of God,*
"The challenging call from God is thus: 'Come, my dear people, you are not
alone.'"[31]

The upshot of all this is that Schillebeeckx also thinks of salvation from
God as another nonantithetical and dialectical relationship. He can affirm
with more and more vigor that *"extra mundum nulla salus est."* However, because of God's eschatological relationship to time, he also denies that this
salvation in the world is definitive or final. The human experience of salvation
in the present is only a fragmentary taste in anticipation of the fullness of salvation, the achievement of the *humanum* which for Schillebeeckx is expressed
under the great biblical metaphors of the kingdom of God, the resurrection of
the body, the new heaven and the new earth, and the *parousia* of Jesus.[32] Nevertheless, without this experience of salvation in the present, the hope for any
future salvation remains purely speculative and subject to ideological distortion. The "burning edge of the present" again is the sole *locus* of the human
experience of God; yet in and through this experience of salvation, human
beings can perceive a real but fragmentary vision of the completeness of
human life in God. In Schillebeeckx's later work, the "reality of salvation" is
not only the mysterious presence of God in history coming to fuller and fuller
expression over time. The focus shifts now to the *eschaton* where this "reality
of salvation" now must be more clearly discerned in its dialectical structure:
salvation-in-the-world as sign of the salvation-to-come from God; hope for
salvation-to-come as grounded in real human experience of liberation and
freedom now.[33]

Because of this dialectical relationship, Schillebeeckx will not attempt to
define the content of salvation. As the preceding discussion has shown, eschatological salvation from God and the attainment of the *humanum* in its fullness are for him very nearly synonymous. Indeed, Schillebeeckx can preface
his most extended exposition of salvation with the maxim taken from Ire-

naeus which could serve as another encapsulation of all of Schillebeeckx's theology: *Gloria Dei, vivens homo,* God's glory is the human being fully alive.[34] However, neither this *humanum* nor a completely positive grasp of God's eschatological salvation is possible for human beings within the ambiguities and finitude of history. Therefore no fixed definition can be given, so to speak, to either the *gloria Dei* or the *vivens homo* in the ultimate sense. Yet, on the basis of the fragmentary experiences of salvation and wholeness that people have in the here and now, one can venture a provisional, parabolic, and metaphorical picture of this reality. In just such an evocative passage Schillebeeckx writes:

> What, then, is salvation in Jesus from God? I would want to say: being at the disposal of others, losing oneself to others (each in his own limited situation) and within this "conversion" (which is also made possible by structural changes) also working through anonymous structures for the happiness, the goodness and the truth of mankind. This way of life, born of grace, provides a real possibility for a very personal encounter with God, who is then experienced as the source of all happiness and salvation, the source of joy. It is a communicative freedom which is actively reconciled with our own finitude, our death, our transgression and our failure.[35]

As one might expect by now, Schillebeeckx refuses to separate God's action from human action in the process of salvation. Salvation does not just happen through some divine fiat; salvation comes from God only in and through human activity, even if the eschatological proviso always relativizes any specific human plan for creating happiness. The human being in Schillebeeckx's thought is not simply the object of God's action but the very symbol of God in the world. Therefore, any human happiness, liberation, and freedom is by its very nature an effective symbol of God's action. Salvation, as in his earlier discussions of "the mystery of salvation" or "revelation in reality," retains a sacramental structure; now the primary symbol is the living human being.[36]

Commentators on Schillebeeckx such as Tadahiko Iwashima and Hilkert agree that the event of salvation has a certain priority in his thought over explicit language of revelation (see nn. 9, 14). However, as Hilkert also argues, this language of revelation (which Schillebeeckx calls in his earlier theology "revelation in word") is a dialectical and necessary counterpart to the event of salvation (which Schillebeeckx calls the "mystery of salvation" or "revelation in reality"). I agree with Hilkert that this dialectic of revelation in reality and revelation in word continues into the later stages of Schillebeeckx's work. Now, though, set within a more fully developed understanding of eschatology, viewed through the second and third epistemological circles, and critically aware of the great difficulties contemporary people have with language about God, this discussion of revelation must take on a greater complexity than the relatively simple relationship of event and explanatory word which Schillebeeckx used in his earlier thought.

What then is revelation and, moreover, why is it necessary to speak of it? First of all, one must recognize that Schillebeeckx continues to use "experience of revelation" almost interchangeably with "experience of salvation." Therefore, revelation is a particular kind of human experience, one which Schillebeeckx describes along the lines of a negative contrast experience:

> This implies therefore that such revelatory experiences lead us through a disintegration of the ordinary to a new, reintegration which makes us happy and which we experience as bringing us salvation or being salvific. We can therefore say that in every human experience which mediates reality we can recognize something of a surprising breakthrough—a "Pascha"—from an initially ordinary integration, through disintegration to a new, differently oriented reintegration. Genuine experiences of reality as a process of self-revelation implies [*sic*] conversion.[37]

This experience of salvation and revelation involves both contact with refractory reality beyond human expectations and plans and an active willingness (conversion) to embrace the reintegration that the interruption of reality imposes.[38] Schillebeeckx argues that these revelatory experiences have different "intensities" for people and that certain of them go to the very heart of what it means to be human.[39] Religious people, as a result of these experiences that reorient lives, bring happiness and salvation, and call for conversion, say that God has revealed God's self in and through these experiences. Revelation, therefore, is not the *nuda vox Dei* proclaiming propositions which form a conceptual "deposit of faith"; it is rather an experience of God's salvation which believers name as coming from God. Why, however, do believers give this name to these experiences? Is it necessary to do so? If people experience wholeness and salvation within the confines of this life, why is naming this as a revelation of God required?

With these questions, one approaches perhaps the central problem that Schillebeeckx has pondered throughout his career: How and why should one speak of God in the modern situation? Without going too far afield, I would argue that in Schillebeeckx's earlier work, the naming of God as the source of the reality of salvation was absolutely necessary to bring that salvation to completion. The later Schillebeeckx is more hesitant about the *necessity* of God language. Confronted with an increasingly secular culture for which such language is seemingly irrelevant for the humanistic task of building up a better society and fighting against oppression, Schillebeeckx argues that God (and therefore God language) is beyond the category of the necessary, useful, or contingent.[40] "God is not to be reduced to a function of human beings, the world or society; in this sense the religious and metaphysical theism in which God stood as an ideological guarantor of a particular view of human beings, society and the world is at an end."[41] The atheist and the humanist can lead meaningful lives without explicit reference to God. Believers and nonbelievers alike strive for the *humanum* in the face of all that diminishes or destroys human beings. Salvific experiences remain ambiguous within the limits of history.

Instead of arguing that human experiences of salvation, liberation, and freedom necessitate the postulation of the existence of God, Schillebeeckx argues only that explicit language of revelation and its accompanying faith are a *plausible* option for human beings. Invoking the concept of "language games" from Wittgenstein's philosophy, he states that the one reality of human life can be expressed through different, and not necessarily commensurate, language games. What the nonbeliever sees and expresses as human liberation, the believer interprets within the language game of faith.[42] What becomes important for Schillebeeckx is not to *prove* that such language is true by some allegedly objective measuring stick, but to show how Christians may reasonably use language about God as a way of seeing and acting in the world. Ultimately, Schillebeeckx will contend that only a critical praxis in the service of the liberation of all humanity can verify this language. However, language about God also will retain a special "surplus of meaning" which will separate it from secular language games, even the language of liberation and freedom.[43]

Therefore, the language of revelation is primarily language used by believers to express their experiences of salvation as coming from God. However, just as God is present only in "mediated immediacy" to the believer and never in a unmediated "direct" way,[44] so language of revelation does not directly name God but only indirectly refers to the divine reality.

All this implies that only in an "indirect revelation" does God manifest and make himself known to human beings as active in salvation history.

Through the intermediary or agency of the liberating conduct of men in quest of salvation-from-God, God reveals himself "indirectly" as salvation for men. It is more especially in surprising, "discontinuous" historical events, experiences and interpretations that God's saving initiative is shown. If God's saving action is both a "here-and-now" and a divine reality, it will be possible to find in our history "signs" of God's liberating concern with man—signs which must be noted, seen and interpreted, because in themselves they are, like every historical phenomenon, ambiguous, ambivalent and calling for interpretation. It is only in the interpretation, only as experienced and verbalized by human beings, that they come to be recognized as signs of God's salvific activity in a history that is nevertheless made by men.[45]

Believers name such experiences as God's revelation because in and through them they become aware of the already given ground of their own existence, which is also an experience of a transcendent and surprising "more" and an experience of mercy and healing. About the first point, Schillebeeckx can say, "At its most profound level, revelation is the non-reflexive pretheoretical givenness (self-giving) of that which has always lain at the basis of and grounds the process of faith."[46] In the experience of revelation, even mediated through shattering negative contrast experiences, the believer comes to recognize the presence of God as fundamental ground of that person's existence and faith. Given Schillebeeckx's theology of creation and eschatology, it is not surprising that he can say this; the human being is never outside of relationship with God, particularly with God's saving intent. Through such an experience of salvation, the believer recognizes this already existing relationship from his or her own perspective.

Second, and inseparably connected with the first, the believer may plausibly name experiences of salvation as revelation from God because these experiences themselves contain a "more" which impresses itself on the believer. God is revealed as not only the ground of existence and faith, but as the ever greater One who transcends the very experience of salvation. Recalling how in all three of Schillebeeckx's epistemological circles, objective reality actively impinges on the active knowing subject to shape knowledge, one can see why he can affirm that although revelation is always an interpreted experience, it is not merely produced by human experience. The event of God's salvation contains within itself elements which call for the interpretation of faith and the explicit naming of revelation.

Christians experience Jesus as the greatest intensity of revelation within the entire history of experiences of revelation. Therefore human experience has a special, irreplaceable value in the religious history of salvation, even though—as is the case of all genuine "revelation experiences"—revelation here is not the result of experience, but rather experience is the fruit of revelation. Thus the faith-statement in no way grounds the revelation on the basis of its own intentionality. Rather, this provides the basis on its own strength for the response of faith. Nonetheless, good reasons must also be given, from which can somehow be deduced, that humans do not allow God to speak, but rather, how and in what way, in and through human experience, God allows Himself to be recognized.[47]

Ultimately Schillebeeckx thinks that believers can name salvific experiences as revelation from God because even at the very limits of human finitude and suffering, experiences of contrast speak of a mercy and healing which is gracious beyond the measure of human expectation. The "no" to suffering and the vague "yes" to the hope for the *humanum* translate for believers into a partial contact with God who unfailingly opposes evil and overcomes suffering.

> So for Christians the fundamental muttering of humanity turns into a well-founded hope. Something of a sigh of mercy, of compassion, is hidden in the deepest depths of reality. . . and in it believers hear the name of God. That is how the Christian story goes. For Christians, the experiences of contrast, with its inherent opposition to injustice and its perspective on something better, becomes that in which the unity of history comes about *as God's gift.*[48]

For all of these reasons, Schillebeeckx thinks that the salvific experiences of believers allow them to speak about God's real revelation. Without engaging in a direct apologetic for religious belief, he argues for the reasonableness of such language.[49] Nevertheless, Schillebeeckx also wants to avoid a type of fideism that justifies the use of language about revelation simply by referring to the inner experience of believers without any connection to the world. Thus, the speech of believers about God's revelation, like all human language, must stand under the conditions of human knowledge and therefore within the three epistemological circles.

As we have seen, the verbal expression of revelation is the necessary but incomplete expression of God's saving presence. Using the perspectivalist epistemology described above, Schillebeeckx can say that the conceptual language of faith gives believers a true direction toward the knowledge of God, which nevertheless remains at a non-noetic, never fully expressible level. As I have said, this perspectivalist distinction will remain constant through all Schillebeeckx's discussions of the language of revelation. For example, as he states in a later work:

> On the reflexive level ("Revelation as category"—K. Rahner) one seeks to bring revelation (in the former, fundamental sense) to verbal expression, which however is never satisfactory or entirely possible. The ground of faith does not allow itself to be so grounded. Nonetheless it has to be *named*. But this naming and thinking never completely brings the inexpressible whence and whither of faith into a conceptual framework or articulation.[50]

Schillebeeckx argues that believers can speak of the revelation of God on the basis of their experience of the world. This speaking, however, like any human language, does not come simply from the subjective experience of the believer but also from the tradition in which the believer already stands, with its pre-understandings and theoretical models. The language of revelation is therefore also an interpretation of a particular experience. As an interpretation, it shares in all the dynamics of experience and interpretation described above. Language of revelation therefore both is *hermeneusis* and requires hermeneutical interpretation, especially in another conjunctural stage of history when the believer no longer lives within the same pre-understanding and theoretical models that informed the original interpretation. Nevertheless, the interpretation of salvific experience in the language of revelation is not purely a subjective or intersubjective affair; Schillebeeckx consistently emphasizes that the experience itself of God's revelation breaks pre-understandings and models as much as it uses them. Particularly when talking about the original Christian interpretation of Jesus, he frequently speaks of how Jesus' actual teaching and way of life reshaped the models available to the earliest Christians from Jewish and Greco-Roman culture.[51] The nonantithetical and dialectical relationship of objective reality and subjective knower applies fully to the language which human beings use to express God's revelation to them.

Finally, language of revelation stands within the epistemological circle of theory and praxis, especially as confronted with the authority of negative contrast experiences and narratives of human suffering. In the contrast itself be-

tween the reality which resists or destroys human beings and the vague anticipation of the *humanum*, there is a disclosure experience of God's revelation.
Yet speaking of this revelation, according to Schillebeeckx, only makes sense
if it is an *actualizing* interpretation, that is, if it arises from and gives rise to a
particular praxis that seeks to overcome the negative experience in favor of the
humanum. Only in this way are both the hermeneutical reception of the past
tradition of language of revelation—and the eschatological expectation of
God's complete salvation of humanity made concretely present. Only in the
present praxis does the believer experience the revelation of God through
"making real" the inherited traditions, concepts, and hopes of the past. But
only in the context of past traditions and future hopes can the believer give
any name to this disclosure experience at all. Human praxis is the actualizing
medium of God's salvation and revelation in this world, and this praxis never
stands without theory. Both theory and praxis never stand in abstraction from
the long narrative of human suffering and struggle for liberation. Any attempt
to use language about revelation without paying attention to these epistemological circles can fall prey to absolutism, ahistoricity, and ideological distortion. Language of revelation, or religious language, although it names in
parables and metaphors the transcendent God who is the ever-greater ground
and future of creaturely existence, is also always a human language and therefore both veils and unveils the reality of God to human beings.

Jesus the Christ as Definitive Salvation and Revelation from God

In Schillebeeckx's theology, creation and eschatology, salvation and revelation,
God and humanity all meet in the person of Jesus of Nazareth. I have argued
so far that there is no single doctrine that dominates Schillebeeckx's theology;
rather each doctrine stands in a nonantithetical and dialectical relationship
with the others. This methodological structure in his thinking can be best seen
with regard to his Christology. Jesus ultimately determines what Christians
mean by God, humanity, salvation, revelation, creation, and eschatology. Yet
this determining power of Jesus' life also cannot be understood except against
the background of these concepts. As an example of this dialectical relationship, take Schillebeeckx's discussion of creation. We have seen that for Schillebeeckx this doctrine did not function as an explanation for the existence of the
world or human beings but as a way of speaking about the salvific will of
God, which is inseparably connected with God's bringing things into existence

and preserving them. Jesus is the mostly fully realized symbol of this divine intent for humanity in creation; he is, as Schillebeeckx often says, "concentrated creation."[52] Hence believers' experiences of Jesus give rise to Christology that in turn provides a more complete meaning to the idea of God as creator. Yet this Christology as "concentrated creation" can only be understood against the already existing idea of God as creator and savior that Christians inherited from the Jewish tradition. Creation and Christology inform each other through a dialectical relationship of promise and fulfillment, hope and realization.

Without dealing with all the other aforementioned doctrines specifically, I would argue that the same relationship also holds for them: Christology is the concentration and most complete actualization of all the language that human beings use of God and themselves, but it always stands against the background of other concepts which both give shape to it and are shaped by its understanding of Jesus. Salvation, revelation, and the epistemological conditions for human knowledge of God find their most concentrated expression and application in Christology. These ideas can be separated analytically, but in Schillebeeckx's theology they cannot be divided.

The first thing to notice in this connection is that Christology, as reflection on the language of revelation, itself stands within the three epistemological circles. Jesus is the definitive *hermeneusis* of God and humanity, the "parable of God and the paradigm of humanity,"[53] but he also requires continual and practical reinterpretation in the Christian communities that follow after him. No Christological interpretation of Jesus is final; all come from a limited perspective, from a particular tradition of language and way of thought; all require actualization in praxis by the contemporary Christian community to demonstrate their validity against the wider tradition and the claims of the poor and oppressed.

Despite the limitations of Christological interpretations, Schillebeeckx also argues that Christology can and truly does name the salvation and revelation that came from God in and through Jesus. In the example cited above, he argues that the church's interpretation of Jesus, though always enmeshed within the conditions of time, culture, and language, also receives an indelible impression from the object of interpretation itself. The career of Jesus in the church's memory and praxis shapes both, even as the latter give shape to the former in everyday life. Furthermore, this process of the ongoing interpretation of Jesus is not simply a matter of remembrance, expectation, and action on the part of human beings; Schillebeeckx argues that God's Spirit, working in and through the lives of human beings, is also an active agent in the church's continuing life.[54] The praxis of the contemporary church is one authentic pole of the critical correlation between situation and tradition that marks Christian theology. Both poles, however, stand under the one source, the living God who works through and in history.[55]

Since Christology deals with the most concentrated or intense form of the experience of salvation and revelation, the person of Jesus of Nazareth, Christology attempts to name most explicitly the *positive content* of any Christian narrative. However, since Christology also deals with a human being living under the conditions of finitude and does so only from within those same conditions, it also can name this positive content only as *limit concepts*.[56] Jesus of Nazareth, according to Schillebeeckx, is the concrete manifestation of the realities that must guide any Christian religious language and any theology. However, he manifests these realities not only positively through his own experience and life, but also negatively as anticipations of an inexpressible fulfillment that his language and life can only suggest. Hence any Christian language to follow must work within this tension of *positive content* and *limit concept.*

What is this positive content and what are these limit concepts? Both content and limit can be expressed together in the following way. First, God is the absolutely gracious One, the pure positivity of life and freedom whose cause is the salvation and wholeness of human beings. Second, this cause of God as the cause of humankind is revealed most fully in the life of Jesus of Nazareth, whose identification with that cause is so complete that a decision for or against Jesus is tantamount to a decision for or against God's cause. Third, the wholeness and salvation of human beings means both their happiness and freedom now and the anticipation of a fullness of life with God that transcends language. God's cause is Jesus' cause is the human cause. They cannot be separated from each other or placed in opposition to each other. The motto *Gloria Dei, vivens homo* finds its fullest expression in the human life of Jesus.[57]

How does the life of Jesus provide the Christian community with both the positive content and the limit concepts of its narrative? Who is Jesus that he can do this? First, it is important to note that this life is both the source of this content and limit concepts and also one of the limit concepts itself. For Schillebeeckx, then, Jesus is both the ultimate norm of Christian interpretation and one who himself can never be fully captured by any interpretation. The believer in the Christian community does not have access to knowledge of Jesus except through the normal means of human knowledge. Even as Jesus and the

Spirit continually work in and through that community, according to Schillebeeckx, this knowledge of Jesus is still perspectival and hermeneutical and still requires practical actualization in the contemporary situation. Therefore, answering the question about who Jesus is and how he determines the limits of Christian language can never be as simple a matter as picking up the New Testament and reading off selected texts as if they were the *ipsissima verba* of God. It requires a more sophisticated understanding of the relationship between the historical figure of Jesus and the community that followed after him. As Schillebeeckx painstakingly explains at the beginning of his *Jesus* trilogy, his task is a both a *fides quaerens intellectum historicum* and an *intellectus historicus quaerens fidem*. That is to say, faith must be accompanied by a rigorous historical investigation lest it fall into a too-easy literalism or supernaturalism; historical investigation on the other hand does not seek to prove faith, but to lead the contemporary believer through the historical process by which the earliest followers of Jesus came to confess him as definitive salvation from God.[58]

This approach has led Schillebeeckx to an acceptance of the historical-critical method for examining biblical texts.[59] Although he opposes Bultmann's radical separation between the "Jesus of history" and the "Christ of faith," he accepts the tension between the two that source and form criticism have discovered in the New Testament. Jesus and the New Testament, according to Schillebeeckx, stand in another nonantithetical and dialectical relationship to each other. The New Testament gives expression in a variety of settings to diverse Christologies, which interpret the significance of the life of Jesus in their present-day communities. On the other hand, this range of interpretations also hearkens back to the *memoria Jesu*, as Schillebeeckx is accustomed to say, to the life, deeds, words, and culmination of Jesus' life in which believers find salvation. There is no access to Jesus except through these early Christian theological interpretations on Jesus, yet there would be no interpretations unless the actual life of Jesus had had this sort of salvific effect on those who followed him. Jesus is known only in his effects, the Christian community itself, but the life of that community also testifies to the reality of the life of Jesus that began it and still influences it.[60]

Thus the only way to answer the questions that I have posed is to embark on a critical examination of this dialectical relationship between the historical Jesus and the early Christian communities formed in his wake. This, in essence, is what Schillebeeckx attempts to do in the first two massive volumes of his Christological trilogy. For us, the heart of the matter is: As reflected in the faith testimonies of the early Christian church, who is Jesus and how does he determine what I have called both the positive content and limit concepts of Christian faith?

Insofar as a historical investigation carried out with the intention of faith can carry one, Schillebeeckx argues that a unique experience of the closeness of God stands at the center of Jesus' life. This is Schillebeeckx's well-known description of the "Abba experience" of Jesus.[61] By reflecting on Jesus' usage of this term of address for God within the whole context of his life, words and actions, Schillebeeckx argues that Jesus experienced God as both intimately present and as "bent upon humanity."[62] Jesus' fundamental experience of God, like any human experience of God, comes through human means of knowledge. In this case the Abba experience is at heart a "contrast experience"—to Schillebeeckx's mind, perhaps *the* paradigmatic contrast experience. He says that Jesus comes to know reality through the same processes that other human beings undergo, through a confrontation with the evil, suffering, and failures that continually dash human hopes. However, along with the negative power of suffering and evil, he also experiences not just the vague hope for the *humanum* that we share but also its fullness. He knows both sides of the contrast because he experiences God as the one who is the Savior of all human beings.

> Such a hope, expressed in a proclamation of the coming and already close salvation for men implied in God's rule—now that we have uncovered the unique quality of Jesus' religious life in terms of his (historically exceptional) *Abba* address to God—in Jesus is quite plainly rooted in a personal awareness of contrast: on the one hand the incorrigible, irremediable history of man's suffering, a history of calamity, violence and injustice, of grinding, excruciating and oppressive enslavement; on the other hand Jesus' particular awareness of God, his *Abba* experience, his intercourse with God as the benevolent, solicitous "one who is against evil," who will not admit the supremacy of evil and refuses to allow it the last word.[63]

Schillebeeckx wishes to leave some room for the mystery of Jesus' life in relationship to God. He argues that the conceptual apparatus developed as a result of the debates and conciliar decisions of the patristic period is a historically true but possibly confusing language for contemporary use, especially if it is used as a sort of chemical formula for explaining how two such diverse substances as "God" and "humanity" can be mixed together. Instead, using the language of relation and identification, Schillebeeckx talks about how the very identity of Jesus of Nazareth as a human being lies in his identification with the cause of the Father,[64] and that, theologically speaking, this identification rests on an even deeper identification of the Father with Jesus.[65] In the end, however, even this language falls short of capturing the mystery of the relationship of God and humanity in Jesus. There is finally a need for "keeping silent in reverence and adoration," because "[a]fter all that we do know of him, in the end we do not know who God is."[66]

Although the ultimate ground of Jesus' identification with God must remain a mystery, Schillebeeckx is more confident in speaking about how Jesus lives from this fundamental identification. Since Jesus' contrast experience is complete on both sides, encompassing both the human situation of suffering and evil and God's saving presence which overcomes them, Jesus is the ultimate source of the *positive content* of Christian faith. Since this positive content, originally expressed by Jesus under the name "kingdom of God," signifies the nature of God as the One who wishes to save humankind and also human wholeness and salvation as the "measure" of God's rule, Jesus' life is the source of these two *limit concepts* of any Christian narrative. Moreover, since Jesus identified himself so much with this message of the kingdom that he died for it, and because his followers experienced him as raised and vindicated by God after this death, he himself became the lens through which later Christians saw the reality of God's kingdom. Jesus becomes the kingdom in its most concrete manifestation and therefore identification with Jesus becomes the criterion for judging one's identification with the cause of God who seeks the salvation and happiness of all people. In this sense, Jesus is also one of the *limit concepts* of Christian faith, even as he is the source of faith's positive content and the manifestation of the other two limit concepts. Again, he is "parable of God and paradigm of humanity."

Can any more substance be given to this positive content of faith? What did Jesus mean more specifically by the "kingdom of God"? On the basis of his analysis of Jesus' preaching, praxis, and passion, Schillebeeckx summarizes Jesus' view:

> The kingdom of God is the saving presence of God, active and encouraging, as it is affirmed or welcomed among men and women. It is a saving presence offered by God and freely accepted by men and women which takes concrete form above all in justice and peaceful relationships among individuals and peoples, in the disappearance of sickness, injustice and oppression, in the restoration to life of all that was dead and dying. The kingdom of God is a changed new relationship (*metanoia*) of men and

women to God, the tangible and visible side of which is a new type of liberating relationship among men and women within a reconciling society in a peaceful natural environment. The kingdom of God is God's revealing and saving presence in the world, a presence of which I have spoken in the two previous chapters. The kingdom of God is "a kingdom of men and women," a human kingdom, in contrast to the kingdoms of the world which are symbolized in Daniel 7 by animals, kingdoms in which the strongest holds sway. The kingdom of God is the abolition of the blatant contrast between rulers and ruled (also where God is seen as such a tyrannical ruler).[67]

Jesus gives shape to this vision through the words and actions of his life. His preaching, conveyed through illustrative and provocative parables, described a God who "does not let himself be claimed by a caste of pious and virtuous people" who know that their faithful following of the law will bring them a just reward. Rather, God in Jesus' parables "comes to stand on the side of those who are pushed aside by the 'community which thinks well of itself': the poor, the oppressed, the outcast and the sinful." This God "lays claim completely on men and women and asks them to follow him with an undivided heart."[68]

Jesus matches these parables of God's reign by his praxis. Schillebeeckx accepts the idea that Jesus and his contemporaries produced "phenomena" which "their contemporaries adjudged to be miracles,"[69] even if they expressed this conviction in language different from modern understandings of these events. What matters for Schillebeeckx, however, is not the sheer fact of miraculous events, but their relationship to Jesus' experience and message of the kingdom of God. Here Schillebeeckx finds an unbreakable connection between the two. Jesus' praxis of healing and restoring wholeness was usually directed at those most marginalized in the society. In a challenge to the prevailing interpretation of the Jewish law, Jesus' actions said that "the poor and the outcast are the criterion of whether the law is functioning creatively or destructively, as the will of God for the benefit of men and women."[70] Righteousness and rules themselves are not a guarantee of God's favor, especially when following them also diminishes or destroys fellow human beings.

In opposition to this restrictive understanding of God's relationship with humanity, Jesus enacted through his own relationships with people a view of God's favor that was liberating and joyful. In addition to the miracles of healing, Jesus' everyday "dealings with people liberate them and make them glad."[71] In Jesus' presence the disciples do not fast, not because he wishes to dispense with the Jewish regulations on fasting, but because he himself "becomes a living dispensation from fasting and mourning."[72] Jesus, as the host of the copious and joyful banquet to which all (especially the marginalized) are invited, represents concretely God's eschatological promise of hope and forgiveness extended to all. Jesus breaks bread with the identified "sinners" in his society and feeds the multitudes as an "invitation to the great eschatological feast of fellowship with God."[73] In this way, Schillebeeckx argues, Jesus again shows with particular force that his "actual way of living is nothing other than the praxis of the kingdom of God proclaimed by him."[74]

Both in parables and deeds, Jesus identifies himself with the action of God. For Schillebeeckx the root of this identification lay in Jesus' unique *Abba* experience, which is also the experiential basis for future Christian language about Jesus' participation in the divine life of the Father. In the more immediate context, this identification with the Father (or with the kingdom of God) meant that Jesus was not just a proclaimer of a message about God's concern for humanity; he also enacted it through his deeds and confronted people with the whole of his person. Jesus took their reactions to his message and praxis as their response, in affirmation or negation, to the reign of God itself.

Jesus' utter identification with God's reign ultimately led to his death. Set up by a collaboration between the Romans and the "Sadducean, pro-Herodian and in fact pro-Roman clan" within Judaism,[75] Jesus was arrested, tried (probably) in an informal hearing before the Roman prefect, Pontius Pilate, and then executed by crucifixion. Schillebeeckx writes that Jesus' complete identification with God's cause and his own self-perception of his mission in relation to that cause led him to silence before the accusing members of the Sanhedrin and the questioning of Pilate and Herod. Recognizing no other authority than God and no other ultimate standard except the reign of God, Jesus tacitly denied the authority of his accusers by his very silence before them. "*Contemptus auctoritatis*, holding Israel's highest authority in contempt, seems to me to be the Jewish legal ground for Jesus' condemnation."[76] Turned over to the Romans when the Jewish authorities could not all agree on such a ground for condemnation, Jesus died on the cross, surrounded only by the silence of the God to whose cause he had unreservedly committed himself. Discerning Jesus' "loud cry" as the only historically warranted word of Jesus on the cross, Schillebeeckx sees in this a sign of the "inner conflict" between "his consciousness of his mission and the utter silence of the One whom he was accustomed to call his Father."[77] Jesus died and to the mind of the disciples, it seemed as if Jesus' vision of the reign of God had died with him.

This was not to be the end of the story. In an unexpected way, Jesus "was seen" by some of the disciples after his death, in an experience of uncalled-for forgiveness, conversion, and reorientation of life. Among the most creative and controversial parts of his Christological writings, Schillebeeckx's treatment of the resurrection stories is a paradigmatic case of the mutually determining nature of objective reality and subjective interpretation. According to Schillebeeckx, the resurrection is neither an experience of some bare objective "fact," such as the empty tomb or the physical vision of the resurrected body of Jesus, nor simply the disciples' own subjective realization of the importance of Jesus' life and message. The resurrection, rather, is God's vindication of the preaching, praxis, and defenseless death of Jesus, a vindication of his whole commitment to God's reign, an overcoming of the pure negativity of Jesus' death by the pure positivity of God. The disciples experience this event as completely unmerited, an unexpected forgiveness in which they have a "disclosure experience" of the true significance of the whole of Jesus' life and the realization that this unbidden forgiveness could only have come from the living Jesus himself.[78] The resurrection, as all experiences, is never a "pure" uninterpreted experience; but, on the other hand, it contains within itself elements that are intrinsically part of the experience itself. In the terminology used in chapter 1, the resurrection experiences contain "interpretative elements" which have their sources both external and internal to the event itself. These elements will undergo further elaboration and reflection (a move from first-level to second-level interpretation) in the various narrative strands that will eventually go in to making the "appearance" narratives related in the Gospels. However, before even the narratives of the empty tomb and the "physical" appearances of Jesus stands the fundamental experience of Jesus' forgiving presence which the disciples understood as the disclosure of the full meaning of Jesus' life and the manifestation of God's vindication on the message, praxis, and entire life of Jesus of Nazareth.

According to Schillebeeckx, because of this fundamental resurrection experience, the disciples begin to see the reign of God, which Jesus spoke about and acted on, through the contours of Jesus himself. Jesus becomes the reign of God for the early church as they interpret, in a variety of ways, the meaning of his whole life in the light of the resurrection. This believing interpretation, done within a community that seeks both to remember Jesus and live out his vision of God's reign in the current time, marks the beginning of the church. With this event of the resurrection, one comes to the most concentrated point of salvation and revelation in Schillebeeckx's theology and the beginnings of his ecclesiology as well. The church in Schillebeeckx's thought is the subject of the next chapter.

The resurrection event is the seal on the salvation and revelation that are the whole of the life of Jesus. His preaching and praxis of the kingdom are normative for any later Christian speech and praxis. Given the discussion to this point, one may list the following qualities of authentic Christian language. First, it is a human language, emerging from and used within the conditions of human life and knowledge of the world. Thus it is always perspectival, interpretative, and subject to possible ideological distortion. Second, it is a language that is inseparably linked with praxis; Christian truth is not mediated in timeless concepts but only expressed in the continually actualizing circle of theory and praxis. Third, Christian language must stay within the limit concepts of any Christian narrative: "God as pure positivity," "Jesus as the definitive revelation of God's cause as the human cause," and "the *humanum* as human wholeness both in actuality and anticipation." Fourth, this Christian language must be constantly and communally actualized in a faithful remembrance of the specific life and praxis of Jesus, as the manifestation of the reign of God. This language must be tested by (and serve as a test for) a praxis which identifies with the poor, marginalized, and forgotten of the world, which brings healing and renewal to the broken and sinful, which resists master-slave relationships of dominance, which remains faithful to this hope even in the grimmest of circumstances, which always recognizes its limitations under the eschatological proviso of the ever-greater God, which always hopes in that yet unfulfilled future. Hence the language of the church, and more specifically the doctrines that the magisterium, theologians, and other believers attempt to formulate for their experience, stand within all these conditions of authenticity.

three | The Church in Schillebeeckx's Theology

The church rarely stands alone as a subject of theological reflection in Schillebeeckx's thought. As I described in the last chapter, Christology is the concentrated form of all the major Christian theological doctrines, which in turn form the irreplaceable background that informs Christology. It is central because in Jesus the Christian finds the most concrete and complete expression of God's creative will and eschatological promise, God's salvation and revelation for the human race. The particular human reality of Jesus leads believers to make Christology the key for understanding these other theological realities.

Ecclesiology both does and does not share this kind of relationship to Christology. The church, of course, does depend on the preaching, praxis, passion, and resurrection of Jesus for its existence. According to Schillebeeckx, Jesus is the source, norm, and guiding presence (through the Spirit) of the community of believers. At the same time, the church is also the historical medium through which the original event of Jesus' life receives (or should receive) its continual reactualization and reinterpretation in history. Jesus and the church stand in a nonantithetical and dialectical relationship in such a way that the church's continuing life provides the "unitive factor" for the diverse images of Jesus both in the New Testament and in later history, but only because the church continually lives out of the "impress" which Jesus himself makes on the church.[1] Ecclesiology hence depends in a certain way on Christology, even if the actual life of the church is also a source for Christology.

In another sense, though, ecclesiology as an area of theology has a different relationship to Christology and to the other doctrines mentioned above. Put perhaps too simply, creation and eschatology, salvation and revelation, talk about *what is mediated:* God's saving presence. Ecclesiology talks about one *structure of mediation,* the Christian church in history. Christology, following this schema, talks about the definitive instance in human history (for Christians) where the mediated presence of God and the structure of mediation, a human life, meet in one. In Schillebeeckx's theology one can never completely separate the mediated and the medium; nevertheless, that which is mediated, the saving presence of God, has a certain determining priority over structures of mediation. Hence, in a way unlike other doctrines, Christology determines ecclesiology, because Jesus is the historical origin of the historical movement of the Christian community. One could conceivably speak about creation, eschatology, salvation, and revelation from God without explicit reference to Jesus; one could not do the same with regard to ecclesiology, since it is reflection on the historical community that arises in the wake of Jesus' life.

As noted earlier, a shorthand form for Schillebeeckx's Christology is the statement, "Jesus is the parable of God and the paradigm of humanity."[2] If ecclesiology is dependent on Christology in the way just outlined, then this means that the church is the continuing historical structure of mediation for all the central elements of Christology captured in this sentence. By continuing to mediate the presence of Jesus, the church also mediates God's presence in the world, while providing a model for the renewal of humanity. Yet because the church always does these tasks within the complexities and ambiguities of human history, it is also related in another nonantithetical and dialectical relationship to the world around it. The world is the arena for the church's mission because it is the context for all God's salvation and revelation. However, the world that provides the context for revelation also ultimately is shaped by that revelation; more specifically, by the revelation of God-in-Christ and by the continuing actualization of that revelation in the church. Just as Jesus and the church form an inseparable dialectical pair, so do church and world. For this reason, therefore, the church is never an isolated topic for theological reflection for Schillebeeckx; he always links ecclesiology with Christology and with an understanding of the human conditions under which all people, not only believers, live.

In both his early and later work, Schillebeeckx uses the metaphor of sacrament to describe the church. If in Schillebeeckx's theology the church always stands in a dialectical relationship with both Christ and world, then it will follow that the church is both *sacrament of Christ* and *sacrament of the world.* Although his writings on the church sometimes give more emphasis to one such sacramental relationship over another, an adequate understanding of his ecclesiology requires the inclusion of both. I will begin with his discussion of the church as sacrament in his early work before proposing that the model of the church as anticipatory sign is the way in which Schillebeeckx translates his early sacramental model of ecclesiology into the epistemological and theological categories of his later work.

The Church as Sacrament

When Schillebeeckx began work on his doctorate in 1946 at L'Ecole du Saulchoir in Paris, he originally intended to write about the translation of the philosophical concepts of particularity and universality into the theological language of nature and supernature. However, because his superiors required him to teach on the sacraments upon his return to the Dominican House of Studies in Louvain in 1947, he instead chose to write on that topic.[3] This dissertation was his attempt, using the *ressourcement* approach of his mentors at Le Saulchoir, to overcome the abstract and essentialist sacramental theology of neo-Thomism with one that was more faithful to Thomas, to the broader tradition, and to contemporary needs. In this work, and in the shorter *Christ the Sacrament of the Encounter with God* that presents the dissertation's main ideas, he does this by raising sacramentality to the level of a fundamental theology, that is, to the level of a general explanation for the relationship between God and the world. Sacraments are not simply quasi-magical rituals performed by the church's priests. They are, rather, a concrete instance of the whole history of God's salvific dealings with humankind. Salvation history itself has a sacramental structure, beginning with the creation, the presence of God in a vague way in the other religions of the world, in the history of Israel, and finally, and definitively, in the life of Jesus himself.[4] Jesus, in Schillebeeckx's language of the time, is the primordial sacrament of humanity's encounter with God because in his visible humanity he is also the effective presence of the Son of God.

> Because the saving acts of the man Jesus are performed by a divine person, they have a divine power to save, but because this divine power to save appears to us in a visible form, the saving activity of Jesus is *sacramental*. For a sacrament is a divine bestowal of salvation in an outwardly perceptible form which makes the bestowal manifest; a bestowal of salvation in historical visibility.[5]

Schillebeeckx continues:

> Consequently if the human love and all the human acts of Jesus possess a divine saving power, then the realization in human shape of this saving power necessarily includes as one of its aspects the manifestation of salvation; includes, in other words, sacramentality. The man Jesus, as the personal visible realization of the divine grace of redemption, is *the* sacrament, the primordial sacrament, because this man, the Son of God himself, is intended by the Father to be in his humanity the only way to the actuality of redemption.[6]

The earthly and visible life of Jesus is the greatest possible human and sacramental encounter with the divine presence. Yet after Jesus is raised up and glorified into the life of heaven, how is the encounter to be continued? Schillebeeckx argues that God never overrides the given human structure of bodiliness as the means of encounter with interiority and grace; rather, God continues to bestow this grace on the human race through visible effective signs, the sacraments.[7] Yet these sacraments do not stand alone but are the most concrete manifestations of the sacramentality of the whole church, which is the primordial sacrament in the world of Christ himself.

Using the "descending Christology" customary to the Catholic theology of the time, Schillebeeckx states that Jesus after the resurrection becomes the glorified Christ, who is himself the deepest reality of the church, in head and members. The glorified Christ who is the church then realizes ("sacramentalizes") himself in history through the earthly reality of the church. Hence the church is a sacrament of Christ because it is the direct bodily (historical) continuation of the reality of the divine and human Jesus on earth.

> In his messianic sacrifice, which the Father accepts, Christ in his glorified body is himself the eschatological redemptive community of the Church. In his own self the glorified Christ is simultaneously both "Head and members."
>
> The earthly Church is the visible realization of this saving reality in history. The Church is a visible communion in grace. This communion itself, consisting of members and a hierarchical leadership, is the earthly sign of the triumphant redeeming grace of Christ.[8]

Schillebeeckx makes no sharp distinction between the inner "mystical" church and the outer church as an institution with its juridical structures.

Reading Pius XII's *Mystici Corporis* in the light of the *ressourcement* theologians,[9] he argues that this encyclical confirms a trend in contemporary Catholic theology that affirms the necessity and unity of both of these aspects of the church. The outer structure is the necessary expression of the inner grace of the union of Christ and the church. In this sense one can talk about the church, as it actually exists in history, as being a sacrament of Christ.

> The visible church itself is the Lord's mystical body. The Church is the visible expression of Christ's grace and redemption, realized in the form a society which is a sign (*societas signum*). Any attempt to introduce a dualism here is the work of evil—as if one could play off the inward communion of grace with Christ against the juridical society of the church, or vice versa. The Church therefore is not merely a means of salvation. It is Christ's salvation itself, this salvation as visibly realized in this world. Thus it is, by a kind of identity, the body of the Lord.[10]

One should also note that Schillebeeckx emphasizes, as much as was possible at the time, that the *whole* church is this sacrament of Christ. Countering the common Catholic ecclesiology of the time that practically identified the church with the hierarchy, Schillebeeckx continues the emphasis of his *ressourcement* mentors and anticipates the Second Vatican Council with his use of the metaphor of the "People of God" as a description of both laity and clergy. He in no way denies that the laity and hierarchy have different roles within the church as a result of Christ's relationship to it, but he also makes clear that the hierarchy consists of believing members within the church, not another class of persons above it.[11]

Because the church is the primordial sacrament of Christ's presence in the world, it is therefore also a continuation of the dynamic of revelation in reality and revelation in word that found its culmination in Christ. However, just as a sacrament both veils and unveils the reality that it represents, the church both reveals the presence of Christ and can possibly hide it as well. On the one hand, Schillebeeckx at this stage can talk about how "the church's word is the personal word of the heavenly Christ in the form of the apostolic word; it is, in other words, the personal word of Christ *in forma ecclesiae* ('in the shape of the church')."[12] In this sense the church bears the *paradosis*, the reality of salvation that the apostles experienced in Christ, although the church also finds its norm in this salvific event.[13] On the other hand, the church is at the same time an earthly reality made up of sinful people and therefore needs the correction of the apostolic witness lest it obscure the event of Christ. In line with theologians like Hans Urs von Balthasar, Romano Guardini, Chenu, and Congar, Schille-beeckx says that the church is not only a motive for faith and an object of faith (both ideas which he does uphold), but it is also a test for the Christian's faith. Yet this weakness of the church, its veiling of the presence of God through its ignorance and sin, is also the occasion for God's grace to triumph over these obstacles, which is the root of Schillebeeckx's understanding of the indefectibility and infallibility of the church.

> The church is great and glorious not because of her power and achievements here on earth, but because the redeeming grace of Christ triumphs in her. Justice is done and, what is more, visible justice is done to the power of God despite human weaknesses and indeed precisely *in* these weaknesses. The church is therefore not only the object of our faith, she is also at the same time a *test of our faith*. She may even be an obstacle and a danger to our faith. After all, believing is not a conviction that is compelled by the evidence of the church's glory. We always believe in the midst of darkness and, viewed in this way, the church's weakness is also a happy fault, causing us to boast only of the glory of God's power.[14]

Despite the human weaknesses of the members of the church, it is still the effective sign, in word and sacrament, of Christ's continuing action in the world.[15] The church is also the sacrament of the world, although Schille-beeckx does not frequently use this terminology before the Second Vatican Council. In the early period of his theology, the church is sacrament of the world insofar as it makes explicit the implicit presence of God already at work in the world. For example, in a very early article on the relationship of religion and the world, Schillebeeckx describes how Christianity can provide a "heavenly humanism" which arises from God's accomplishment of salvation in Jesus. This humanism identifies the true dimension of human existence that only comes to partial expression in the contemporary humanism of existentialism. The event of Christ, as borne in history by the church, therefore brings the most complete humanization to the world by both including the world within his redemptive act and by transcending it in eschatological expectation. In this sense the church exists to draw the world to its true humanity by offering it a life that both transcends and includes the ordinary course of history. The church is to be the living sign of this true humanism.[16] To borrow the terminology of Chenu and Jean-Baptiste-Henri

Lacordaire that so influenced Schillebeeckx at this time, the church fulfills its mission of being a sacrament of Christ by its *présence au monde*.[17]

The Second Vatican Council and Schillebeeckx's Ecclesiology

This framework for the relationship of church and world will remain constant in Schillebeeckx's thought during the period preceding the Second Vatican Council (1962–65). The council itself will both legitimate the ecclesiological ideas that he and other more progressive theologians held before the council and will provide the impetus for further reflection on the church as both sacrament of Christ and sacrament of the world. A brief examination of some of Schillebeeckx's main ecclesiological writings from this transitional period will illustrate this point.

Later in his career, Schillebeeckx is able to look back on the period of the council both with great appreciation for the pivotal role it played in the renewal of Catholicism and with a clear recognition of its limitations. On the one hand, he argues that Vatican II marked a real and significant break with the medieval and Tridentine conception of the church, a break that did not mark a betrayal of the essence of Christian faith but rather its rediscovery.[18] On the other hand, he also recognizes that Vatican II opened Catholicism toward the modern world precisely at the time when modernity began to undergo its own crisis of identity. The council, which focused primarily on ecclesiological issues, did not address the great Christological and theological questions that would become the central concern in such a rapidly and radically changing world.[19] Using a phrase that will almost become a slogan in his later works, Schillebeeckx argues that the church now needs an "ecclesiology in a minor key" which directs less attention to the church itself and more to the central three realities of the Christian narrative: God, Jesus the Christ, and the wholeness of humankind.[20]

However, at the time the conciliar ecclesiology heralded a new era for the Catholic Church, according to Schillebeeckx. Although all the council's documents reflect in their own way this spirit of change and renewal, the two great constitutions, *Lumen Gentium* and *Gaudium et Spes*, are the main sources of a new ecclesiological vision for Catholicism.[21] Commenting on the first, Schillebeeckx notes many new elements, such as the use of biblical imagery, the placement of the church within the history of salvation, and the dialectical tension between the kingdom of God and the church, as well as that between the Catholic Church and the church of Christ.[22] Of particular importance is the definition of the whole church as the "People of God" and the council's approval of the collegial government of the church by the bishops with and under the primacy of the pope.[23] For Schillebeeckx these changes provide the basis for the other new ideas contained in the document: the acceptance of non-Catholics, non-Christians, and even nonbelievers within the extended boundaries of the church; the new emphasis on the role of the laity; and the possibility of creating a "theology of the local church" that respects differences within the unity of worldwide Catholicism.[24]

Perhaps the most important sentence for Schillebeeckx in *Lumen Gentium* comes at the beginning of the document. There the constitution states:

> Since the Church, in Christ, is in the nature of sacrament—a sign and instrument, that is, of communion with God and of unity among all men—she here proposes, for the benefit of the faithful and of the whole world, to set forth, as clearly as possible, and in the tradition laid down by earlier councils, her own nature and universal mission.[25]

Here the council uses the sacramental analogy for the church in a twofold manner, one that echoes Schillebeeckx's earlier work and sets the direction for his future writings on ecclesiology. The church is a sacrament not only of the communion with God, accomplished fully in Christ, but also of the "unity of all men." Naming this second aspect of the church's sacramentality signifies a shift in ecclesiology of momentous proportions. No longer will the world simply be the implicit field of God's action that the church's teaching and life make explicit. The world no longer exists simply to be drawn into the church; rather, the church exists to be a sacrament of what the world should become in its graced autonomy. Of course, the drafters of *Lumen Gentium* and Schillebeeckx had no intention of setting these two aspects of the church's sacramentality over against each other, but the clear recognition of the value of the world in relation to the church will change the direction of Catholic theology in the postconciliar period. Schillebeeckx recognizes this shift early on and sees the connection between *Lumen Gentium* and the other groundbreaking ecclesiological document from the council, *Gaudium et Spes*.

> Finally, although the term is not used, the church is *sacramentum mundi*, the sacrament of the world, "sign and instrument of unity among

men." Thus church and world are brought into contact and the *Pastoral Constitution on Church and World* is ushered in—a remarkable expression which appears in the very first paragraph of this dogmatic constitution.[26]

Regarding the Pastoral Constitution, Schillebeeckx notes the new spirit of acceptance of the historicity of human nature, and the willingness both to give to the world and to receive from it. Of paramount importance is the constitution's embrace of the autonomy and goodness of secular reality; it is the end, as Schillebeeckx puts it, of the "'syllabus' mentality of Pius IX."[27] This acceptance of the goodness of human historicity, corporeality, culture, and learning is then the basis for the specific reflections of the second part of the document on the contemporary problems of marriage and family, culture, society, and economy.[28]

Although the inner renewal of the church is of great interest to Schillebeeckx, I would argue that he saw the changed relationship between the church and the world as the most revolutionary result of the whole council. He wrote not long afterward: "The characteristic of Vatican II is that its basic theme concerns the question of religious existence in a world that is changing, abandoning sacral for human forms."[29] While still affirming the uniqueness and fullness of the revelation given in Christ and its preservation within the Catholic Church,[30] Vatican II also says that the other Christian communities and the other great traditions of the world bring salvation to their members. The Catholic Church abandons any claim to possess a monopoly on all forms of religiousness, all forms of Christianity, all forms of the church. Furthermore, it abandons all claims to control over every aspect of ordinary human life and recognizes the proper autonomy of the world and the right of persons to organize their lives according to their deepest convictions.[31] Yet because the church is still the bearer of the fullness of revelation, the problem of the relationship of church and world still remains. Schillebeeckx believes that the council, especially as addressed by *Gaudium et Spes,* maintains the appropriate tension between the rightful claims to autonomy of human life on earth and the ultimately transcendent goal of human existence, as promised in the resurrection of Christ.[32] The council's answer to the question of the relationship of church and world ultimately has its source in *Lumen Gentium,* which describes the church as both sacrament of Christ and sacrament of the world. The church is an effective sign of God's presence in the world insofar as it both mediates Christ's presence and presents the world with a realization of the universal community that the world itself is supposed to become.

In this sense the church already is the presence of salvation in our midst, and thus conceived she also has a value of her own. But, sign and mediating realisation are one. As a sacrament the church experiences in advance what still needs to be given concrete shape in the whole human fellowship. This means the church achieves a fellowship of men because she herself is already a community: God's people and, therefore, a community of brothers. She is "a sign set among the nations." The *Pastoral Constitution on the Church in the World of Today*, as the intrinsic consequences of the *Dogmatic Constitution on the Church*, has recognised the existential link between the religious Christian and the world as a link which is essential to the church yet fades into an unfathomable mystery.[33]

Schillebeeckx will continue to develop his ecclesiology along these lines during and after the council. Perhaps his most in-depth reflection on the theme of the church and world in the conciliar period is "The Church and Mankind," which he wrote before the final session and which appeared in the premiere issue of *Concilium*.[34] Here he plumbs the implications of the council's language about both the openness of the church to the world and the presence of God in the world outside the visible boundaries of the church. Because of this presence, he can name all human beings as the "people of God" insofar as God has already implicitly redeemed and destined them for a unity that he calls the *communio sanctorum*.[35] This implicit redemption and hoped-for unity come to their fullest, if proleptic, expression in Jesus himself and continue in the church. As he did in his preconciliar writings, he relies on an implicit-to-explicit relationship to picture the relationship of world and church. However, although the church is the place where "Christ's triumphant grace becomes a plain, historical and recognizable fact,"[36] the church also stands in a dialectical tension to the world. Schillebeeckx argues that the church is where the people of God, possessing perhaps only an inchoate sense of God and their redemption, become the Body of Christ, the only living link between Jesus and the world. Because even the postresurrection Christ is absent from the world, the church is the only real and complete sacrament of Christ for the rest of the world. Yet Schillebeeckx also recognizes that both church and world are also *in via* toward their eschatological fulfillment. Since neither are complete, and the world and its people are also filled with the gracious presence of God in an implicit form, Schillebeeckx must also state that there is a certain fluidity in the boundaries of church and world. Because of the example of Christ, who accepted his own truly human life as the medium of God's communication and revelation, those who accept the mystery of their own existence make an act of "God-centered faith."[37] This act of faith only can come to its complete fruition within the church of Christ, but it signifies again that the church cannot see itself as the only "sacred" reality surrounded by a hostile world. Rather, Schillebeeckx says:

> This means that in the plan of salvation the concrete world, by definition, is an *implicit Christianity;* it is the objective, non-sacral but saintly and sanctified expression of mankind's communion with the living God; whereas the Church *qua* institution of salvation, with her explicit creed, her worship and sacraments, is the direct and sacral expression of that identical communion—she is the *separata a mundo.*[38]

The dialogue between the church and the world is not between two opposing or alien realities, but "is rather a dialog between two complementary authentically Christian expressions of one and the same God-related life concealed in the mystery of Christ."[39] Although the anonymous or implicit Christianity that exists within the structure of secular reality also contains a drive for full manifestation in the life of Christ and the church, during the current earthly existence of the church the two remain in the aforementioned dialectical tension. "Eschatologically, Church and mankind coincide fully,"[40] Schillebeeckx writes, but the current life of both world and church can only partially reflect this coincidence. This eschatological proviso serves, as it does in other areas of Schillebeeckx's thought, as both a caution against any putative final or complete picture of the Christian faith and as a spur toward active renewal and reform.

Because the church is both sacrament of Christ and sacrament of the world, and because the two realities of church and world are not opposed to each other, Schillebeeckx can also describe the church as the sacrament of dialogue.[41] In distinction from the monological attitude that characterized the Catholic Church before Vatican II, *Gaudium et Spes, Lumen Gentium, Dignitatis Humanae,* and other key conciliar documents endorsed an entirely new approach: that of dialogue with the world. Following the lines of argument outlined above, Schillebeeckx says that the church must become such a sacrament of dialogue because it is also *sacramentum mundi;* the church's new task, as a service to the world, is to serve as a model for open communication for the world.[42] In an interesting twist on the old maxim of *extra ecclesiam nulla salus est,* Schillebeeckx also argues that the church cannot make such a claim to universality except through such a dialogue with the world. This is so both because the church cannot preach its message about God in Christ without an awareness of the world that will receive that message and because the eschatological proviso again warns the church away from thinking that it has achieved its final form or its most complete expression. The world, as he argued in the earlier *Concilium* article, is also a source of God's presence and God's summons through the lives of contemporary people. The church can only fulfill its role as sacrament of Christ's presence if it maintains this constant and real interchange with the world around it, which is also the world in which it lives.[43]

The Church as Anticipatory Sign

Taking his lead from these ideas, Schillebeeckx embarked on a nearly decade-long critical dialogue with the intellectual currents of the contemporary world. This dialogue, as I noted in the first chapter, led Schillebeeckx to move away from the phenomenological and personalist Thomism of his earlier career toward an eclectic approach heavily influenced by the hermeneutics of the humanities, linguistic analysis, and critical theory. Combining these philosophical explorations with an intensive reading of contemporary theology and biblical studies, Schillebeeckx aimed at continuing the dialogue initiated by the council by offering a full-scale reappraisal of the significance of Jesus for the contemporary world. Although he has written copiously on many topics since the time of his "clear break" with De Petter in 1966, the "Christological trilogy" has been the backbone of his mature work. There Schillebeeckx shifts the focus from explicitly ecclesiological concerns in favor of this reconsideration of the basic elements of the Christian narrative in the current context. Even the third volume of the trilogy, which was originally supposed to be an ecclesiological reflection on the themes developed in the first two volumes, became instead a restatement of fundamental theological themes.[44] Schillebeeckx has apparently followed his own advice and treated ecclesiology in a minor key in his later works.

Because of this deemphasis on ecclesiology, and because of his tendency to describe the church only in its dialectical relationships with Jesus and the world, Schillebeeckx does not construct a systematic doctrine of the church in the second major period of his thinking. However, his treatment of the church in relationship to other topics, when seen against the background of his new approach to theology, provides the reader with many suggestive directions for the construction of such a doctrine. A synthetic reading of these suggestions, extrapolated from the material that Schillebeeckx has provided, offers a more complete picture of a critical ecclesiology. I will argue that Schillebeeckx's later thought provides the basis for an ecclesiology built around the central image of the church as anticipatory sign.

Schillebeeckx's nonantithetical and dialectical method of thought drives him to link all the theological *loci* together in a series of mutually informing relationships. Creation and eschatology, revelation and salvation, Christology and ecclesiology can only be understood within the web of these relationships, because they each in their own way bear witness to perhaps the fundamental doctrine of his theology: God's salvific will for humanity. Although all of these connections play an important role in the development of his ecclesiological thinking, of particular importance to begin with are the relationships between creation, Christology, and eschatology. As we have seen, creation is not an explanation for the cosmos along the lines of scientific knowledge but rather a statement of God's creative and preserving relationship to humankind, which ultimately signifies that God wishes to be a God of human salvation.[45] Similarly, eschatology is not simply a catalogue of the catastrophic events at the end of history but a statement of the utter historicity of human nature and both God's immanence within and ultimate transcendence of history. In the person and work of Jesus, Schillebeeckx sees the concentration of these ideas of creation and eschatology: Jesus is the fullest expression of Israel's trust in God's creative presence as well as God's promise for the future. Ecclesiology, because it is theological reflection on the community of disciples of Jesus, has a specific historical focus and dependence that the other theological *loci* do not necessarily have. Schillebeeckx expresses this status by consistently describing the church as a sacrament: the sacrament of Christ in the world and the sacrament of the world, signifying how the church should bring to full expression both the active presence of God in the world and the latent potential for the unity of the human race. This understanding persists into his later thought; however, it takes on a different character within the paradigms of that thought.

Because the church is the sacrament of Christ in the world, it is also by extension the sacramental representation of the creative and eschatological relationships between God and humanity that came to fullest expression in Christ. In other words, within the narrative structures of human historicity, within the dynamics of remembrance, action, and trusting hope, the church is a sign both of God's creative and salvific intent for the human race and the eschatological culmination of human history. As Schillebeeckx puts it, the church that follows after Jesus is the eschatological community.

> What he did leave—only through what he was, did and said, simply through his activities as this particular human being—was a movement, a living fellowship of believers who had become conscious of being the new people of God, the eschatological "gathering" of God—not a "sacred remnant" but the firstborn of the gathering together of all Israel, and eventually of all human kind: an eschatological liberation movement for bringing together all people, bringing them together in unity. Universal *shalom*.[46]

Because this eschatological community takes its origin from Christ and is the sacrament of Christ in the world, its language and actions fall within the linguistic, practical, and theological limits of Christian language and praxis that were described in the first two chapters. The church can only be the anticipatory sign of the eschaton if it is at the same time a remembrance and actualization of the message and praxis of Jesus, who embodied most completely this eschatological hope.

I would like to focus on these three aspects of the church—remembrance, actualization, and eschatological hope—in order to explicate more fully the model of church as anticipatory sign. These dimensions of the church's life are necessarily interconnected and interpenetrating, but it will be useful to isolate each one momentarily in order to understand it better. Each of these dimensions illustrates how Schillebeeckx develops the church-world relationship from his earlier thought within the paradigm of his later theology.

Although the church is anticipatory sign of the eschatological fulfillment of God's intention for humanity and the world, it does this only as a community of remembrance, of *anamnesis*. The church's historical dependence on Jesus signifies that part of the church's essence is the recollection of its own origin in the message and praxis of Jesus that should continually criticize and reanimate it. As Schillebeeckx is fond of writing, one of the church's main functions is the critical appropriation of the *memoria passionis et resurrectionis Christi*. In one of his more concise definitions of the church, he uses primarily this language of remembrance.

> The church as a visible community of faith arises as a community of people who stand in the tradition of Israel and Jesus of Nazareth and

who on basis of this confess the same faith, celebrate this community and finally allow their behavior to be determined by the guidelines of the praxis of the Kingdom of God, a kingdom of justice and love among all human beings who find their salvation in God: a community of people of God gathered round the God of people as he is revealed in Jesus Christ.[47]

One immediately notes that this anamnetic dimension of the church's life is in no way a slavish traditionalism that preserves the memory of Jesus in the ossified form of one particular moment of history, even the moment of Jesus' own life. Schillebeeckx argues that the church's praxis, its *sequela Jesu,* to use his phrase, is the living anamnesis of Jesus. This memory-in-praxis, as it were, must find purchase within each period of history. On the other hand, this praxis and memory also stand under the critical and corrective force of that memory of Jesus.

The church is a community of remembrance; it is bound to the recollection, critical reappropriation, and practical living out of the message and praxis of Jesus. This commitment entails a corresponding relationship to the world: the church is the place that keeps alive the name of God. Schillebeeckx has from the beginning of his career been concerned with the question about belief in God in a world growing more secularized every year. Particularly after his contact with the theology of secularization in the 1960s, and the dramatic changes in religious practice among the Dutch (and other Europeans) in the wake of that turbulent decade,[48] Schillebeeckx has sought to discover the significance of this move toward secularization (rather than simply condemning it), while simultaneously arguing for the fittingness of naming God in this new situation. The church is a primary location of this naming in the modern world, because it is the community that addresses God through worship and prayer. Before theological and philosophical reflection on this language of God, there is first the language that people direct to God, in praise, prayer, celebration (and curse).

First of all the word God is used by communities of faith and within a specifically religious activity, which we can sum up as an articulate confession of belief in God, the witness and the ritual, cultic or liturgical activity of the celebrating community, and finally ethical admonition (on a smaller or larger scale). This in fact means that the human use of the word God belongs primarily in a context in which people do not so much talk about God as to God and therefore in a context of worship and reverence and further in a context of confessing and witnessing to God; and finally in the praxis of "following God."[49]

By their continuing address to God, Christians, both socially and individually, keep the name of God alive in the world. This naming cannot be either an antiquarian or an insular exercise. The church performs its anamnetic task both for itself and for the world not only by remembering the story of Jesus and addressing God in prayer, but by its concrete action in the world.

This brings us to the second dimension of the idea of church as anticipatory sign: the church as a community of celebration and praxis in the present situation. During my earlier discussion of Schillebeeckx's view of revelation, history, and eschatology, I noted that God's presence is continually made real only in the concrete present moment. God's revelation is not only mediated to human beings through created realities; it must also be *enacted* by human beings through their praxis.

This practical theology of revelation applies even more so to the life of the church. Schillebeeckx sets this present-day actualizing aspect of the church, that is, its role as both sacrament of Christ and sacrament of the world, within the dialectic of mysticism and politics.[50] He defines the terms of this pair in the following way: "I use the term mysticism here to denote an intensive form of experience of God or love of God, and politics to denote an intensive form of social commitment (and thus not the political activity of professional politicians *per se*), a commitment accessible to all people."[51]

Schillebeeckx argues that in the contemporary situation both mysticism and politics are necessary components for an authentic Christian life. In opposition to a form of piety that would either exclude political involvement or radically separate it from prayer, Schillebeeckx asks that Christians develop a form of "political holiness" that both integrates prayer and praxis and offers a critique of both the individualistic excesses of personal spirituality and the often deadening earnestness of political activism. "Politics without prayer or mysticism quickly becomes grim and barbaric; prayer and mysticism without political love becomes sentimental and irrelevant interiority."[52] Not only do they provide the necessary complement to each other, but they also provide the occasion for the enriched experience of both. Resisting the negative contrast experiences of human history through political praxis can itself provide a mystical experience of union with God; conversely, mystical prayer leads one to embrace fully the ambiguity of the human situation with a hope that transcends any purely political solution.[53]

This dialectic of mysticism and politics for Schillebeeckx does not refer only to the experiences of the individual believer, but also to the ecclesial community itself. The result of this Christian life of mysticism and politics is the liturgical worship of the Christian community and the concrete service the church offers to the wider human community.

Communal liturgy and worship, according to Schillebeeckx, are the most concentrated forms of the church's life as anticipatory sign. The experience of God's transcendence in and through the human overcoming of suffering naturally leads to liturgical worship and prayer.[54] This worship not only celebrates God's salvation occurring in the present, but also recalls the fundamental narrative of Jesus' life and symbolically represents the eschatological hope for the fullness of the human future, which transcends and completes the fragmentary experiences of happiness in the now. All three of these aspects come into play in the central event of worship, the sacraments.

In his early phase Schillebeeckx's sacramental theology provides a framework for a general fundamental theology. Although later his focus certainly shifts away from the sacraments,[55] the model of the church as anticipatory sign that I am developing here derives from an analogous translation of his later, fragmentary, sacramental theology into categories of ecclesiology. For example, near the end of the *Christ* book Schillebeeckx writes:

> As long as there is still a real history of suffering among us, we cannot do without the sacramental liturgy: to abolish it or neglect it would be to stifle the firm hope in universal peace and general reconciliation. For as long as salvation and peace are still not actual realities, hope for them must be attested and above all nourished and kept alive, and this is only possible in anticipatory symbols.[56]

This passage (and others similar to it) provides the starting point for Schillebeeckx's reconsideration of the meaning of the sacraments within his new theological paradigms. Sacraments are "anticipatory, mediating signs of salvation, that is, healed and reconciled life."[57] In the context of the community's worship, they proleptically represent the fullness of human life in the eschatological future, celebrate human fragmentary experiences of wholeness in the present, and through the contrast of these two elements also provide the basis for criticism of that which does not bring about salvation and peace. In his new book on the sacraments (see n. 55), he describes them as metaphorical celebrations which interrupt the human profane story with the equally human story of "the 'eschatological *dromenon* or drama' fulfilling itself, especially [in] the 'worldly' event, completed in our profane history, of the course of the life of Jesus of Nazareth, which ends in the historical, humiliating fiasco of an execution."[58] As in his earlier works, the sacraments are not quasi-magical events in some mythical sense but encounters in the world with God's presence through the mediation of the worldly. Schillebeeckx thus reinterprets previous insights through both the hermeneutical and critical frameworks already discussed. Because of the necessary dialectical interrelationship between mysticism and politics, between theory and praxis, between church as sacrament of Christ and sacrament of the world, the sacraments as metaphorical celebrations also link the Christian church with service to the world and the furtherance of the *humanum*. Schillebeeckx writes:

> What, finally, is a "metaphorical celebration"? For that is what the
> church sacraments are, and in such a way that, on the one hand, the
> metaphorical "Eucharistic breaking" of the bread becomes an empty shell
> without the human basis of our actual "fraternal sharing with others"
> in the sphere of our earthly, everyday reality; while on the other hand,
> the naive optimism of worldly-political solidarity, because of repeated
> historical failures, becomes a deceptive ideology without liturgical cele
> brations and hopes. Moreover, *can* we still celebrate? Even: *dare* we still
> celebrate? And above all, *what* do we celebrate?[59]

The church's sacraments therefore not only celebrate God's presence in midst of the current assembly but also concretely represent the church's role in the wider world, as a sacrament of human unity, a living sign of the redeemed and peaceful human community. The actualizing aspect of the church must necessarily extend to the whole world that it serves.

That is to say: the restricted, well-defined brotherhood of the Christian community is at the service of a universal brotherhood. Thus the universal brotherhood is effectively mediated by a historically particular limited brotherhood. Therein lies the profound importance of the performative utterance of the Second Vatican Council, when it declared that "the Church is a sacrament, that is, an effective and operatively mediating sign of the unity of mankind." Both theologically and sociologically this would appear to be a justifiably performative statement, calling upon Christians actually to live out their Christian brotherhood as serving the project of universal brotherhood among all people, and as a way of life anticipating in miniature what on a larger scale must be the goal of all human endeavour.[60]

The church therefore must also be an agent for political and social change in any situation that threatens the flourishing of human life. However, the church's call to political involvement, although an essential part of its mission, is not absolute. Schillebeeckx argues that the church's involvement in politics has two dimensions. The first is concrete actions in solidarity with those who also seek the *humanum*. He asserts that the church in the current situation cannot create its own political solutions to problems (a reference to the disappearing Dutch social structure of *verzuiling*, or pillarization) but must cooperate with others who are likewise committed to a just world for all. The second is that the church cannot simply be another political party or contestation group on the political scene. The church must bring a particularly religious and theological quality to the problems of the current society and their attempted solutions.

This quality of the church's involvement in society provides a segue to the third aspect of the church as anticipatory sign. The church not only keeps the name of God alive in the world's memory and liturgically celebrates the presence of God in the here and now but also hopes for the final fulfillment of the human race in the *eschaton*, which is God's future. Because of this expectation, the church also warns against any premature identification of this final state; all human attempts at liberation, all naming of salvation in the present, can only be partial because they stand under the eschatological proviso.

> In other words, religion, even Christian faith, is politically relevant, in that it opposes a *complete identification* of human salvation with politics. God's proviso, which for men takes the form of an eschatological proviso, makes it impossible for the believer to absolutize politics. Christianity *desacralizes* politics.[61]

Because God's salvation for human beings ultimately transcends the bounds of history, no experience of human liberation is itself ultimate. For this reason, no human project of emancipation and liberation can claim divine sanction without this eschatological reservation.

> God cannot be used as a means for human ends, any more than man can be used as a means for divine ends. Religion and mankind transcend

the category of the usable and the functional—which does not prevent religion in this respect from being "highly functional" for the advancement
of human dignity generally.[62]

On the other hand, the church's eschatological aspect is not simply a negative warning against making absolute any human project. The church's memory of Jesus and its celebration of God's presence also provide a positive,
if fragmentary, content for the church's eschatological hope and its contemporary praxis. In the church's action in the present, one also sees a glimmer of
the eschatological future, toward which God is drawing the whole human
race.[63] Also in a broader sense the church can see in human experiences of salvation a sign of God's ultimate salvation, even if they cannot be identified
completely with each other. Therefore the church's eschatological nature and
its concurrent proviso do not weaken the church's anamnetic or actualizing aspects; rather, only its eschatological nature gives the church the freedom to
engage in its critical remembrance of Jesus in the present situation and to act
in worship and justice as the situation demands.

The church as a community of remembrance, praxis, and hope is also a
community in and through which God works. In his earlier period Schillebeeckx relied on the theology of the sacrament as encounter to explain how
the human actions of the church's worship were a medium for God's prior
action on human beings for our salvation. In his later theology this activity of
God in the church is less easily discernible because Schillebeeckx places
greater emphasis on the autonomy and concrete historicity of human beings.
Yet God's activity and human activity in history are never opposed to each
other in any phase of his thinking. According to Schillebeeckx, the history of
human overcoming of evil and suffering is also a history of God's liberating
and cooperating presence. Schillebeeckx calls this active presence in both
church and world the Spirit of God.

It is ironic that the Spirit plays such an important role in his later ecclesiology, because Schillebeeckx rarely talks directly about pneumatology. For example, in the previous chapter, I argued that Schillebeeckx's theology has
three "limit concepts" that provide both boundaries for any authentic Christian narrative and positive content for that narrative. These limit concepts
were, in short form: the pure positivity of God; the manifestation of God's
cause as the human cause in the life, death, and resurrection of Jesus; and the
humanum, or human flourishing, as God's ultimate aim for humanity. Although it would be anachronistic to accuse Schillebeeckx of a certain form of

"binitarianism," one can certainly ask what role the Spirit of God plays within this framework. In his earlier work Schillebeeckx rarely deals explicitly with Trinitarian theology,[64] and this tendency continues in his later theology as well. In an interview recorded in *I Am a Happy Theologian*, Schillebeeckx affirms his belief in the Trinity but also expresses his reluctance to engage in any speculative reflection on such a mystery.

> Christianity speaks of the divine Trinity. But I personally am somewhat reticent about the Trinity. I am afraid that saying that God is three persons risks producing a kind of tritheism: three Gods, three persons, like a kind of family. I hesitate to do speculative theology on the three persons and the relations between them. Through Jesus Christ, Son of God, there is the relationship with God the Father; after his resurrection, Christ is from God in the form of the Spirit, as an eschatological gift of God and God's. One can talk of the Trinity, but what does it mean to say three persons? I accept the personality of God, but we do not know the divine mode of this personality. The Trinity is God's mode of being personal. In this I am fully orthodox and in harmony with dogma.[65]

Particularly concerning the Spirit, Schillebeeckx maintains this sort of modesty, which he does not hesitate to label an "almost agnostic" position.[66] Yet this "agnosticism" pertains only to the possibility of human knowledge about the inner-Trinitarian relationships; for Schillebeeckx human beings know the Spirit through the Spirit's effects on the church and human history. As he describes it in the quotation above, the Spirit is God's presence in salvation history and the church as an eschatological gift. Without wishing to say much more, Schillebeeckx affirms that the Spirit is the God of Jesus Christ continually present in the concrete circumstances of history.

> I fully accept the creed, but the three divine persons are not in the profession of faith. I believe in almighty God, in Jesus the Christ, the beloved of the Father, Son of God *par excellence;* I believe in the Holy Spirit, who is the greatest problem for me. In the Bible the Spirit is a gift, not the third person; it is the very mode of being God, who gives himself to human beings. It is always the personality of God, but the personality of God in the history of the church, in the history of salvation.[67]

This continuing presence of God's Spirit in history and the church is the final element in Schillebeeckx's ecclesiology of the church as anticipatory sign.

The church is a community of anamnesis, actualization, and eschatological hope not only through its own efforts but also through the work of the Holy Spirit within it. Consistent with his overall theology of creation and revelation, Schillebeeckx affirms that this dialectical interrelationship of God and human in the church cannot be simplistically divided into God's action and human response. Although God's saving and revealing activity is ultimately prior to any human action, this salvation nevertheless only comes mediated through the life of Jesus and the lives of believers in the community. As always, Schillebeeckx refuses to play the divine off against the human. The Spirit works in the church, but only within the humanity of the church's believers. Thus the church as anticipatory sign of God's reign is always and at the same time a purely human institution with its limitations and flaws. This nonantithetical and dialectical interrelationship of Spirit and the church community is the background for Schillebeeckx's understanding of ministry and authority in the church in both his earlier and later theology.

four | The Apostolicity of the Church in Schillebeeckx's Early Theology

The discussion in the previous chapter focused on Schillebeeckx's general ecclesiology of the church as sacrament. Essential, of course, to the Catholic understanding of the sacraments is the idea that they are visible signs through which the church mediates the grace of God. This emphasis on the mediation of grace through visible, external signs holds no less when one applies sacramental theology to ecclesiology. The community of the church itself, especially as it expresses itself most concretely through its liturgical worship and institutional structure, becomes a sacramental sign and mediator of God's continuing presence. For this reason Catholic ecclesiology has customarily seen both "internal" spiritual life and "external" institutional structures as necessary elements for any complete theological discussion of the nature of the church.

However, this ecclesiological approach contains certain tensions and dangers. In a sacramental ecclesiology the fundamental tension is found in the relationship between the mediator and the mediated; because the church is both human community and place of the divine presence, the fundamental danger lies in collapsing the distinction between the mediator and the mediated so that the mediating structure becomes simply identified with the divine.

The institution of official forms of ordained ministry and teaching authority in the church exemplify in a particularly clear way the problems possible in a sacramental ecclesiology. For, as they have developed in the Catholic tradition, both ordained ministry and magisterium lay claim to being special places of mediation. The former has the power to administer sacramental grace; the latter has the power to judge in the light of God's revelation in Jesus what is or is not an authentic mediating expression (doctrinal, liturgical, or ethical) of that revelation. The fact that Catholic doctrine explicitly links ordination to ranks of ministry with magisterial authority makes the tension and danger all the greater.[1] The problem can be expressed best as a paradox: God's presence in the church is always mediated through the human reality of the church community. Yet one part of this ecclesial community (the ordained, hierarchical magisterium) can judge what is an authentic mediation in the wider life of the church. But the hierarchical magisterium is also part of the human reality of the church and therefore of the structure of mediation. How can this mediating structure judge another aspect of the mediating structure of the church without claiming to be the mediated itself, that is, the divine presence?

With this question in mind, it is necessary to focus more strictly on the different elements involved in preserving the apostolicity of the church—particularly the ordained ministry, the magisterium, and theologians—before approaching the question of theological dissent and critical communities in the church. In this chapter I will focus on Schillebeeckx's early thought, particularly concerning: the general structure of the church; specific ideas about the Petrine and episcopal ministry and the idea of infallibility; the role of theologians in the church; the possibilities for dissent and critical communities within the church; and the concept of the indefectibility of the church. Throughout this discussion I will use Schillebeeckx's understanding of the truth status of the various levels of discourse used by these different offices and people within the church as a way of clearly demarcating their respective roles and authority.

The Hierarchy and Laity as Essential Expressions of the Church's Apostolicity

In his early phase Schillebeeckx describes the church as the sacrament of the primordial sacrament, Jesus Christ, the Son of God. Setting the sacramental nature of the church within a general understanding of the sacramentality of all salvation history and revelation leads Schillebeeckx to conclude that the church is the community and institution necessary for making concrete the presence of Christ in the world after the resurrection.[2] More specifically with regard to the structure of the church, Schillebeeckx argues that although the whole church is this continuing sacrament of Christ, the church does have a division between the apostolic office of the hierarchy and lay believers based on the different aspects of Christ's relationship to it.

We remarked that this visibility of grace defines the whole Church; not the hierarchical church only, but also the community of the faithful. The whole Church, the people of God led by a priestly hierarchy, is a "sign raised up among the nations." The activity, as much of the faithful as of their leaders, is thus an ecclesial activity. This means that not only the hierarchy but also the believing people belong essentially to the primordial sacrament which is the earthly expression of this reality. As the sacramental Christ, the Church too is mystically both head and members. When the twofold function of Christ becomes visible in the sign of the Christian community, it produces the distinction between hierarchy and faithful—a distinction of offices and of those who hold them. Even though the hierarchy, on the one hand, are themselves part of the believing church, and the faithful, on the other hand, share in the lordship of Christ and to some extent give it visibility, the sacramental functions of hierarchy and faithful differ within the Church and show the distinction.[3]

This statement, presaging Vatican II's renewed emphasis on the role of the laity in the church, indicates Schillebeeckx's acceptance both of the traditional distinctions between clergy and laity and his relatively progressive stance toward what was then called the lay apostolate. Given the structure of the church as hierarchy and laity, Schillebeeckx argues consistently that the laity have a mandate within the church that does not simply derive from the hierarchy.[4] In distinction from the early forms of Catholic Action, which saw the layperson's role as an extension of the hierarchical apostolate, Schillebeeckx argues that the laity have a mission separate from the hierarchy which requires them to be witnesses to the Gospel through their ordering of secular life.[5]

Although he does attempt to balance the roles of the laity and the clergy in his early theology, Schillebeeckx still follows the pattern of the day in placing a great deal of emphasis on the ministry and office of the ordained in the church,[6] particularly priests, bishops, and the pope. For Schillebeeckx the most basic definition of ministry or office in the church is: apostolic and sacramental participation in Christ's headship over the church.[7] This office or ministry, which is also the paradigmatic priestly office in the church, is held by the bishops as successors to the apostles.

The sacramental and earthly manifestation of the Lord in his capacity as head of the people of God is carried out, and that exclusively, in the apostolic office, whose postapostolic continuation is the episcopal hierarchy, although within the *closed* apostolic "traditio Domini." In this respect the ecclesiastical hierarchy or the "ordo episcopalis" stands sovereign *over against* the whole church community of faith, and that in such a way that this distinction between "clerical" hierarchy and lay community is of divine origin. Only the apostolic office officially represents Christ-as-head-of-the-church (as Pope Pius XII also repeatedly suggests in *Mediator Dei* in connection with the priesthood: the priest as liturgical leader acts "in persona Christi *capitis*").[8]

Since they possess the fullness of the "sacerdotium" given to the church by Christ, they are primarily responsible for both the word and sacrament; that is, recalling the earlier discussion of the theology of revelation, the bishops are the ones commissioned to continue the apostolic task of transmitting and keeping alive in the church the dialectic of revelation in reality and revelation in word which culminated in Christ.[9] From their primary task of oversight over word and sacrament flows their teaching authority, which Schillebeeckx characterizes as simply an organized and official exercise of that task.

> The priestly function of the people of God, which is present in all who are baptized and confirmed, is present in the episcopate in mode of guiding authority, and hence as the immediate representatives of Christ in his role as Head of the Church. Hence this priesthood is manifested in the mode of ecclesiastical authority, in which quality it is distinct from and constituted above the *laikoi* or the members of the priestly People of God. Authority as such implies jurisdiction and the power of government, and therefore in a religious context is called pastoral authority or office. But in virtue of the character of the ecclesial community this authority is also the principle of the administration of the sacraments and of the preaching of the Gospel (teaching authority). The various divisions of authority in the Church, the hierarchy, are derived from her authority over sacrament and word; they are merely the systematic organization of the one underlying reality: the apostolic office or the episcopal priesthood.[10]

Because the ministry's teaching authority over the laity involves the power to make judgments on the doctrinal language, liturgical practice, and ethical behavior of the other members of the church, the laity ultimately do not have an independent "power" of interpretation, judgment, or action. Although Schillebeeckx is an early advocate for the more complete participation of the laity in their own mission in the church, this activity does not yet include a share in the teaching ministry or office which is the prerogative of the hierarchy.

The Teaching Office of the Hierarchy and the Role of Theologians in the Church

According to Schillebeeckx, the teaching authority of the hierarchy rests on their possession of the apostolic office of maintaining the living dialectic of word and sacrament in the church. This magisterium therefore has a positive and a negative aspect. Positively, the hierarchy has the role of expressing the fundamental reality of salvation that has occurred in Christ; the bishops and pope are the chief preachers of the word in the church. In a negative or limiting sense, they also possess the authority to judge whether a particular language, practice, or behavior falls within the parameters of the reality of salvation; in other words, the hierarchy judges whether some ecclesial language or practice preserves or strays away from the "deposit of faith."[11]

The hierarchy of the church exercises this magisterium in different ways with differing levels of authority. In addition, not all of the church's language has the same claim on truth (and hence obedience), because different forms of language and different sources of that language have different levels of the "reality of revelation" expressed within them. In preconciliar Catholic theology, these distinctions in the authority of language became the object of a complex series of classifications known as "theological notes." Schillebeeckx describes a list of such notes (which he also calls "qualifications") in order to shed more light on the teaching authority of the magisterium and the role of theologians in relation to the magisterium.[12] This discussion of levels of authority in doctrinal and theological language ties in to Schillebeeckx's first circle of epistemology. Schillebeeckx develops that epistemological understanding in an attempt to overcome a purely propositional approach to the truth of doctrinal statements. Hence, although the system of theological "notes" primarily refers to different types of propositions, Schillebeeckx's early theology gives greater nuance to this discussion by relating the truth of statements (and the truth of the judgments made about statements) to the dynamic and historical reality of salvation and revelation which underlies them.

At the highest level are "propositions which are of *divine and Catholic faith*" or "dogma."[13] Schillebeeckx gives a more complete definition of "dogma" in another contribution to the same theological encyclopedia.

In the time of Renaissance it [dogma] first obtained the classical status it still has. Dogma is therefore: any truth revealed directly by God, be it explicitly or implicitly, which is thus contained in Holy Scriptures or in the oral Tradition, and moreover is expressly held up to believers as divinely revealed, either by the extraordinary or the ordinary teaching authority of the church. The [First] Vatican [Council] calls these truths "divine and Catholic faith" (Denz 1792).[14]

Dogmas are true in the highest sense, that is, infallibly, because they have their source in God's direct revelation in Scripture and tradition and have been judged as such by the highest authority in the church (the extraordinary and ordinary magisterium). Determining the truth of a theological proposition requires a consideration of both its source and the source of the judgment about it. Statements that arise from different sources or do not have the same judgment of approval therefore do not possess the same quality of truth. Schillebeeckx encapsulates this idea in a short formula: "The dogmata [collection of dogmas] are therefore the ecclesial, authentic representations of a truth of revelation."[15]

However, Schillebeeckx also argues that the nature of human knowledge and the intellectual status of concepts render even dogmatic propositions subject to the limitations of language and open to the possibility of development. Concepts are true not because they somehow simply capture the truth within themselves but because they point in an objectively true way to the reality that is incompletely expressed in that concept. Dogmas are therefore true expressions of the reality of revelation, but their linguistic and conceptual content is not that reality itself.[16]

Concerning the possibility of development, Schillebeeckx argues that because of the true but inadequate nature of dogmas, these concepts can be the subject of greater clarity, depth, and complexity of expression. Since the community of the church experiences the reality of revelation in different conditions and periods of history, the dogmatic language of the church can change and develop as historical circumstances compel the church to explore more fully and elucidate more clearly the inexhaustible content of the one mystery of faith.[17] This process of the development of doctrine is a complex one where human beings, actively engaged in their tradition and their historical situations, strive to bring to a more complete expression the reality of salvation and revelation which they both inherit from the past and experience in the present. This striving is not a purely human effort; true development of doctrine only takes place through the light of faith and ultimately under the impulse and guidance of the Holy Spirit.[18] Within the church itself, it ultimately falls to the teaching authority of the church to judge whether a particular development of doctrine is true.[19]

Dogmatic truths are those both revealed by God and defined as such by the highest authority in the church. However, revealed truths and truths defined by the teaching office are not a coterminous set; there are truths which belong to either category but not necessarily to both. Next in the order of theological notes are "doctrines of faith" ("geloofsleer"), which Schillebeeckx defines as "truths whose character as revelation cannot be doubted, but which have not yet been so declared as dogma with infallible certainty by the church's teaching authority."[20] Hence the scope of revealed truth is broader than official definitions of it, although an official and infallible definition does raise a doctrine of faith to an even higher level of certainty, that of dogma.

Next come two notes which refer to propositions that are either connected in some direct fashion to the truths of revelation or that are not with certainty known to be part of those truths. The first, a "dogmatic fact," is "a fact which is not revealed, but connects closely with the doctrine of faith: for example, the legitimacy of this or that Pope."[21] The church can decide these truths, but not infallibly.[22] Then there are the "almost doctrines of faith," which Schillebeeckx describes as "the propositions, which according to the general opinion of theologians are really implied with regard to their content in the sources of revelation, but about which the Church has not yet spoken, so that [their] revealed character still can be doubted."[23] The role and authority of theologians varies with the level of statement concerned; at this level the general consensus of theologians about the revelatory nature of some truth is indicative but not determinative of that truth.

The infallibility of the magisterium extends further than revealed truths (although the sum of revealed truth is also greater than magisterial declarations of it). The next note is

> [a] truth not to be believed, but to be held: ("veritas tenenda, non credenda"): natural, non-revealed truths, which have been defined as truth by the Church infallibly, because of their close connection with dogma. The infallibility of the church always extends further than the formally revealed. Under this heading fall above all the natural foundations of the faith. Sometimes these are called "catholic truths" or "authentic church doctrine."[24]

In another place in the same encyclopedia, Schillebeeckx expands on what is covered by these "foundations of the faith."

> Infallible ecclesial definition is broader than the ecclesial definition of faith. . . . So the Church can solemnly and infallibly define the truth of purely natural truths, of historical facts, of ecclesial practices, and so forth, which are closely related to revealed truths.[25]

In this sense the infallible authority of the magisterium extends not only to the speculative theological connections between dogmas but to the practical dimension of the church's life as well. Schillebeeckx does not define "ecclesial practices" or "practical" connection much further, but one could argue that practices that would fall within the purview of such infallibility would include the basic structure, offices, and authority in the church, since these pertain directly to how the truth of revelation expressed in the deposit of faith can continue to be a living reality within the whole church community.

The final two theological notes refer more specifically to the work of theologians. The first, "theologically certain propositions," "are truths which in one manner or another follow from truths of faith and are theologically-scientifically responsible, although they are not formally revealed."[26] This may be Schillebeeckx's expanded definition of the neoscholastic "theological conclusion," which involved a premise drawn from dogma, a syllogism based on that premise, and a conclusion which could then be held as "theologically certain."[27] The second is the "common opinions of theologians," referring to propositions, "which, apart from the particular nature of their connection with the doctrine of faith, are generally accepted by theologians."[28]

What does this discussion show us about the power of the magisterium itself? The magisterium of the church, both extraordinary and ordinary, is exercised by the bishops and the pope, and it has the gift of infallibility to define dogmas of the faith and also other truths that form the foundation of these dogmas. The magisterium can also define other truths that have a close connection to doctrines of the faith, even if it does not do so in an infallible manner.

Schillebeeckx at this point accepts the distinctions between the extraordinary and ordinary magisterium and between the episcopal and papal exercises of magisterial authority. The extraordinary magisterium of the church only occurs when the pope himself makes an infallible dogmatic definition under certain particular circumstances[29] or when a properly convened ecumenical council, under papal authority, does so.[30] This extraordinary magisterium of the pope with the bishops is a particular form of the ordinary and universal teaching authority of the whole hierarchy, whose infallibility Schillebeeckx also accepts.[31] Likewise, he agrees with the classical distinction between episcopal teaching authority and the particular teaching office of the pope, although he also recognizes that papal infallibility also occurs only under restricted circumstances and only in relation to the fundamental reality of revelation.[32] Schillebeeckx carefully nuances the various levels of the authority of church statements and argues, on the basis of his epistemology and understanding of language, that even dogmas are not themselves simply the truths of revelation. In so doing, he takes an orthodox but minimalist posture toward the magisterium. The shifts in both his theological presuppositions and the church's situation after the Second Vatican Council will test even this minimalist reading.

From the list of theological notes given above, it would seem on first reading that Schillebeeckx confines the theologian's task to the "lower" end of the scale of authoritative language. The final two notes concerned propositions that either were considered "theologically certain" because they followed logically from dogmatic truths or were simply considered true on the basis of their general acceptance by theologians. In neither case does theologians' work enjoy any privilege of infallibility or any claim to be revelation in itself.

However, these notes refer only to the value of theologians' language *in itself*; the actual task of theologians in the church and their relationship with the magisterium is far more complex. In order to describe this task and this relationship, it is necessary first to give Schillebeeckx's understanding of theology as a scholarly discipline within the context of the church.

In this early phase of his work, Schillebeeckx gives the most complete overview of his understanding of theology in an article originally written for the *Theologisch Woordenboek* and later included in *Revelation and Theology*.[33] For him, "theology is really the scientific, conscious evaluation and expression of the content of the church's experience of faith."[34] Beginning with the last part of the definition, Schillebeeckx argues that theology derives from faith because the act of faith itself means both consent to revealed truth and a desire to know more about the truth to which one has consented.[35] However, one makes the act of faith in response to the revelation which culminated in Jesus Christ and which the life of the church continually makes present. Hence theology both depends on and presupposes faith and also recognizes the history of salvation and revelation, which is the human medium through which God's offer and the human response of faith occur.

Although theology is therefore based on faith in the God revealed in the history of salvation, it is also a scientific activity that requires, as Schillebeeckx puts it, insight, research, and methodical precision.[36] This is true because the object of faith is the revelation of God's own self in and through the conditions of history. This revelation is objectively real and "external" to the believer, and so it can be a subject for investigation and exploration. Because this revelation is meaningful as a solution to the mystery of human life, it "implies a certain intelligibility and is therefore open to reflection."[37] Therefore theology can be a intellectual and scientific discipline that both draws on faith and yet remains in a certain sense separate from it.

Schillebeeckx makes a distinction between two functions, or aspects, of theology: the "positive" and the "speculative."[38] Positive theology is the study of the "sources of revelation and the various testimonies of the faith throughout the centuries" in order to determine the content of revelation "as purely and as integrally as possible."[39] More than a "pre-theological preliminary stage of speculative theology," positive theology is a necessary function of theology that should examine all stages of salvation history, including the present situation of the church, in order to discover the *loci theologici* in each era.[40]

The other function of theology, the speculative, depends and builds on the positive. Consistent with the epistemology described in the first chapter, Schillebeeckx argues that speculative theology is not simply the discovery of the interrelationships and ordering of dogmatic concepts but the reflection on the one mystery of faith to which dogmatic and theological concepts projectively point. Because the one mystery of faith only comes to human beings through the mediation of salvation history, culminating in the event of Christ, speculative theology should have a Christological focus. Yet since theology ultimately is thinking about the mystery of God, speculative theology also has a theocentric and Trinitarian focus. However, Schillebeeckx argues (again in opposition to the excessively conceptual neoscholasticism of the day) that the theocentric task of speculative theology only comes into focus through the lens of Christocentric salvation history. "Theology is undoubtedly concerned with the intelligibility of the living God, and the history of salvation is the only way toward this understanding."[41]

For Schillebeeckx, speculative theology has several main tasks. First, speculative theology can show the "mutual connections between the mysteries of faith."[42] Second, it can provide a "deeper insight into the intelligibility of the separate truths of faith."[43] Third, it draws "theological intelligibility from the saving value of the content of revelation."[44] That is, it reflects on the concrete experience of salvation as narrated in the history of salvation and from that reflection expresses its understanding of the God who brings salvation. Finally, speculative theology can reflect on the *preambula fidei* and so bring about "a deeper knowledge of faith through the theological study of the natural basis of faith."[45] Especially in an age that has a greater critical consciousness, discovering and explicating those truths of faith that can be understood from a secular perspective as well would prove very useful.

As one can see from this overview, theology and the theologian's task focus on the fundamental realities of faith and their conceptual and scientific expression. Although theologians themselves only have authority within the scientific and fallible limits of their discipline, the subject matter of their work is the very reality of salvation and revelation that the church's dogmatic and infallible statements attempt to capture. Hence, as Schillebeeckx points out several times in his essay, theology is a science of the content of faith, "of which the immediate norm is the church."[46] More specifically, since the work of theologians pertains to the development and explication of the deposit of faith, this work falls under the judgment of those entrusted with the task of defending and preaching that basic deposit of faith, the bishops with the pope. Theology is a human, fallible service of critical authority in the life of the church, but the "official critical authority" in the church is vested in the magisterium.[47]

In the final analysis, then, the theologian is under the authority of the magisterium, which has the obligation and the power to judge the theologian's language. For Schillebeeckx this does not mean that the theologian's role can be reduced or subsumed under that of the hierarchy. Because of the particular scientific and exploratory nature of theological work, theologians are a "living organ of reflection" who have a certain freedom to pursue their work beyond the simple exposition and defense of magisterial statements. As previously noted, the function of positive theology includes an investigation of the *loci theologici* in the world and in the present-day life of the church. Similarly, with regard to the speculative function of theology, the theologian should be engaged in the world and be aware of modern thought so that the church can make its teaching known within the language and forms of thought of contemporary life. For this reason, Schillebeeckx can say, even in this pre–Vatican II period, that theologians should be a progressive element in the church.

Theologians have therefore to be the "antennae" with which the church feels modern thought, so as to assimilate those elements of it that can be used and to reject what cannot. The theologian is called to stand at a dangerous crossing of the roads—at the point where faith comes into contact with modern thought and the whole of the new philosophical situation, but where no synthesis has as yet been achieved. It is he who is expected to provide the synthesis. Living theology is always a step ahead of the official theology of the church and ventures along paths where it is still unprotected by the church's teaching authority. . . . In this sense, theologians are by definition the progressive factors in the life of faith and the thought of the church. They are the catalysts, since as Aquinas himself has said, nothing is so paralysing as habitual thought which makes us adhere firmly to traditional views that, on critical analysis, frequently turn out to be false views.[48]

Nevertheless, for Schillebeeckx this progressive and catalytic nature of theology does not yet give the theologian any right to dissent. I define "theological dissent" as the publicly expressed disagreement by a theologian or a group of theologians with an official and noninfallible teaching promulgated by the magisterium. Schillebeeckx's understanding of theology allows the theologian to explore "paths . . . unprotected by the church's teaching authority"; however, these explorations are ultimately subject to that authority and cannot contradict, to pursue his metaphor, the areas already mapped by church dogma. This understanding corresponds to my analysis of the theological notes, where the theologian's own views are at the lowest level of authority without sanction by the magisterium. It is possible that the magisterium may raise a theologian's understanding of some element of the deposit of faith to the level of infallibly proclaimed dogma, but, of course, this does not fall within the power of theologians themselves.

The idea of the critical community also seems largely absent from this early period of his thought. "Critical community" may be simply defined as an intentional gathering of Christians outside of the regular boundaries of parish and diocesan organization which has the express purpose of seeking to live out Jesus' message of the reign of God to the fullest and to offer that community life as a challenge to both the rest of the church and to the world. In a later interview, Schillebeeckx mentions that he had been involved with a theology critical of the dominant Roman school from 1957 onward.[49] However, judging from his theological writings in this early period, it seems that this critical theology was not directly associated with what he will later call "critical communities" because the institutional and ecclesiological "space" for these did not yet fully exist.

Within the narrower confines of thought and practice that governed the pre–Vatican II church, Schillebeeckx does not openly attempt to create a theological justification for dissent or the creation of alternative community structures. I would argue, however, that his approach to dogma and church authority are themselves implicit forms of theological dissent. Insofar as Schillebeeckx strove to combat the highly conceptualist model of dogmatic theology with one which recognized the limitations of theological language and the importance of salvation history, he also undermined the claim that the truth is contained in dogmatic formulations which the magisterium simply repeats and theologians apologetically defend and conceptually nuance. Similarly, because of this careful exposition of the relationship between dogmatic truth and the various levels of dogmatic and theological language, he also delineates the amount of adherence that believers need give to different statements. This stance thus argues against any "creeping infallibilism" (as it will later be called), which accords absolute authority to any and every statement that proceeds from the pope and bishops. Not every denial of a magisterial statement is a heresy, and even the rightful antiheretical statements produced by the church's authority run the risk of one-sidedness.[50] In other words, Schillebeeckx attempts to give as much latitude as possible to the development of doctrine and the role of theologians within the church. He remains resolutely orthodox in his acceptance of magisterial authority, but he also recognizes the complementary roles that theologians and even the laity play in the development of Christian teaching.

The Indefectibility of the Church

This complementary interplay between laity, theologians, and the magisterium ultimately stands under the protection of the Holy Spirit, who is the final guardian of the church's preservation in the truth. In both his earlier and later work, Schillebeeckx affirms that the Spirit is the ultimate source of authority in the church, even if that authority is also mediated through the apostolic office of the hierarchy. However, this mediation of the Spirit also has a dialectical aspect; the teaching office, and indeed the whole church itself, is both *sancta* and *semper reformanda*. Instead of describing the teaching office as simply the direct mediator of the Spirit's presence, Schillebeeckx prefers to speak about the Spirit's preservation of the church in truth, despite the errors and limitations of the church members themselves, even the officeholders.

This is in essence Schillebeeckx's doctrine of the indefectibility of the church. The church remains in the truth because God's salvific and revelatory message must be carried forward in history until the time of eschatological consummation. Because of the limitations and weaknesses of the church in history, this preservation of the church in truth is also a continual process of renewal and purification. Writing near the time of the close of the Second Vatican Council, Schillebeeckx says that the church's indefectibility rests in the Spirit's power to renew it constantly in and through its efforts to renew itself.

> Precisely because of her promised indefectibility, the church is in the concrete the church which is always purifying and reforming herself. To put it in a different way, the Church's constant reformation of herself in faith is the historical modality of her indefectibility. What is at once clear from this is that the indefectibility is not something that displays itself in triumphalism, but something that consists of a weakness in which God's grace triumphs.[51]

He adds:

> The basis of the indefectibility of the Church is not purely the fact that the people of God has been constituted into the body of Christ since Easter and Pentecost, but the fact that this body is the dwelling of the Holy Spirit. The Spirit is in fact effectively and irrevocably the eschatological gift and it is he that therefore leads the Church from within towards fulfillment.[52]

> This indwelling of the Spirit in the church which leads to its indefectibility is first of all a matter of the spiritual lives and holiness of all the members of the church; because the church's attempt at self-renewal, which is also the Spirit's prompting toward renewal, proceeds from a conversion to a life led in greater harmony with the theological virtues, this indefectibility is more than any specific office or structure in the church.

> This indefectibility, which functions within faith and the church's correction of herself in faith, cannot, however, be objectivised juridically, be-

cause the essence of the church as founded by Christ implies the existential experience of the community of salvation precisely as the fruit of the redemption. . . . It is in and through faith, hope and love which constantly impel us to *metanoia* and renewal that the promise of indefectibility—which is therefore not a purely juridical or forensic promise—is interiorised in the church.[53]

With this we have come full circle. In the previous chapter I discussed how the idea of the church as sacrament rests on the nonantithetical and dialectical working of the Spirit and the human situation of the church. With specific reference to the structure of the church, he argues that one can then make distinctions between the hierarchy and the laity on the basis of their relation to the apostolic charism given to the church by Christ and continued in the Spirit. With regard to dogmatic language and ecclesial authority, these different relations to the apostolic charism give the hierarchy the particular power to define dogmas as belonging to the fundamental deposit of faith and to judge the agreement of other language and practice in the church with that deposit. Theologians have their own specific and scientific task in relation to the church's experience of salvation and revelation in Christ, but ultimately theological language stands under the judgment of the magisterium. In the final analysis, though, the Spirit's working in the church is not a matter purely of guaranteeing the hierarchy's power of judgment or giving theologians insight into the mysteries of faith. It is a matter of conversion, one that is communal and continual. It is for this purpose that the authority of the magisterium and the scientific discipline of theologians exists.

five | The Apostolicity of the Church in
        Schillebeeckx's Later Theology

This harmonious picture of the ministry of the magisterium working with the scientific efforts of theologians to develop the deposit of faith (all within the preserving power of the Spirit) becomes a *quaestio disputata* in the years following the Second Vatican Council. Although initially buoyed by the optimistic spirit of the conciliar decrees, Schillebeeckx will later argue that the view of ministry and authority expressed there has not become an actual institutional reality in the Catholic Church.[1] Instead, the church has entered a period of the "anti-Council,"[2] where a reactionary outlook has attempted to slow, stop, and reverse the advances made by the council. Therefore Schillebeeckx's discussion of ministry, office, and authority is not an abstract exercise in theological speculation but reflects the actual tensions and conflicts of the postconciliar church. More specifically, his theology of ministry and his understanding of authority arise from the struggles within the Dutch Church after the council, particularly its experimentation with more democratic forms of church governance and the development of alternative forms of ministry within the critical communities there. This ecclesial and political situation will meet with his changes in epistemological and theological presuppositions to produce a series of occasional (and thought-provoking) works on ministry and authority. My task now is to synthesize from these various works an overview of his thought concerning: a redefinition of ministry and office in relation to the nature of the apostolicity of the church; the criteria for the orthodox transmission of Christian faith; the status of dogmas; the role of the magisterium; the role of theology and theologians; critical communities and their role in the church and world; and other sources of authority. All of these factors are necessary elements in Schillebeeckx's understanding of the apostolicity of the church in his later theology. They will provide the immediate context for my final synthesis on theological dissent and critical communities in the church.

Ministry and Office as Expressions of the Church's Apostolicity

Schillebeeckx's early ecclesiology foreshadowed elements of the Second Vatican Council's teaching on the church, which in turn Schillebeeckx integrates and emphasizes in his later ecclesiological writings. If the model of church as sacrament still defines his later thought, but in the sense of the church as "anticipatory sign," then this shift in theology will also affect how Schillebeeckx sees the structure of the church as an expression of that sacramental relationship. Earlier, the sacramental nature of the church translated directly into a necessary distinction between clergy and laity, between those who sacramentally represent the Body of Christ and those who represent Christ's headship over the church. Later, however, following the conciliar teaching on the primacy of the common membership of all believers in the church,[3] he will come to emphasize more and more this basic commonalty of membership which precedes any hierarchical distinction or any office. He will also join this emphasis with another leitmotif drawn from the council's language: the importance of the local church. On the other hand, he will also always argue that the church requires a ministry of leadership, even if in his later thought he distances himself from the idea that this leadership need necessarily have the same official structure and method of operation in every period of church history.

Not long after the council (1969), Schillebeeckx sets forth the basic paradigm for much of his postconciliar thought on ministry and office in the church. Recognizing the hermeneutical problem of the mutual relationship of past experience with the present, he begins by arguing that past practices and the current situation must critically inform each other in order for the church to reach a clear understanding about the question of ministry. Even before the council he steered away from any sort of ahistorical or excessively juridical notion of office; he now has begun to move away from a purely developmental or organic understanding.[4] In continuity with his earlier thought, Schillebeeckx will here argue that office in the church (and therefore the distinction between officeholders and nonofficeholders) rests upon the apostolic office of the first disciples. However, in distinction from his preconciliar period, he will also more clearly argue that this office developed in the church according to "sociological laws" which nevertheless reflect the inner working of the Holy Spirit in the whole Christian community.

> The offices in the Church, which certainly emerged from the community of the Church according to sociological laws, nonetheless owe their emergence to the community of the Church as set in order by the apostles—in other words, to the community of the Church as authoritatively guided by the apostles from the very origin of that community. What, then, is at the origin of the sociological process of growth (in which the Spirit of God is active) is not a community that was initially without authority, but the apostolic community itself.[5]

Schillebeeckx will concede that there is "no direct link" between the contemporary three-tiered understanding of office in the church and Jesus himself, but the historical process of the emergence of these offices is nonetheless "the work of the Holy Spirit, the Spirit of the exalted Christ."[6] However at the beginning of this process stands the apostolic witness, which Schillebeeckx will argue is the criterion for any later understanding or reinterpretation of ministry.[7] As in his earlier work, apostolic charism lies at the root of church office and authority; this concept will persist, even as Schillebeeckx redefines the character of "apostolicity." Indeed, one could argue that his entire understanding of ministry in the church in any form rests on his understanding of apostolicity. His reinterpretation and broadening of the meaning of that term will have far-reaching implications for his understanding of magisterial authority and the role of theologians in the church.

In traditional Catholic doctrine, the authority of the magisterium derived from proper ordination in apostolic succession, which endowed the recipient with the threefold office of teaching, governing, and sanctifying the rest of the church.[8] Schillebeeckx accepts this basic understanding but also attempts to combat an excessively juridical or mechanical view of apostolic succession by locating it within the general apostolicity of the church and under the impulse of the power of the Spirit.

> The foundation of the apostolic succession in the office of the church is, in the first place, the apostolicity of the community itself, because it is precisely in the apostolic Church that the Holy Spirit is active. The apostolicity of a Christian community implies the apostolic faith and an office which proceeds from the apostolic Church. The pneumatic character of

the apostolic community of the Church is therefore also the primary basis of the apostolic succession and thus of the validity of the office of the church. The apostolicity of the community of the Church, that is, belonging to one of the empirical communities of the Church which, in mutual "ecclesial recognition," claim to be the "Church of Christ," is the basis of the apostolicity or validity of the office of the church.[9]

Because of this general apostolicity of the church and its pneumatic basis, Schillebeeckx can also assert here that it is possible to conceive of a legitimate apostolic succession *praeter ordinem*, that is, "outside valid church order, but which is nonetheless valid in the church." This could occur "under the charismatic impulse of an apostolically founded community which finds itself in a state of emergency."[10] That is to say, a community leadership can arise and be recognized as valid even without the imposition of hands or formal ordination. Although here he narrows the range of applications of this idea to situations in the missions, the principle also admits of further development in his later thought.

In *Ministry* and *The Church with a Human Face*, Schillebeeckx both expands and carefully refines his understanding of the apostolicity of the church and of church office. In these works, which reflect Schillebeeckx's in-depth exploration of New Testament criticism and exegesis during the writing of the two *Jesus* books, he gives a lengthy exposition of the various forms of church leadership in the different New Testament communities.[11] This presentation supports his basic contention that every church community needs leadership and that "apostolicity" is the criterion of validity for that leadership, even if it takes on different forms in different communities or eras in the church.

In response to Pierre Grelot's criticism of *Ministry*,[12] Schillebeeckx refines his understanding of apostolicity in the second work to include four dimensions: First, he regards as "the fundamental dimension of the apostolicity of the churches the fact that these churches are founded or built up 'on the apostles and prophets' (Eph. 2.20; 4.7–16, see already *Ministry*, p. 14)."[13] Second, "There is above all the apostolic content of 'tradition,' *paratheke*, the gospel of the pledge entrusted, in other words the apostolic tradition. Here the New Testament writings are a permanent foundation document (see already *Ministry*, p. 17)."[14] Third, "There is also the apostolicity of the Christian communities of believers themselves, as called to life by the apostles and prophets on the criteria of the apostolic content of faith, what is handed down (see (i) and (ii)). The *sequela Jesu* or the praxis of the kingdom of God is an essential part of this, i.e., following Jesus in his message, his teaching and his actions (see already *Ministry*, p. 13f.)."[15] Finally, "There is the apostolicity of the church ministries, the so-called apostolic succession (see already *Ministry*, pp. 17–18)."[16] Because of the richness of this concept of apostolicity, it cannot be reduced, as Schillebeeckx sees Grelot and others doing, to the last dimension, the succession of ministerial office. Rather, these dimensions of apostolicity continually inform each other (in another series of nonantithetical and dialectical relationships) over the course of the church's history.

Within this whole process of tradition, ministry is important, but it is only one of many authorities which are concerned to preserve and keep alive and intact the gospel of Jesus Christ and therefore of apostolicity. So we cannot reduce the apostolicity of the church to the one dimension of the apostolic succession. Moreover, the four dimensions of apostolicity stand in permanent reciprocal relationship. The *successio apostolica* is not to be isolated from the rich reality, nor must it be formalized, with all the unecumenical consequences which ensue.[17]

This broadening of the definition of apostolicity allows Schillebeeckx to argue that the whole church has a commission to carry forth the apostolic tradition and that this commission is fundamentally prior to the ministerial office and its specific task. Indeed, according to Schillebeeckx, the ministerial office, as it develops historically into the combined functions of presidency at the Eucharist and magisterial authority over Christian doctrine and practice, should only be seen as a concrete instance of the apostolicity of the whole Christian community, given to it in its baptism by the Spirit.

In this process of official, specialized concentration we see that the prophetic function is gradually bound up with or drawn nearer to the *presbyteros;* it is concentrated even more in the presidency of the presbyteral council and ultimately in the monoepiscopate. What is also involved here is the expansion of the church and therefore also some fading of the first enthusiastic pneuma christology and of the general experience in the church of the power of the baptism in the Spirit, the foundation of prophetic, pneumatic and even ecstatic phenomena. However, it emerges from the whole of this development that what is later rightly called *sacramentum ordinis* is a specific, viz. diaconal or ministerial heightening or crystallization of the baptismal gift of the Spirit. This has theological consequences, as we shall see.[18]

Schillebeeckx then spends the greater part of *The Church with a Human Face* on a careful historical examination of the development of ministerial and magisterial office within Catholicism, with the aim of showing how this Spirit-given and multidimensional apostolicity of the church became more and more isolated within the office of the priest and bishop and how these offices were defined increasingly in sacral, substantialist, and juridical categories. The ultimate goal of this biblical and historical study is to argue for the legitimacy of the development of new forms of ministry in the contemporary situation that seek to preserve and carry forward the general apostolicity of the church.[19] These ministerial forms can be both a renewed understanding of traditional offices, such as that of priest and bishop, and the emergence of entirely new forms of ministry uncalled for in earlier periods of the church's history.

Preserving the Church's Apostolicity: Criteria of Orthodoxy

Before turning to the question of how Schillebeeckx views the specific forms and functions of the official ministry, one needs to first discuss how he deals with the problem of the preservation of the apostolicity of the church as a whole. He argues that the apostolic nature of church office is rooted in the more fundamental apostolic origin and commission of the whole church. How then does the church maintain this apostolic identity?

The early Schillebeeckx locates this continuity in the development of dogmas that truly express, however inadequately, the mystery of salvation and revelation contained in the deposit of faith. This continuity in development is guaranteed by the church's magisterium, whose task it is to preserve, define, and teach these doctrines, and ultimately by the Holy Spirit, whose guidance preserves the magisterium from error and overcomes the fallibility of the church's human members. This doctrinal development does not equate continuity with the simple repetition of dogmatic definitions from the past but allows for the possibility of new conceptual expressions that clarify and refine the church's earlier understanding in new contexts. Theologians in particular have the role of advancing this scientific understanding of the faith, even if their conclusions always stand under the judgment of the magisterium.

Schillebeeckx eventually distances himself from a developmental model of doctrine. Because of the epistemological turns of his later theology, in order to name this apostolic continuity, he will instead opt for *a hermeneutical, critical, and practical translation of Christian experience from one historical era to the next.* Because this translation of experience in the church is itself the line of apostolic continuity, it is also the bearer of "orthodoxy." The church's status as anticipatory sign and the dialectical presence of the Spirit in the church mean that this translation is also always done under the eschatological proviso and the continually formative power of the memory of Jesus.

Therefore any discussion of Schillebeeckx's later understanding of dogmas and doctrines must necessarily depend on his understanding of this process of the translation of experience. One sees, for example, that the use of the "theological notes" or "qualifications" entirely disappears. When Schillebeeckx discusses infallibility in a very late work, he can even show a certain impatience with all the different nuances of the truth of theological propositions developed in preconciliar theology.[20] In place of these notes, Schillebeeckx develops at several points a framework and criteria for more clearly understanding this critical translation of Christian experience. This general framework in turn has implications for a whole range of ecclesiological issues: the meaning of dogma or doctrine, the role of the magisterium, the role of theologians, other sources of teaching authority in the church, and the role of critical communities.

In *The Understanding of Faith*, his seminal description of this framework and criteria, he attempts to maintain the apostolicity and orthodoxy of the church by placing it within the criterion of the proportional norm, the criterion of orthopraxis, and the criterion of the reception by the whole people of God.[21] Of these three, the latter two are specifications of the first criterion, which is his most encompassing explanation for how this process of the critical translation of experience should take place.

The criterion of the proportional norm begins with the recognition, now basic to Schillebeeckx's theology, that any purely theoretical understanding of the faith, whether simply conceptual or even hermeneutically nuanced, is impossible within the epistemological conditions of human historicity.[22] Because the criterion for orthodoxy does not rest in such a theoretical construction, or even with the idea that there is one essence of faith which is simply clothed in different conceptual forms, Schillebeeckx argues that continuity in the understanding of faith comes from the act or intentionality of faith itself in relationship to the various referential contexts in which that act occurs. There is only one saving mystery of Christ that elicits the inward act of faith, but that saving mystery both expresses itself (through the biblical *kerygma*) and is received and understood in the course of the church's history in a variety of different contexts and through a diversity of "structurising elements."[23] The constant factor, therefore, is neither the act or intentionality of faith itself nor the "structurising" elements that are used to express it, but rather it is the proportional relationship between the two, as they both shape the understanding of the one saving mystery of Christ.

> The norm is therefore proportional, consisting in the relationship between the intentionality of faith and a given (and changing) referential framework. The relationship must also remain the same in different referential frameworks. This means, therefore, that the truth that was expressed in the definition of Chalcedon must remain sound in every other referential framework which structurises the datum of faith. The criterion for orthodox faith is therefore not an unchangeable formula and not even a homogeneous one, just as, on the other hand, any new character is no indication as such of a wrong development in faith. The criterion consists of a certain proportion in which subsequent expressions (in their different contexts) find themselves with regard to the intentionality of faith as inwardly determined by the mystery of Christ. In conceptual expression, it should be possible to recognise a reflection of the balance that exists in the mystery of Christ and the christian experience of faith.[24]

Because Scripture is the first such "structuring" of the relationship between the mystery of Christ and Christian experience, it has a normative value in the determination of the later proportions of orthodoxy.[25] However, this is not recourse to an ahistorical fundamentalism. This criterion makes it clear that the mystery of Christ and the response of faith in the whole of Christian life and praxis is greater than any theoretical expression of it; therefore the Scriptures are the paradigm of the proportional relationship, not a fixed deposit of concepts. This conclusion will also lead Schillebeeckx toward his second criterion of orthodoxy, the orthopraxis of believers.

Schillebeeckx consistently maintains this proportional understanding of the translation of orthodoxy throughout his later work. For example in *Theologisch Geloofsverstaan*, his 1983 retirement lecture from his teaching chair at Nijmegen, Schillebeeckx employs the same idea to describe how theology, hermeneutically and critically aware of the poles of tradition and situation, maintains an identity of meaning.

> That identity-of-meaning is only to be found *on the level of the corresponding relationship between the* original *message* (tradition) and the *situation,* dif-

ferent each time, then and now. That is what is meant by what used to be called the "analogia fidei." The fundamental identity-of-meaning between the successive periods of Christian understanding of the tradition of faith does not refer to corresponding *terms*, for example, between the situation of the Bible and our situation . . . , but rather to corresponding *relationships* between the terms (message and situation, then and now). There is thus a fundamental unity and equality, but this has no relationship to the *terms* of the hermeneutical equation, but to the *relationship* between those terms.[26]

He then goes on to illustrate this complex set of relationships by arguing that the "*given* articulation or relationship" between Jesus' message and his sociohistorical context is equal to the proportional relationship between the New Testament message and its sociohistorical context.[27] This relationship is then reproduced in the proportional relationship between the patristic understanding of faith and its sociohistorical context, between the medieval understanding of faith and its sociohistorical context, and so on. Finally, it must be reproduced in the current situation lest the understanding of faith become frozen in an earlier relationship and no longer address the contemporary situation.[28]

Only in this relationship and its continual translation can one find Christian identity.

> The equal relationship between these articulations bears in itself the Christian identity-of-meaning. That equal relationship of relationships throughout the Christian tradition is a norm, an orientation and inspiration, the model on whose ground we now, in evangelical trust, can nevertheless put into words the contemporary meaning of the Christian message here and now. We thus never look the Christian identity-of-meaning directly in the face; moreover, this is never laid down once and for all. But that does not mean arbitrariness. Christian identity, the one and the same, is thus never *the equal*, but *the proportionally equal*.[29]

This understanding of Christian identity as the translation of experience is not simply the hermeneutical reinterpretation of a past tradition so that it bears meaning in a new situation. Rather, as Schillebeeckx's second criterion of orthodoxy points out, orthopraxis itself is part of the translation of the understanding of faith. This criterion is the logical outgrowth of the shift in

Schillebeeckx's epistemological framework from the second to the third circles that I described in the first chapter. He argues with regard to this specific question of orthodoxy that the "pre-understanding" which is common to all human beings and thus can serve as a ground for continuity cannot be the "positive" philosophical anthropology advanced by hermeneutics. Such an understanding is still too narrow and reduces the possibilities for Christian theology down to this one framework. Instead, Schillebeeckx argues that the negative dialectics of Adorno and the *humanum* concept of Ernst Bloch are better grounds for any "universal pre-understanding of all these different views of man" and therefore can serve as a "universal pre-understanding of the Gospel."[30]

Schillebeeckx argues that the universal resistance to that which diminishes or destroys human life provides a negative but real source of hope for human fulfillment. This negative and diffuse hope is made positive and concrete in the life of Jesus himself. "The *humanum* which is sought, but always threatened, is proclaimed and promised in Jesus Christ. The Kingdom of God is the *humanum* which is sought, but now promised in Christ, made conceivable and really assured for us in grace."[31] However, because of the dialectic between past event, present actualization, and future promise, this fulfillment of the *humanum* in Christ is also a continuing task for the Christian in the current situation.

> The object of christian faith is, of course, already realised in Christ, but it is only realised in him as our promise and our future. But the future cannot be theoretically interpreted, it must be done. The *humanum* which is sought and which is proclaimed and promised to us in Christ is not an object of purely contemplative expectation, but also a historical form which is already growing in the world: at least this is what we have to do, in the perspective of eschatological hope. Christianity is not simply a hermeneutic undertaking, not simply an illumination of existence, but also a renewal of existence, in which "existence" concerns man as an individual person and in his social being.[32]

Therefore the "basic hermeneutic problem of theology" is not simply the relationship of past and present, but the relationship "between theory and practice,"[33] which exist in such a nonantithetical and dialectical relationship that the one serves as the *disclosive source for* and the *critical test of* the other. In this particular case, it means that orthodoxy becomes truly *orthos* in orthopraxis, and vice versa. "Christian orthopraxis, or 'right doing,' then, is not a consequence of a previously given, communal unity of faith, but the manner in which such a communal unity and conviction is realised. The way in which this is effectively realized is also the conscious assurance of orthodoxy."[34]

Schillebeeckx does not think that praxis is self-authenticating. Whether a particular ecclesial praxis is *orthos* must be investigated against the witness of the broader tradition by the whole church, particularly through its theologians and teaching office.[35] Therefore, Schillebeeckx wishes to hold both of these ideas together in dialectical tension; in his view this dynamic relationship of theory and praxis must continue if the church wishes to preserve the apostolicity and authenticity of its message and life.

This interrelationship of theory and praxis leads then to Schillebeeckx's third criterion for orthodoxy, the acceptance by the people of God. Relying again on the ecclesiological motifs of the Second Vatican Council, Schillebeeckx argues that the church, as the people of God, is a community of shared discourse and communication which has a certain priority over both any distinctions between clergy and laity and any individual theologian or local community. "The subject sustaining the hermeneutics is not the individual theologian, but the community of the church as a whole."[36] Within this community there are various roles which interact with each other through a "tested dialectical process" to ensure the orthodoxy of the transmission of the faith.[37] This process of transmission (or translation) is the responsibility not only of the magisterium but also of the theologians and the whole community as well. In this belief Schillebeeckx is in agreement with his earlier writings; however, here, following Vatican II and his epistemological shifts, he also argues that this communal process consists of a series of mutually critical relationships, including those between theologians and the magisterium, between the local church and the other local churches of the wider community, and also between local churches and their leaders, including the pope. Even if the local community must see itself always in relationship with the wider church and ultimately under the judgment of the bishop of Rome in his capacity as successor of Peter, this does not mean that the local church may not be a source for a new interpretation of faith for the entire church.

> The local communities of God are therefore essentially subject to the criticism of the other local churches and, ultimately, to that of all the leaders of the local churches with the "president of the bond of love" among them—the bishop to whom the office of the primacy of Peter is entrusted

within the college of bishops. Assuming this, then, the consciousness of faith of one local church which accepts a given interpretation of faith may well be a *locus theologicus,* a source for theology within the universal church, an indication of the Holy Spirit, on the basis of which the given interpretation may be regarded as a safe guiding principle.[38]

Because of these mutually informing relationships, the specific praxis and understanding of faith of a local community which gains acceptance in the church as a whole are themselves signs of orthodox continuity.

> Acceptance by the community of faith or, seen from a different point of view, the *sensus fidelium* or consciousness of faith of the community, thus forms an essential part of the principle of the verification of ortho-doxy. Because this orthodoxy is, as I have said, the theoretical aspect of christian praxis, the "acclamation" or "amen" forms an essential part of the structure of the christian liturgy in which orthodoxy is above all to be found: *lex orandi, lex credendi.*[39]

Nevertheless, this criterion of acceptance, like the criterion of ortho-praxis, is not absolute nor is it to be identified with the concept of "reception"; simple "reception" by the community is in itself not a sufficient guarantee of apostolic continuity.[40] The understanding of "acceptance" that he presents here includes the dialectical process of mutual criticism and recognition of the role of the church's teaching authority as a part of that process. Moreover, even this complex process of acceptance by the community, both leaders and nonleaders, will also stand under both the eschatological proviso and the con-tinually normative memory of Jesus. Therefore, in order to preserve apostolic orthodoxy, the community must continually translate and reenact the ac-cepted understanding of faith of an earlier era within its own.

The Status of Dogmas

Schillebeeckx no longer locates the "constant unitive factor" of the apostolicity of the church in the preservation and development of dogma, but in the criti-cal translation of Christian experience from one historical period to the next.[41] What then is the status of dogmatic affirmations in Schillebeeckx's later work and how are they related to this critical translation of experience?

Although one could argue that all of his works in the post–Vatican II period, particularly the Christological trilogy, give an implicit answer to these questions, only in two relatively recent essays does he make this answer explicit. In the most general sense, Schillebeeckx maintains continuity with his earlier understanding of dogmas; they are expressions of the essential truths of the Christian faith. "Generally and ecumenically speaking (so that this also holds for non-Catholic, Christian churches), dogma means the Christian teaching of the faith in so far as that cannot be given up, because it goes back to the word of God."[42]

However, this "teaching of the faith" is not a timeless set of propositional statements that captures the whole reality of salvation in conceptual form. Schillebeeckx's first epistemological circle already militates against such a view of dogma; now in the light of his later epistemology, he will argue that dogmas can only be understood as linguistic expressions of the experience of faith which fall within the hermeneutical, critical, and practical limits of all human language. This definition does not undermine their truth, but it does limit their role in the translation of the experience of faith. Continuity in dogmatic expression does not necessarily guarantee continuity in the experience of faith. To repeat a passage cited in the introduction to this work, "Continuity can therefore also be only apparent-continuity. A certain *break*, such as that of Vatican II, can really mean a rediscovery of the deepest tendencies of the Gospel."[43]

Using the understanding of cultural and historical change that he previously employed in the *Jesus* book,[44] Schillebeeckx argues that these breaks are a necessary part of the transmission of a living Christian faith. He then engages the question about how dogmas can remain true even through these shifts and breaks in dogmatic formulations. Drawing on concrete examples from the history of Christian doctrine, he illustrates several factors which can create such shifts and which can therefore be helpful in determining how a dogma should be reinterpreted in the current situation. An examination of these factors will show how Schillebeeckx locates dogmatic language within his three epistemological circles.

First, one needs to recognize "the expressive power of the language which is used for a definition of dogma."[45] The meaning of a language is not always the same in all situations and all cultures; thus the terminology of the dogmatic definitions of Chalcedon or of the papal condemnations about Jansenism (to use Schillebeeckx's two examples) might not bear the same power to express meaning now. Second, one must recognize "the inevitable tension between reality and our merely conceptual, expressive, even metaphorical and symbolic verbalization of the-reality-of-revelation-as-known-by-us."[46] He cites the apparent contradiction between the exclusivist theology of salvation enunciated by the Council of Ferrara-Florence in 1439 and the teaching of the Second Vatican Council. Interestingly enough, Schillebeeckx here reverts to his perspectival epistemology to explain how these two statements could both be expressions of the truth, however "filtered" through the different perspectives of the speakers.[47] Third, one must recognize "the tension between the faith and the socio-cultural, as well as ideological and situational contexts."[48] The example he offers here comes from the Fourth Lateran Council in 1215, whose dogmatic definition about demons and angels had little to do with proclaiming their existence (because all people believed in them in that period), but with asserting God's creation of all beings, good and evil, against a certain Manichean style dualism of creations.[49] Knowing the cultural and ideological assumptions of a particular period can therefore clarify the intention of any dogmatic statement. This in turn can allow for a change in understanding if one recognizes what the dogma intended to define and what it actually left open for further examination.

Schillebeeckx continues with this discussion of shifts in dogmas by noting a theological concept given full expression at the Second Vatican Council: the hierarchy of truths. Some Christian beliefs, whatever the differences in their form of expression, must be seen as basic truths, whereas others are less central. Schillebeeckx makes the comparison between basic beliefs, such as those in Jesus as the Messiah and in the Trinity, with secondary beliefs about church structures and practices which have grown up over time. In this latter category he includes even the Tridentine reaffirmation of the number of sacraments and the necessity of a particular form of church governance, namely, episcopal or presbyterian.[50] The purpose of this distinction, which he elaborates with the example of the difference between the belief in eternal life with God and the idea of the immortality of the soul, is to argue that theologians, who may be labeled as heretics because of their apparent denial of a secondary doctrine, are actually seeking to preserve the heart and soul of the faith at a fundamental level.[51]

A fifth factor involved in creating the need for shifts in dogma is "the structure of communication of church proclamation."[52] Hearkening back to a theme present in his work from the very earliest days, Schillebeeckx argues that mere repetition of verbal formulas is not the same as the transmission of dogma to a new generation. If dogma is to remain living in the church—that is, if it is to be the real vehicle of an act of communication between the past tradition and present situation—it may need to be reformulated so that it truly addresses the questions of that situation. Indeed, since every dogma is part of a dialectic of question and answer which is located in a specific historical and linguistic context, the possibility remains real that a dogmatic formulation can become irrelevant; it becomes the fixed answer for a question that no one is asking anymore.[53]

Finally, Schillebeeckx argues, "a purely theoretical question about meaning often can be a reason to relativize the immobility of a dogma and to stimulate a reformulation."[54] What he means by this statement is that "human growth in consciousness and knowledge," with the new opportunities and crises that this brings, necessitates "a more clearly refined, more nuanced and more contemporarily satisfactory expression of the dogmas which have been handed down."[55] He illustrates this point with the doctrine of original sin and argues that the growth in the understanding of human nature beyond the medieval and patristic worldview makes such a term now seem "absurd" if there is no attempt to understand the meaning of such a concept in the contemporary situation.[56]

My purpose for laying out these six factors involved in creating shifts in dogma is to show how Schillebeeckx now places dogmatic affirmations within the later circles of his epistemology and understanding of revelation, as well as within the more specific criteria of apostolicity. Although I would argue that his presentation of these factors is somewhat unsystematic and does not fit perfectly into his framework for epistemology and fundamental theology, it is clear that the language of dogmatic affirmations must be both historically located and continually subject to hermeneutical reinterpretation lest it take on the appearance of some timeless truth. Furthermore, to include the circle of theory and praxis, Schillebeeckx concludes by saying that "each doctrine *must go through human experience* again and again and can never go past the experience of faith of the believing community."[57] This brings us back to the point at which I started this discussion of dogma; in Schillebeeckx's later thought dogmatic affirmations are expressions of this critical translation of Christian experience and not the bearer of that translation itself. They are "legitimate, but contingent and often not necessary developments from the New Testament, although they are not in conflict with it."[58]

Schillebeeckx's thought might seem to imply that because once-meaningful dogmas can become irrelevant in later periods, then the church can leave them aside, or at least leave aside the dogmatic formulations which attempted to express that truth about the Christian experience in a different era. But does he actually imply this? I would argue that by setting dogma within the epistemo-logical circles and the theology of revelation outlined above, he also sets it within the ecclesiology of the church as anticipatory sign. If this is the case, then dogmas are linguistic expressions that also serve as anticipatory signs. They therefore fall within the threefold dynamic of past remembrance, pres-ent actualization, and future hope. This idea is what Schillebeeckx means when he describes dogmas as primarily "doxological."[59] Because dogmatic statements (and, in general, theological affirmations of the understanding of faith) "express the content of a definite act of trust in God," they more speci-fically express a faith in the God of the promise whose action in and through Jesus is an anticipatory sign of the eschatological fulfillment of the human race. Schillebeeckx can conclude:

> Every dogma must have an orientation towards the future and be open to the sphere of the future. This has consequences for our conception of dogma itself, since truth then becomes, for us now, something whose full-ness belongs to the future; to the extent that its content is already realized, it discloses itself essentially as a *promise*. The present, itself a sphere of in-terpretation of the past, must be caught up in a sphere of promise, or the past will not be seen clearly for what it is. What is ultimately and pri-marily in question here is conceiving both the present and past as open-ended, orientated towards a new reality—what is still to come. Dogma thus becomes the proclamation of the historical realization of God's promise, which of its very nature implies an openness to the future and to new historical realizations.[60]

Despite this doxological and future-oriented quality of dogma and de-spite the need for their critical reinterpretation in successive eras, Schille-beeckx does not think that the church can simply dispense with past dogmatic formulations. Because they express doxologically the Christian experience of faith within the parameters of a particular time, they are abiding elements of the church's continuous tradition. New experiences (including new experi-ences of faith) always occur within the tradition of past experiences, including the general frameworks or models that unify experiences into an entire world-view. Hence even if the language of these past affirmations cannot be affirmed in the current situation without critical translation, this language, as the true expression of an earlier experience of faith, must be valued within the context of its particular time and recognized also as a bearer of that experience of faith to the next era.[61]

The Teaching Office of the Hierarchy

This exposition on apostolicity, the criteria of orthodoxy, and the status of dogma will serve to frame a presentation of Schillebeeckx's understanding of the role and authority of the magisterium, theologians, critical communities, and believers in general within the church. It will be my argument that his understanding of the latter group of topics flows from his understanding of the former; the magisterium, theologians, and believers all participate in a "tested dialectical process" which, under the ultimate guidance of the Holy Spirit, allows the church as a whole to preserve, enact anew, and hope for the fulfillment of the message of Jesus' life: God's salvific will for all humanity. This interrelationship between roles and authorities in the church is another example of the nonantithetical and dialectical relationships that pervade all of Schillebeeckx's thought. My purpose below will be to explain these different roles and their relationships to the other elements in the church, with particular emphasis on the question of authority and dissent.

First, Schillebeeckx in his later theology will continue to affirm the necessary role of the magisterium in the translation of Christian experience. However, he will always locate its authority within the broader context of the apostolicity and current experience of the whole church. This placement, coupled with his epistemological shifts, will accentuate his earlier "minimalism" about official church authority to such an extent that, especially with regard to the issue of infallibility, Schillebeeckx will have extreme difficulty affirming this authority in any traditional sense. He will struggle to preserve the language of earlier pronouncements on magisterial authority but will use increasingly metaphorical language to explain it.

Schillebeeckx never denies the need for the magisterium in the church. He sees the ministerial office, including its teaching functions, as a legitimate "crystallization" or concentration of the apostolic "pledge" and task given to the whole church.

> The Sovereignty of Jesus Christ is exercised in the Church through the Pneuma or Spirit; the Church's teaching authority is pneumatically-christologically grounded. It must be so organized that the enduring

presence and liberating authority of the Lord Jesus continually and effectively comes into the life of the Christian faith community. Rather than formal authority, the Church's fundamental norm is the *"paratheke"*—the entrusted pledge of 1 Tim. 6:20 and 2 Tim. 1:14—which is to say, the Gospel (1 Tim. 1:11; 2 Tim. 2:8), as the apostles interpreted it. The fundamental norm in the Church is the *"didaskalian tou soterios humon theou,"* the teaching of God our Savior (Tit. 2:10).[62]

The magisterium's role is subordinated to the service of this "entrusted pledge." "The magisterium, therefore, is appointed to serve the life of the ecclesiastical faith community. It serves, now as always, on the basis and according to the direction of the essential biblical documentation on the lives of Jesus Christ's first witnesses and followers."[63]

This grounding of the magisterium within the broader context of the apostolicity of the whole church also means that the magisterium is not the sole or even immediate norm of the orthodoxy of the church. The church's teaching office is not one of the three criteria of orthodoxy, although it does have a role to play in maintaining orthodoxy. In distinction from his earlier thought, Schillebeeckx will now criticize the magisterium when it pretends that it is itself the "regula proxima" of faith.[64] This move is significant, because now Schillebeeckx does not see the magisterium (and its official teachings) as belonging primarily to the *interpretandum* of the Gospel which the theologian must take into account, but as part of the process of interpreting the Gospel within the whole church. The magisterium hence is not a purely independent source of dogmatic teaching; it is not primarily a source for the church's language and theological expression but is instead the office charged with the pastoral obligation to watch over the church's language.[65] As such, the magisterium should only bring to definitive expression the belief of the whole church; its role is not to create new doctrines, but to evaluate critically the language and practice of the church in order to discern if it really proceeds from the *sensus fidei*.[66]

This shift in the understanding of the magisterium comes to its clearest expression when Schillebeeckx confronts the idea of ecclesial and papal infallibility. As I suggested above, he will not directly deny either doctrine, but he will take two approaches to understanding infallibility that cumulatively lessen its claims. First, he will argue that infallibility, particularly that of the pope as proclaimed at Vatican I, cannot be understood as an isolated power divorced from the wider church. Here he is following a line of moderate or minimalist thinking about Vatican I that begins there and receives particular expression in Vatican II's doctrine of the *sensus fidei* of the whole church.[67] However, even with Vatican II's more balanced ecclesiology, after the council Schillebeeckx will have more difficulty in affirming even the moderate traditional language used in this doctrine, because his epistemological and theological presuppositions will make it nearly impossible to do so. As time progresses, Schillebeeckx's language will become more and more fragmentary and metaphorical with regard to infallibility, particularly the papal variety. This, of course, will have a corresponding effect on his understanding of the role of the theologian in the church and the legitimacy of theological dissent.

Like magisterial authority in general, Schillebeeckx locates the infallibility of the magisterium, particularly papal infallibility, within the general indefectibility and infallibility of the church. In this way, he consistently argues that the infallibility decree of the First Vatican Council can only be rightly understood in the light of the ecclesiology of the Second Vatican Council, which more clearly spoke about the infallibility of the *sensus fidei*.[68] But the infallibility and indefectibility of the church rest on the Holy Spirit's continual renewing power working in and through it and therefore cannot be considered an inherent or "static" quality of the church itself.[69] Rather, the indefectibility and infallibility of the church flow from God's promise to preserve the church in truth; this promise in turn extends to the magisterial office in the church.[70]

This promise does not mean that the magisterium's authority works automatically or quasi-magically, or that magisterial statements are somehow exempt from historical location and the possibility of critical distortion. Schillebeeckx argues that the magisterium's location within the community of faith and the very humanity of its members means that even infallible decisions can only be reached through "the free will, understanding and experience of the human office bearers."[71] This fact also leaves open the possibility that this mediation of the Holy Spirit can be distorted either through the manipulation of those in office or through their negligence. In either case the magisterium can produce poorly formulated or one-sided doctrines that need correction in the context of the wider Christian tradition.[72]

Beyond even the possibility of distortion or one-sidedness on the part of the office bearers, ecclesial or papal infallibility cannot exceed the bounds of human language and knowledge. In a 1973 *Concilium* article, Schillebeeckx invokes both the perspectivalist and hermeneutical circles as parameters for any dogmatic language,[73] and he argues that the traditional doctrine of infallibility itself can only be affirmed through the following reinterpretation.

In its offices or ministries (the papacy, the episcopate, etc.), the Church is able, at a given moment and within a concrete historical context of under-standing, to express the Christian confession of faith *correctly, legitimately, faithfully* and with authoritative *binding* force. It can do this even though such concepts as "infallible," "irrevocable" and *ex sese* are disputable as his-torically situated terms implying a certain view of truth and belonging to a certain ecclesiological context. It can also do it although no concrete for-mulation or articulation (*enuntiabile*) can claim to stand up to the test of time.[74]

This qualified definition says much. Schillebeeckx here demonstrates again a dynamic that goes back to the earliest stages of his work: the nonanti-thetical and dialectical interrelationship of objective truth and subjective knower. In this case, the objective truth of God's revelation can be expressed through the subjective context of the members of the church's teaching au-thority. Yet, even as he accepts this idea of infallibility, he also continues his "minimalist" approach by locating that "power" in the context of a whole series of "withins." It must be exercised within the perspectival and hermeneutical limits of language, within the thought forms and questions of a particular his-torical period, within the context of the whole church's *sensus fidei*, within the dialectic of past tradition, present actualization, and future hope, and within the very human possibilities of willful distortion, ignorance, and negligence.[75] With all these hedges around the law, so to speak, it is not surprising that Schillebeeckx will argue that the very terms of the traditional doctrine that seem to imply that infallibility reaches beyond these "withins" are themselves highly problematic and should possibly fall into disuse.

The term "infallibility" is itself the most problematic, because it is "sur-rounded by ideological and sociological difficulties which seem insoluble."[76] At a later point he will argue that "freedom from error" or, better yet, simply "true" are more adequate qualifications for dogma than "infallible," a term that adds nothing real to the quality of judgment about a doctrine, save a questionable "heightened appearance of certainty."[77] The problematic nature of this term becomes even greater when set in the context of the First Vatican Council's definition of *papal* infallibility. As noted above, Schillebeeckx argues that Vatican I can only be properly understood within the ecclesiology of the people of God and the doctrine of collegiality promulgated at Vatican II. This ecclesiological framework, however, coupled with his epistemological parame-ters, makes the terminology of Vatican I, especially the phrases "irreformabilis ex sese" and "non autem ex consensu Ecclesiae," particularly difficult to accept in any maximalist sense.[78] Since this combination of changes raises problems for the whole idea of infallibility, *a fortiori* Schillebeeckx argues in an increasingly forceful manner against the idea of an independent (or specific) papal infallibility.

> It would therefore be better that we no longer speak of "papal infalli-bility" (the expression is elliptical and misleading), but rather of the "in-fallibility" of the world episcopate together with the pope as head of that college, and this therefore only in specific, determined actions. Moreover, Vatican II places all this in a still greater perspective, but this council did not work this out further; namely—and now I am citing from the theolo-gian Ratzinger before his career as bishop and cardinal—as follows: this vision involves a moral bond between the pope and the world episcopate and the voice of the people of God. The pope with the bishops must also listen seriously to the voice of all the community of faith before solemnly promulgating a dogma. I would add: in order also to rightly give this form in concrete structures, particular organs of representation of the people of God would have to be called into existence.[79]

Because of his location of papal infallibility within the infallibility of the whole church, and his location of infallibility as a whole within the epistemo-logical conditions of all human knowledge of the truth, Schillebeeckx will treat this idea as he literally does in the previous quotation: he will put it in quotes. He does accept the idea of the magisterium and even its decision-making ability, but he restricts the proper usage of such magisterial authority to very rare and specific circumstances, and only as last resort for the sake of the preservation of the whole Christian message. Even these rare pronounce-ments also are only boundary markers or "road signs" for a particular era; since dogmas are the linguistic expression of a critical translation of Christian experience, even an "infallible" dogma can never completely or permanently capture that experience for all time. Even "infallible" dogmas are open for fur-ther reflection, reinterpretation, and criticism.

> Moreover, the Roman Catholic Church itself has always directly resisted sectarian assertions that the community of faith alone is "a church of the pure," a "church of the holy remnant." That goes just as much for its pastoral-doctrinal and disciplinary-governing authority. What it names

"infallible statements" are only single, rare and sporadic "road signs" on its historical course of life; mostly course corrections in the many-sided movements of the churches.[80]

Schillebeeckx's bracketing of the traditional language of infallibility results in his use of more metaphorical language for that doctrine as well as for the function of the magisterium in general. For example, "particular papal or conciliar decisions taken in the name of the whole church community at the level of challenges which are vital for Gospel faith can indeed be "infallible," i.e. in a more or less happy way they nevertheless give historical expression to Christian truth."[81] Or, similarly, the magisterium "in *very exceptional and definite cases* is gifted with the *same* "infallibility," that is, stability of the exchange rate, as that with which the whole Christian community of faith is gifted."[82] Because of the rare nature of these interventions (and perhaps, in Schillebeeckx's mind, because of the epistemological doubts he has about the possibilities of such statements), the magisterium, especially in its Petrine office, should normally be the court of last appeal, not the sole or first voice heard in the church. "I agree that it is good that the local church of Rome has a leader, its bishop, who has the function of Peter and ultimately sees to it that there is unity between the other local churches. But that is the only function of the church of Rome—to be a kind of appeal court, so that, in the last resort, the local churches can make an appeal to the Petrine office."[83]

Similarly, the magisterium's chief function, along with its regulation of the language of the church, is actually to facilitate communication and institutional freedom in the church so that the consensus of all believers can emerge.

> In view of the new situation in which the christian community is placed since the emergence of so many different interpretations of faith, the teaching office must above all serve as a means of communication within the community itself and guarantee an institutional freedom in which open dialogue can take place and in which all views can be heard. Any attempted manipulation must be prevented by that teaching authority so that a free consensus of opinion can come about within the community of believers.[84]

As time progresses Schillebeeckx is less and less sanguine about the possibility that this vision of the magisterium will become a reality. Nevertheless, even if his later language about the actual exercise of authority by the current Roman administration becomes harsher, he strives to maintain the idea, based on his understanding both of Vatican II and the nature of dogmatic language, that the magisterium is a necessary pole in the ongoing dialectic of preserving the apostolic witness in the church. Yet, as but one element in the process, the magisterium in Schillebeeckx's later thought always works within a series of nonantithetical and dialectical relationships with other elements in the church, including theologians and the general experience of believers.

Theology and the Role of Theologians in the Church

Another important element in this ongoing dialectic of preserving the apostolic witness in the church is the scientific work of theologians. In his earlier period Schillebeeckx defines theology as "the scientific, conscious evaluation and expression of the content of the church's experience of faith."[85] Later, Schillebeeckx would still generally accept this definition; however, because of the development of his second and third epistemological circles and the accompanying changes in his fundamental theology, his definition of theology (and hence of the theologian's role) will come to be more encompassing: "the reflective and critical self-consciousness of Christian praxis."[86] The method most appropriate for this critical reflection on Christian praxis is the "correlation" between "tradition" and "situation."[87]

To unpack both this definition of theology and of theological method, first one should note that the theologian's work is located within and directed toward the Christian experience and praxis of the wider church. Just as the magisterium is not an authority somehow set above the Christian community, so theologians are not independent intellectuals who operate outside of it.[88] Rather theologians find their object of reflection, so to speak, in the contemporary experience, praxis, and questions of believers.

> Theologising or the theological understanding of faith is always a second, reflexive undertaking in relation to what is here and now going on, being believed and being thought in the Christian communities of faith. On the other hand theological reflection can also anticipate and be a preparation for the *coming* proclamation of the churches as the "congregation of God," for the simple reason that theology takes as the object of its study not only the current or the always limited present, but also the broad

spectrum of the entire Christian tradition of faith, with its Christian experiences within many social and cultural forms.[89]

The dialectical interrelationship of theologians and community is clear from the start. On the one hand, the theologian's task is always a "second step" into relation to the community's belief and praxis; theologians have the obligation to reflect on the current praxis and belief of the Christian churches and to bring the contemporary understanding of faith to clear and self-conscious expression. On the other hand, the theologians' purview extends to the entire tradition of faith, which they can then use to enrich and critique the contemporary understanding and praxis of faith. Theology brings the experience of the whole Christian tradition to bear on the present so that the present situation, or the present community, does not become isolated from the church extended throughout history. In this sense theologians are the mediators between the contemporary communities and the wider tradition and therefore have a certain critical responsibility for the "flow" of reflection between the two sources.

> Academic theology has the task of *integrating* the new experiences and the new praxis and reflections of local communities and basic groups into the whole complex of the "Church's memory" and into the great reserves of experience and faith of the entire Church. It therefore at the same time prevents these new experiences, in which a new and increasing "consensus" is manifested, from remaining merely sporadic or from tending to disintegrate the church. In this way academic theology "mediates" the rich traditions of the Church's experience throughout the centuries down to the basis and at the same time prevents that basis from becoming cognitively isolated as a sect. It is even enriched itself as academic theology by these new experiences, reflections and forms of consensus that are made manifest in this so-called non-academic theology.[90]

This citation comes from a discussion of the relationship between formal, academic theology and the "non-academic theology" developed in the base and critical communities in the church; however, the principle applies more broadly to the theologian's task in general. Theologians and the community as a whole are both active subjects in the process of understanding the faith (as is the magisterium); their roles in this process differ even as they interact.

Theologians not only mediate between the current situation and praxis of the Christian churches and the wider historical traditions of the church but also between the specifically religious understanding of the world and humanity and other fields of knowledge. Like the interrelationship of theologians and community, the interrelationship of theology as a discipline with other forms of learning and thinking is also nonantithetical and dialectical. Following the direction of the Second Vatican Council, with its emphasis on dialogue with the modern world, Schillebeeckx will argue that theology (or theological reasoning) is not the same as the critical or scientific reasoning of the Enlightenment and the period afterward,[91] but neither is it an isolated branch of knowledge which can learn nothing from modern thought and science. Rather, using again ideas drawn from Wittgenstein, Schillebeeckx says that theology and the other disciplines of human knowledge apprehend the same object, the reality of human life in the world, under different language games. Thus theology and other forms of human knowledge and reasoning can neither be collapsed into each other or radically separated. The knowledge that each offers can be a source of new insight or even an "alien prophecy" which spurs critical reflection within the discipline of theology itself.[92]

By the same token, theology and theologians do not have the same role as the magisterium in the church. Schillebeeckx will consistently note how theologians must recognize the magisterium's function in the church but must also have the legitimate freedom of inquiry and expression which accompanies theology as a distinct discipline.[93] They thus work at the intersection of several dialectical relationships: with the church community as a whole, with the other disciplines of human knowledge, with the magisterium of the church. As those charged with the task of bringing to critical self-consciousness the praxis and beliefs of the Christian community, theologians perform this role more specifically through what Schillebeeckx calls "critical correlation," a method of theologizing which encompasses the epistemological circles and understanding of fundamental theology which forms the framework of all of his later thought. In other words, theology is that reflection and self-consciousness of Christian praxis which is avowedly hermeneutical, ideological-critical, and always linked to an authenticating and actualizing praxis itself.

I will illustrate this definition by examining his most complete exposition of theological method, *Theologisch Geloofsverstaan anno 1983*. In its dialectical and mediating role, theology has to do with the two poles of "tradition" and

"situation." "Tradition" for Schillebeeckx is a code word for the complex hand-
ing on of "tradition of revelation, faith, experience and interpretation," which
has two important facets. First, this multilayered tradition can still disclose
meaning for people today through the meeting of its narrative with the contemporary situation.

> *The tradition of faith opens a horizon of possible experience also for us now.*
> *But this is primarily not about a theoretical unpacking of meaning, but first of*
> *all about a narrative revelation of meaning, which nonetheless even in the Old*
> *and New Testaments was continually accompanied by at least a beginning of*
> *theological reflection. Narratology, or the science of narrative, has revealed the*
> *structures of this in broad outline.*[94]

Along with the meaning-disclosing aspect of tradition comes its libera-
tive and transformative power.

> *On the other hand,* that tradition of faith is a religious tradition of
> meaning *with transformative, renewing and liberating, and finally saving*
> *power.* The meaning-disclosing tradition of faith is at the same time a
> summons to a well-defined, practical way of life. However the specific-
> characteristic of what is named "liberation" can also be filled in within
> the different great human traditions, those traditions promise through
> their own disclosure of meaning salvation and liberation to human
> beings: *truth* concerning life-as-human-beings. Ultimately it is a matter of
> the flowing together of two stories: the story of the evangelical tradition
> of faith and our personal and communal story of life.[95]

Notice that Schillebeeckx invokes here the distinction, discussed in the first
chapter, between "meaning-disclosing" and "meaninglessness-transforming"
models of truth. The tradition must bear both kinds of truth into the present
in order to be a really living tradition.

The other pole of the "critical correlation" which frames the theologian's
work is that of the "situation." Schillebeeckx defines it first in the following
way: "As standing over against tradition, I name 'situation,' in a general sense,
the social-cultural and existential context of human beings to whom the
Gospel is proclaimed here and now."[96] In the more specifically Christian sense,
he defines the term as

the present-day context in which an answer, or several answers, are given to the question, how do Christians properly as Christians concretely live in this common modern culture and society and how do they take over its categories of thought and experience: by conforming to them? by legitimating them? by criticizing them? Or by entirely rejecting them? In other words, what is, here-and-now, their praxis of faith and their actual understanding of faith? [97]

As one would expect, Schillebeeckx argues that the "situation" is not simply the passive recipient of the truths of the tradition but is itself theologically significant.

Moreover, the current situation is not only the *bed* for the "stream" of faith which is handed down. That worldly situation is itself also *theologically relevant*. For, according to the understanding of faith of just this Christian tradition, all history stands under God's plan of liberation and redemption.[98]

Although he does not explicitly state it here, Schillebeeckx therefore sees the current situation as also having the potential to bring forth both "meaning-disclosing" and "meaninglessness-transforming" experiences of truth. In the light of this polarity, the theologian's task is to correlate critically these experiences of truth found in both tradition and situation. This correlation, however, does not mean that the theologian simply harmonizes past and present. "Correlation" covers a range of meanings from continuity to rupture.

One can use the term "method of correlation" for this process of interrelation between tradition and situation. Yet that seems ambiguous to me. In any case I mean by "correlation" very generally "interrelation." This term allows for all sorts of differing possibilities, from likeness and [simple] correlation to conflict and confrontation; in short, all the broad spectrum that lies between on the one hand "identity" (it clicks), and on the other hand "non-identity" (it clashes).[99]

Further on, Schillebeeckx comments that even this multivalent term "correlation" is not entirely accurate. Given the possible range of interrelationships between tradition and situation, and given his underlying theology of revelation which states that God saves and reveals through the historical and practical mediation of human life in every era, Schillebeeckx prefers "to speak of the 'encounter of cultures' which live out the Christian substance of faith and 'acclimatize' this in their own cultural setting."[100] He goes on to explain this "encounter of cultures" using the criterion of the proportional norm (or analogy of faith) described above. Recall that the apostolicity and orthodoxy of the church and its dogma require a critical translation of experience from one historical era, with its cultural paradigms, to the next. It is not a simple matter of the translation of terms but the translation of the relationship between the understanding of faith and its accompanying social-cultural context.

Although this translation of Christian experience is a task for the whole church, theologians have a special role to play in it. As the ones who reflect on the current situation of the church in the world in the light of contemporary human knowledge and the greater Christian tradition, theologians have the responsibility both to bring to conscious expression the current forms of the translation of Christian experience and to submit those forms to criticism. Theologians must consciously and scientifically engage in the hermeneutic task and continually bring to the church's awareness the need for reinterpretation of the understanding of faith in different eras.[101] They also need to criticize current praxis and belief when they either do not fit within the Christian tradition, broadly conceived, or when they do not address the current situation. Theological assertions "must be able to be justified through an appeal to the Christian tradition of faith in which the theologian stands" and "must also be justified by an appeal to the analyzed and interpreted contemporary situation."[102]

This critical aspect of theology also means that the theologian has the obligation to unmask ideological language and praxis in the church's life, as well as in the society in which the church lives. Schillebeeckx's understanding of ideology refers to the manipulation, monopolization, and distortion of language by those in power to maintain that power over others.[103] The "de-ideologizing" function of theology is the "unmasking of the naive idea that *being* and *language* (= thinking and speaking) . . . should always correlate to each other according to their content."[104] This unmasking of false consciousness applies to the church as a whole and to theologians themselves. Even as they perform their hermeneutical and critical tasks, theologians must also become aware of their own social-political location and the possibility that their language is an attempt to preserve their own, usually privileged, place in society. Ultimately the theologian also stands within the epistemological limits of human knowledge and the limit concepts of Christian faith. Thus the theologian's expressed understanding of the faith also requires the actualizing test of praxis; and the theologian's work itself remains limited and open to the criticism of the wider church under the impetus of the subversive memory of Jesus, the cumulative narratives of human suffering, and the eschatological proviso of God's fulfillment of the *humanum*. Theologians, like the magisterium, stand under the authority of the Gospel, even as they perform the indispensable task of publicly interpreting its significance for the current situation by mediating the church's tradition, contemporary knowledge, and critical awareness in an ongoing dialogue with the current community.

Critical Communities and Their Role in the Church

The critical impulse in theology does not proceed only from the learning of the individual theologian (or even community of theologians) who confronts the contemporary church with the wider tradition. Rather, this critical or "de-ideologizing" aspect of theology derives from the power of negative contrast experiences and the protest that they evoke. In the most mature form of Schillebeeckx's epistemology, the complex event of reality's resistance to human aspirations and human protest and action against this destructive reality is the disclosure experience par excellence. These negative contrast experiences at the heart of the circle of theory and praxis most clearly come to expression in the cumulative history of human suffering and active struggle for liberation. Hence the critical impulse in theology is rooted in the greater critical impulse of negative contrast experiences, which are primarily communal.

For this reason, it is not surprising to see that Schillebeeckx links the development of critical theology with the growth of critical communities in the church and society. Although he recalls that he was critical of the official theology of the church even before the Second Vatican Council, only during the period of tumultuous change after the council does Schillebeeckx come to associate himself sympathetically with the growing movement of critical communities within the church.

> Even before 1957, when I was teaching in Louvain, I was quite critical of the official theology of the Church in my own theology. I was very influenced in those days in my reaction to the Roman theology by Rahner and Congar. But after the Second Vatican Council and especially when the

reactionary forces in the Church paralyzed all progress—that was from about 1969 or 1970 onwards—it became not just a theological question for me, but a really existential question: How should I proceed?

I looked around and saw various critical communities emerging in the Church. That was decisive for me. A marginal critical movement that was nonetheless spreading throughout the whole Church. I wanted to go along with that movement and, as it were, supervise it theologically, because I realized the future of the Church was in it. If the Church is ever to change at the top, I thought, it has to recognise that it is in fact becoming more and more a top without a base—the base, that is, people themselves, have gone their own way. It is only in this way that the top can change. And it will change![105]

The critical communities in the church therefore form the immediate background for Schillebeeckx's own theological journey after the council. His identification with them will continue throughout the rest of his work; for example, the two books on ministry directly address questions raised by the praxis of these communities,[106] and the *Church* book is dedicated to those laboring and suffering in these communities.[107] However, beyond the significance of critical communities for his own theological work, Schillebeeckx sees in these communities the ecclesiology of the future. Understanding their role in the church will therefore be necessary for a complete consideration of the central question of theological dissent and magisterial authority.

What does Schillebeeckx mean by a "critical community"? As William L. Portier argues, Schillebeeckx's basic understanding of this term originates in the progressive, politically active, small church communities which grew up within Dutch Catholicism, particularly in university settings, after Vatican II.[108] I would argue that on the basis of this model Schillebeeckx would define "critical community" as an intentional gathering of Christians outside of the regular boundaries of parish and diocesan organization which has the express purpose of seeking to live out Jesus' message of the reign of God to the fullest and to offer that community life as a challenge to both the rest of the church and to the world. Schillebeeckx's task as a theologian in a dialectical relationship with these communities has been to listen to their critical voice and in turn to provide a certain kind of "oversight" for them in relation to the mainstream church.

The first aspect of that dual task is asking the question about the very Christian and ecclesial nature of the critical communities themselves. In distinction from other emancipatory movements which base their struggle for justice in the world on Marxist or neo-Marxist thought, Schillebeeckx argues that these critical communities, even though the scope of their task overlaps with their secular counterparts, must draw their inspiration from the Gospel.

> Because of the present historical situation and a new understanding of the historical Jesus, these critical communities on the one hand long for freedom, humanity, peace and justice in society and, on the other, resist the power structures that threaten these values by repression or oppression. What J. Jüngel has called "a Kingdom of God mindful of humanity," a rule that has been handed down to us in the tradition of the Old and New Testaments, inevitably makes Christians feel at one with contemporary emancipation movements, although they have a critical attitude toward their violent and one-sided tendencies and subject them to the criterion of the "life praxis of Jesus."[109]

This criterion means that the Christian critical community, although it takes its origin from the same negative contrast experiences and histories of human suffering that create other emancipatory movements, lives out of the concrete eschatological vision that Jesus proclaimed and enacted. The Christian's guiding principle is not the Marxist or the secular "utopia" but the critical memory and practical anticipation of God's reign.[110] On this basis alone should the Christian community found its freedom movement; without this connection the critical community becomes indistinguishable from the secular political party.[111] In a concrete application of the interrelationship of mysticism and politics, Schillebeeckx argues that the critical community must also be a community of liturgical celebration and prayer, because these actions, just as much as political activism, are the necessary forms of praxis in anticipation of the kingdom of God.

The critical community is therefore, within the general ecclesiological dynamic of remembrance, praxis, and hope, particularly committed to the living out of Jesus' vision of God's reign in the light of the current situation of suffering. In this sense the critical community is the church as a whole writ small. What distinguishes the critical community from the mainstream church is its intentionally dialectical relationship with the wider church and with the political and economic structures of the world. As a group committed to the emancipation of humanity in the light of the Gospel, the critical community expresses and lives out a criticism of both the world and the church when the structures of either bring suffering and diminishment to human beings. Because the church is a social institution as well as a spiritual one, it can succumb to ideological distortion and thus is liable to criticism.[112]

In Schillebeeckx's later works, his (usually occasional) discussions of critical communities focus more directly on how these communities both preserve their ecclesial identity and act as a critical leaven for the wider church. The concern with their criticism of the structures of society is not lost, but Schillebeeckx writes more about the relationship between critical community and the wider church, because the critical communities have come under greater fire from Rome for their experiments in specific ecclesial form and ministerial practice. By the time of the *Ministry* books he can also link the critical communities of the Netherlands with the base communities developing in the Latin American context and also around the world.[113] Their alternative practices become both a voice that Schillebeeckx thinks should be heeded and an object of careful investigation on the part of the theologian. The theologian's task here is to act as critical mediator between the contemporary church and the tradition. Thus, on the one hand, he can say to the first meeting of the Acht Mei Beweging (the 8th of May Movement), a coalition of critical communities and church reform groups in the Netherlands:

> This day, on the Malieveld at the Hague, 8 May 1985, may be something of a day of jubilee. It is not as if we were celebrating that we are right, but it is so that we may (and with all of us here *can*) show another face of the church and say: judge whether we, as people of God in the footsteps of Jesus Christ, are contributing to making people whole and freeing them in the gospel. We too all know that a healed church in a healed world is not "of this world"; but that the church and world contain an imperative to work here and now towards the making whole and healing of both the world and the church, a making whole of . . . people. In these attempts we may and can, as believers, see fragile but real prefigurings of the final consummation we have dreamed of, of the God who is concerned for human beings: in the gesture or the hand-wave of individuals, in the liberating action of our many dear fellow men and women as it opens up communication. We just live by God's liberating word and action: you and I, all of us, have a right to be there![114]

The critical community therefore is a specific and local manifestation of the church, which therefore stands under the same mandate that the whole church does, to be a sacrament and anticipatory sign of God's reign in favor of humanity. On the other hand, the critical community also cannot detach itself from the wider church either by a sole dedication to political activism or the isolation of their life of prayer and ministry from the basic parameters of the Gospel as expressed in the Scriptures and tradition. Schillebeeckx can therefore join his vigorous defense of critical communities in the church with a critical reminder to them about the need to keep themselves in a relationship with the whole Christian community.

> Precisely because of the danger that as a result of our actions, in place of a living tradition of faith, indwelt by the life-giving Spirit, tradition can also rigidify into well preserved mummies, interesting to have a nostalgic look at, but not appetizing to live from, we need basic communities within and alongside the great, perhaps somewhat cumbersome and "traditional parishes," basic communities which are nevertheless in the form of a community of Jesus, the Christ. The theology of the local communities needs a theology of the universal church, as the bond of many communities in love. It needs this precisely so that your new experiences and your new praxis can be integrated into the great tradition of the church's experience, which will be enriched by it. At the same time this prevents these new experiences and this new praxis, in prayer and political commitment in keeping with the gospel, from remaining just sporadic, from failing to stimulate the church community as a whole, and ultimately from beginning to have a disintegrating effect, so that the critical community is driven in the direction of a ghetto or sect either through a lack of self-criticism or through a failure of the church hierarchy to understand. Permanent mutual brotherly and sisterly admonition is therefore an element in the health of the Christian identity.[115]

This dialectical relationship between the critical communities and the universal church thus stands at the root of Schillebeeckx's investigation of the forms of ministry developing in their context. This praxis itself is not self-authenticating; it requires reflection by the theologian in the light of the tradition and the theology of the universal church just mentioned. On the other hand, these new forms of ministry, arising both in the Dutch Church and around the world, are a very specific expression of the needs and complaints of the people of God in the current situation. After his careful consideration given to the history of the development of the ministry in the church and an examination of those current needs and complaints, Schillebeeckx concludes that these alternative practices in the ministry are legitimate possibilities for the church; they may be *praeter ordinem,* so to speak, but they are not *contra ordinem.*[116]

The legitimacy of such alternative practices means that their existence, despite their "illegality," is itself a criticism of the church's current order. According to Schillebeeckx, critical communities therefore do not simply criticize the defects or abuses in the church along the lines of a political party or pressure group but by actually enacting in its fullness the alternative vision of the church of the future. For ultimately the people of the critical community are the ones most sensitive to the eschatological nature of the church and its accompanying proviso, because that community attempts to create within its own life a glimpse of that future community which is the culmination of both church and the world.

> For this reason, I regard the critical alternative communities as ferment in a universal process [in] which Christian consciousness is being formed and therefore as a necessarily exceptional position within the one great union of the apostolic churches. They occupy a marginal position, continuously stimulating Christian consciousness, so that the great Church will be made ready to receive another Church order which is more suitable for the modern world and its pastoral needs and which will give a contemporary form in our own times to the apostolic character of the Christian community.[117]

Schillebeeckx's Redefinition of Authority

Throughout this discussion of the preservation of the apostolicity of the church, it is clear that all the specific factors and roles—the definition of apostolicity itself, criteria of orthodoxy, status of dogmas, the respective roles of the magisterium and theologians, the special function of critical communities— only have meaning in a nonantithetical and dialectical relationship with each other and, most important, with the entire Christian community as a whole. That community—past, present, and future—is the essential reference point for all such discussions. In this sense not only must one recognize the particular authority vested in the various role players in the church, but one must locate this authority within the experience of the entire Christian community. All discussions of authority must therefore take seriously the voice of the whole community, in all its diversity. The *sensus fidelium* is not an empty phrase; it is the name for the actual teaching authority of all believers.[118]

Because of this complex dialogue of universal church, office bearers, theologians, and critical communities, Schillebeeckx no longer can locate absolute authority in any one place, nor, given his fundamental epistemological and theological framework, can he even define "authority" in any sort of traditional sense. He never systematically deals with the topic, but based on his usage of the term, I would argue that Schillebeeckx redefines "authority" as the critical, cognitive, and productive force of an experience or a tradition of experiences.[119] Those experiences have authority which rest on the truth in such a way that they unmask ideological distortions (the critical aspect), they provide a disclosure of meaning (the cognitive aspect) and they effect a liberating praxis (the productive aspect). Because authority truly comes from experiences that have these qualities, it does not inhere in people (or in offices themselves for that matter) in an "essentialist" way, but in the dialectical relationships between people and offices that create these experiences.

In the first chapter, I argued that Schillebeeckx locates the greatest concentration of the revelation of truth in the authority of the narratives of human suffering. This anthropological assertion converges with the theological assertion that the Spirit of God is the source of all authority in the church.[120] For the narratives of human suffering are the most intense revelation of the *humanum,* in both negative experience and positive hope. This *humanum* as God's cause and the cause of Jesus is the heart of the Christian gospel. Hence the Spirit of God, who works in and through the church in all its dialectical interrelationships,[121] leads the church back to this basic message time and again and thus leads the community to that prayer and praxis in Jesus' memory and hope which is also the positive vision of the *humanum.* One can therefore say that the critical, cognitive, and productive power of the Spirit can be discerned in the church most clearly in the church's own identification with the history of human suffering and its praxis to overcome it in order to become an anticipatory symbol of the reign of God to come.

six | Symbols of the Church to Come

Theological Dissent and Critical Communities
as Sacraments of the Future Church

At the beginning of this work, I stated that ecclesiology, both in theory and practice, is often an expression of a more fundamental theological understanding of revelation. The very structure of a church reflects its understanding of the process and location, so to speak, of God's revelation to it. In turn, such concrete structures mediate and shape theologies of revelation as circumstances and contexts change in the life of any particular church. In the postconciliar Roman Catholic Church, the struggle over the interpretation of the council undertaken by various parties in response to a series of controversies has led to the development of seemingly irreconcilable ecclesiologies. If my original statement holds true, these ecclesiologies in turn really reflect in part the theological shifts in the understanding of revelation that have marked recent Catholic thought. Hence the drama of postconciliar Catholicism can in part be explained by the emergence of multiple, internally coherent, and nearly incommensurable theologies, which inhabit the same church and claim the name Catholic, but which seemingly dwell in very different worlds.

In the light of this situation in the church, and in order to illustrate the connection between ecclesiologies and underlying theologies of revelation, I have interpreted the theology of Edward Schillebeeckx. In the course of synthesizing a more systematic ecclesiology from his writings, we have seen how such an ecclesiology coheres with his epistemology and theology of revelation. So construed, his theology can now offer a tentative way forward from the impasse in which much Catholic theological discussion finds itself today. This solution is no easy "via media," but a call for a break in the Catholic Church with what Schillebeeckx would call an antiquated view of itself in favor of church that can both serve humanity in its suffering and remain faithful to its original inspiration in the Gospel.

Of great interest here are the specific problems of theological dissent and the development of critical communities in the church. They are significant phenomena in themselves, but, most important, the way in which Schillebeeckx's theology treats these problems indicates how his theology offers that way forward from the impasse.

Theological dissent, as generally understood within contemporary magisterial pronouncements and theological writings, is a concept of relatively recent coinage.[1] One could argue that such a term could only develop within the structures of authority and understanding of dogma prevalent in Catholicism from the Council of Trent onward, particularly after the First Vatican Council and its proclamation of papal infallibility. For dissent in its most basic sense means the refusal to give assent to the exercise of authority by another, either by rejecting one specific action of that authority (whose legitimacy in general is not questioned) or, more radically, by rejecting the authority all together. The question about the possibility and range of legitimate dissent only arises when there exists a person or office which has a presumptive claim to (absolute) authority; in the Catholic case, the magisterium's claims to authority reach their zenith during the last century and a half, since Pius IX defined the doctrine of the Immaculate Conception of Mary on his own authority.[2] However, the question of theological dissent only emerges from subtle manualist discussions into the public forum after the Second Vatican Council and the watershed event of Paul VI's *Humanae Vitae*.

The controversy about *Humanae Vitae* framed the debate about theological dissent largely in terms of a traditional, propositional understanding of the truth of dogmatic statements, the various levels of authority attached to dogmas (see chapter 4), and the corresponding forms of assent and obedience owed to each type of statement. In this framework, the definition of theological dissent is: theologians, on the basis of their scientific work and judgment, publicly expressing disagreement with a noninfallible doctrine promulgated by the magisterium. For example, the National Conference of Catholic Bishops in the United States issued a statement about theological dissent soon after the controversy over *Humanae Vitae* erupted. The statement allows for prudent dissent from noninfallible, authentic teachings of the magisterium, but only under certain conditions.

When there is a question of theological dissent from non-infallible doctrine, we must recall that there is always a presumption in favor of the magisterium. Even non-infallible authentic doctrine, though it may admit of development or call for clarification or revision, remains binding and carries with it a moral certitude, especially when it is addressed to the universal Church, without ambiguity, in response to urgent questions bound up with faith and crucial to morals. The expression of theological dissent from the magisterium is in order only if the reasons are serious and well-founded, if the manner of the dissent does not question or impugn the teaching authority of the church and is such as not to give scandal.[3]

The West German Bishops, the International Theological Commission, and prominent theologians like Charles Curran all agree in principle on what theological dissent is. What they disagree about is: the range of subjects liable to an infallible declaration (e.g., are concrete applications of moral theology drawn from the natural law so subject?); whether previous magisterial declarations are in fact infallible (e.g., is *Humanae Vitae* really infallible because it has been taught by the ordinary and universal magisterium?), whether the *obsequium religiosum mentis et voluntatis* owed even to noninfallible statements precludes any dissent; and what are the proper methods, if any, for expression of dissent (public, organized dissent? writings and lectures in restricted academic settings? internal dissent only?). Even a very restrictive document like *Donum Veritatis*, the 1990 statement by the Congregation for the Doctrine of the Faith, works within the same paradigm, even though it practically rules out any possible conditions for legitimate dissent.[4]

It is not surprising, given Schillebeeckx's central theological concerns after the council, that he rarely engages directly in a discussion about theological dissent within the basic paradigm just described. In fact, not even in his writings about the Vatican's investigations of his own work does he use the term "dissent."[5] The sole discussion of theological dissent that I was able to discover comes in his late article about "breaks in Christian dogma."[6] Schillebeeckx there deals with the question in a section concerning "[t]he attitude of believers with regard to non-*ex cathedra* statements of the so-called *magisterium authenticum*."[7] Writing particularly in response to John Paul II's *Veritatis Splendor*, Schillebeeckx opposes himself to the "maximalizing" tendency he sees at work in this document, which replaces the old distinction of "ordinary" and "extraordinary" teaching office—itself not used by Vatican I or II—with a distinction between the "infallible teaching office" and the "*magisterium authenticum*." Citing Cardinal Ratzinger in this regard, Schillebeeckx notes that this distinction is intended to invest even "noninfallible" statements with the aura of infallibility because they follow "in the logic of" infallible statements.[8]

In the face of this trend, Schillebeeckx argues for what he sees as the traditional right to dissent from fallible doctrinal statements. "However it is of old an unshakable custom in the Catholic tradition that a fallible doctrine remains open for serious and public, albeit respectful, dissent and discussion concerning it."[9] In response to *Veritatis Splendor*'s treatment of dissent (which echoes *Donum Veritatis*), Schillebeeckx agrees that theologians have the obligation to present the complete doctrine of the church, but they also have the right to express their criticisms publicly.[10] The claim that the act of faith includes a presumption of inner assent to all teaching of the magisterium strikes Schillebeeckx as excessive. "Moreover, is it really psychologically possible to give an inner consent to something which you see as white, while the pope demands that you must see it as black, when it is properly a matter of rational arguments?"[11] This attempt to elevate all magisterial teaching to the level of infallibility contradicts Vatican II as well; using those documents and the commentary on them by one of their authors, Monsignor Philips, Schillebeeckx argues that the council recognized the differences in assent owed to differing types of pronouncements. Furthermore, the *obsequium religiosum* owed to even "noninfallible" statements cannot be rendered simply as "submission." Rather, it means "respect," a respect that recognizes the more than rational authority of the magisterium but also leaves open the possibility for dissent.[12] With all these arguments in mind, Schillebeeckx can conclude that, in line with Vatican II, the church recognizes "the right in the church of dissident opinions in regard to noninfallible teachings of the church's teaching office,"[13] and that therefore dissent, particularly that which is prudently voiced by experts, is possible from documents such as *Veritatis Splendor*.[14]

Theological Dissent and Critical Communities in the Church

The "standard paradigm" for understanding theological dissent depends on a traditional view of dogmatic language and magisterial authority. Even from the beginning of his career, Schillebeeckx has argued against the sufficiency of such a propositional view of dogma and against any "maximalizing" of the claims of the magisterium. By viewing the "standard paradigm" through the lens of Schillebeeckx's three epistemological circles and his understanding of salvation, revelation, and ecclesiology, a synthetic projection of how Schillebeeckx would reinterpret that paradigm takes shape.

To start with, theological dissent is the public expression by a theologian or group of theologians of a possibility for authentic Christian experience that differs from the official formulations of the range of possibilities of that experience received from the past and defined by the magisterium of the church. This statement is based on Schillebeeckx's redefinition of all the elements in the standard paradigm as stated above: theologians, on the basis of their scientific work and judgment, publicly expressing disagreement with a noninfallible doctrine promulgated by the magisterium. For Schillebeeckx "theologian," "scientific work and judgment," "public disagreement," "noninfallible," "doctrine," and "magisterium" all take on different meaning because of the changes in his epistemology and fundamental theology.

Since Schillebeeckx defines "theology" as "the critical self-awareness of Christian praxis," the theologian's task is the critical mediation between the praxis of local communities and their experience, the accumulated experience and interpretation of the wider church, and the forms of human knowledge available in the current situation.

This move toward the centrality of experience and praxis applies to the meaning of "doctrine" as well. In Schillebeeckx's thought, doctrines are linguistic expressions of the interrelationship between Christian experience at a certain time and the historical and social context of that experience. Therefore, doctrines are not themselves the central focus of the theologian's work and judgment, or of the magisterium's for that matter; the authenticity of Christian experience that comes to expression in doctrine is the main concern. For this reason, and because of the particular nature of their task, theologians have the responsibility to examine new forms of Christian praxis and experience in the light of Scripture and tradition, and also to speak on behalf of these new forms when they are judged to be real possibilities for Christian life.

The received doctrines of the church do reflect the accumulated experience and wisdom of the church and therefore cannot be dismissed, but these doctrines cannot enjoy any absolute or fixed status since they are the expression of an experience, not the experience of salvation and revelation itself. Hence Schillebeeckx's theology actually radically questions the distinctions between noninfallible and infallible doctrines and the classifications of the various authorities that can produce them. He will still occasionally employ these classical distinctions, but his basic epistemological and fundamental paradigm precludes any absolutization of linguistic expression or praxis. The magisterium's role is no longer to be the "regula proxima" of the understanding of faith, but to be instead the guarantor of open communication in the church, the supervisor of the church's language and the court of last appeal. According to Schillebeeckx, then, theological dissent is not an act of defiance aimed at the magisterium; only the "classic" paradigm, which assumes a propositional understanding of dogma and the magisterium's control over it, would understand dissent in that way. Rather, theological dissent is aimed at the received range of possibilities for authentic Christian experience. This range, expressed customarily in doctrine and preserved by the magisterium, can also be found in liturgical customs, ethical norms, and popular piety. The theologian's dissent can and should address the whole range of the church's received life, not just the doctrinal statements of the tradition. Therefore, theological dissent is also an ecclesial and thus public act of the theologian. Because of this understanding of the theologian's interrelationship with the community, Schillebeeckx will argue against any attempt to quash dissent because of the alleged "confusion" that it causes among the "simple" faithful.

Theological dissent is circumscribed by a variety of conditions and should always be voiced prudently and respectfully, but this aspect of the theologian's public role in the church remains legitimate. Theologians have the right to such expression because of the nature of human knowledge and salvific divine revelation, the nature of the church and the nature of the process of the preservation of the church's apostolicity. These justifications also place limits under which it can occur, including the authority under which theologians stand. Concerning these conditions of possibility and their limits, first one must recall the epistemological frameworks that determine human language. Schillebeeckx's three epistemological circles each in their own way argue for the possibility of human knowledge of objective reality, which is expressed only in a limited fashion through human language. The first circle showed how knowledge is perspectival; linguistic concepts are therefore always limited in relation to the reality they intend to capture. The second circle showed how knowledge comes through an interpretative understanding of the world carried out in an irreducible hermeneutical circle; language is therefore always limited by its tradition and historical location. The third circle showed how knowledge comes through negative contrast experiences, which disclose not only the interruptive power of reality on human plans and flourishing but also the hope for the *humanum;* language is therefore subject to the authority of these experiences which both expose ideological distortion in it and ground it authentically in praxis that overcomes suffering and brings about human fulfillment. Taken as one, all of these epistemological conditions indicate for Schillebeeckx that no language can claim a universal, timeless, and unimpeachable status.

As a condition of possibility for dissent, all the church's language falls within these circles. Since therefore no church language can legitimately claim absolute status, theologians always have the right to investigate this language critically. As a limit on dissent, these epistemological criteria indicate that the theologian's language also cannot claim absolute status; it too must recognize its perspectival, hermeneutical, and ideological location. It too must stand under the authority of negative contrast experiences and the disclosive test of praxis. Thus theological language is inherently limited and must have a critical counterbalance, both within and without the community of theologians.

In Schillebeeckx's theology, God's salvation and revelation to the human race, as most concretely expressed in the life, death, and resurrection of Jesus, provides the "positive" content of specifically Christian language. This positive content also supplies further conditions for the possibility of theological dissent and further limits as well. Since Christian language must stay within what I called the three "limit concepts" of the Christian narrative—"God as pure positivity," "Jesus as the definitive revelation of God's cause as the human cause," and "the *humanum* as human wholeness both in actuality and anticipation"—the theologian can both authentically express possibilities for Christian experience which do not transgress these boundaries, even if they transgress official church doctrine and practice, and criticize official (or other) expressions which actually do violate them. Conversely, the theologian's expression always stands under the authority of the same Christian narrative. Furthermore, this narrative ultimately finds its disclosive test in orthopraxis; hence theologians both can recognize authentic Christian praxis that manifestly makes real the substance of the Christian narrative at a particular time and must submit their judgments to the test of praxis itself in the wider community.

The nature of the church as anticipatory sign provides more specific grounding for the possibility of theological dissent as well as sets more limits on it. Since Schillebeeckx thinks of the church as the community of believers who make real the Christian narrative in the present in a dialectical relationship with remembrance of the past and anticipation of God's future, theologians in their role as critical mediators can dissent from the received language and praxis of the present by arguing that current church doctrine and praxis do not actually take into full account the subversive memory of Jesus. Alternatively, theologians can also criticize any absolutization of language or praxis in the church in the name of the eschatological proviso. Since the church should be the anticipatory sign of the redeemed and just human community (and thus is the sacrament of the world as well as sacrament of Christ), theologians particularly have the obligation to criticize the church when it falls short of making real the just human community that it is supposed to represent proleptically. They also stand within the same dialectic of anamnesis, actualization, and hope and within the same dialectic of church and world. Thus theological dissent is limited by the same subversive memory of Jesus and eschatological proviso that marks the church. The theologian's language, like the church's narrative as a whole, must find constant actualization in the present, and this actualization must disclose an experience of the just and harmonious human community which is the *telos* of both church and world.

The most specific context for theological dissent is the preservation of the apostolicity of the church. Of central importance here for Schillebeeckx is the apostolic mandate (the "entrusted pledge") that falls upon the whole Christian community, particularly as each local church lives it out in mutual connection and criticism with all the other local communities in the world. Thus criteria for orthodoxy, the meaning of dogmatic statements, the respective roles of magisterium and theologians, and the purpose of critical communities all must refer to this wider ecclesial context for their legitimacy. In this sense the nature of the preservation of the apostolicity of the church allows for theological dissent by recognizing the particular role that theologians play in the critical translation of orthodoxy from one era to the next. As mediators between the current communities, wider tradition, and contemporary knowledge, theologians have the responsibility to articulate in a self-consciously critical way the relationship between Christian experience and its social-historical context. This task may lead theologians to express and defend formulations of that experience that go beyond (or against) the received expressions for possible experience in the church contained in doctrine and magisterial teaching. This is Schillebeeckx's understanding of theological dissent within his more general theological paradigm. The nature of the apostolicity of the church also limits dissent in that the theologian's work cedes a certain priority (but not an absolute one) to the current praxis and life of the Christian community. Since the community as a whole is the bearer of the apostolic mandate, the community's life has this priority because it provides the *subject* of the theologian's work, even if the theologian may also have to criticize that community life. Schillebeeckx thus argues that theological dissent cannot be an abstracted or academic exercise or the product of the theologian's intelligence alone. The theologian's work must ultimately have a public, ecclesial reference; "private" or purely "internal" dissent would be an oxymoron to Schillebeeckx.

Other counterbalancing forces also limit theological dissent within the church. One, which Schillebeeckx rarely talks about directly (perhaps because its existence is assumed), is the community of professional theologians who can criticize each other's work. The theologian's work is also subject to the judgment of the magisterium of the church, but Schillebeeckx does not see the magisterium itself as a standard of orthodoxy nor can he accept its claims to infallibility without serious qualifications. Because of this relocation of the role of the magisterium within the church's apostolic mandate, it is difficult at times to see what authority the magisterium actually has over theologians. Schillebeeckx prefers to speak of a necessary tension between theologians and the magisterium as part of the normal functioning of the church.[15] They stand in a nonantithetical and dialectical interrelationship whereby theological dissent and magisterial admonition are in continual interplay within the life of the church. Does the magisterium's authority, in Schillebeeckx's framework, extend any further?

I would argue that Schillebeeckx would concede that the magisterium has the Spirit-given authority to censure a theologian's work or to declare it as not falling within the limit concepts of the Christian narrative. However, this magisterial authority is also situated within the same limits and dialectical interrelationships that define the theologian's task. Therefore such a decision could not be reached independently of the experience of faith of the wider community and the critical work of other theologians. Moreover, this declaration could only be a last resort after all other methods of dialogue had failed and if the results of the theologian's work were manifestly damaging to the well-being of people in the church (and world). It seems obvious to me that for Schillebeeckx these criteria of "last resort" and "manifestly damaging to the well-being of people" mean that the censure of theologians by church authorities should be an extremely rare event; the other limits and counterbalances in the church's life should act first to curtail drastically the possibility of such occurrences. Nevertheless, one should note that this sort of language is also used by the magisterium to justify its interventions against theologians, which have become much more frequent in the last three decades. Who decides what is really "manifestly damaging to people" and when more extreme "last resort" measures should be taken? What if no decision can be reached and an impasse occurs? This possibility for a breakdown in the dialectical interrelationship of theologians and the magisterium (or the attempt to collapse the dialectic through authoritarian pressure or radical disconnection) leads to the question of democratic structures in the church.

Critical communities in the church are the necessary *disclosive source for* and *critical test of* theological dissent and exist within the same range of possibilities and limits that mark theological dissent. In every level of Schillebeeckx's thought, every theory (or language) must find its source and disclosive test in praxis, and vice versa. The most concentrated form of this circle of theory and praxis is the negative contrast experience contained within the narratives of human suffering and resistance. In the Christian narrative, Jesus' own life is the negative contrast experience par excellence, giving the church that follows in his path both a clear sense of the suffering and evil which the world causes and a very real experience of *Abba,* the saving God who is the "positive" and always greater overcoming of the negation of the world. The church as a whole has the task of reactualizing this contrast experience of Jesus in its own life and times. The critical community stands in a dialectical relationship with the wider church community because it intentionally lives out its Christian life from a heightened awareness of these negative contrasts and a heightened commitment to the reign of God as God's future for humanity. They thus act as a critical leaven for church and world by their alternative praxis. These communities find both their conditions of possibility and their limits in the same basic paradigms that theologians do for their own work. The church's life and praxis is the immediate subject of the theologian's work; by extension one can argue that theological dissent, as expression of a possibility for Christian life outside the received order, has as its main source and disclosive test the communities which actually attempt to create a new form of Christian life from their intense awareness of negative contrast in both church and world. The theologian who dissents must be connected to a community that dissents, and yet both must be connected to the wider church.

The exchange between the theologian and critical community is dialectical. The theologian analyzes the praxis of the critical communities in relation to the wider tradition; the critical community in turn attempts to create as authentic a *sequela Jesu* as possible based on both its own shared experience and the work of theologians. Although Schillebeeckx gives priority to the community over the individual thinker, he also recognizes that theological research can in fact influence church life and should find expression in that life as a test of its "evangelical" authenticity.[16] Thus the theologians have a dual role: to analyze the praxis of the critical community but also to contribute through their work to the realization of that critical community, because each stands under the same memory, mandate, and hope.

From this necessary and dialectical interrelationship it follows that theological dissent and critical communities not only need each other, but they are a necessary part of a living church. This idea follows most clearly from the concept of the church as anticipatory sign. Because the church lives in the complex tension of past, present, and future, a living church cannot allow itself to be trapped by an excessive weight given to any one element, either to a traditionalism of the past, an opportunism of the present, or a "futurism" of the world-to-come. Schillebeeckx's theology would argue that critical communities and theological dissent represent (sacramentally, I would suggest) the eschatological or future element in the church's life. He proposes that they prepare the church for the future by trying to make actual an example of that future in the present as a witness to the rest of the church. Especially in the current situation of, as he puts it, "restorationism," Schillebeeckx would argue that dissent and critical communities are the desperately needed alternative vision to a church whose authorities seem intent on turning the clock back to premodern Christianity.[17] In any case they are necessary elements because they enact in a particularly intense way (again sacramentally) the eschatological proviso for the whole church. Both critical theologians and critical community also stand under that proviso, which reminds them that God's future is ever greater than even their attempts to express it in words and deeds.

As we have seen, in his later theology Schillebeeckx shifts the location of authority in the church from the Spirit-given charism of the magisterium over the church community to the working of the Spirit in the whole church through the continuous interplay of community, theologians, and magisterium. For Schillebeeckx authority comes first from experiences of a particular kind, those with "critical, cognitive and productive" power. The experiences with the greatest power (and therefore the greatest authority) are the negative contrast experiences, which capture both the reality of evil that destroys people and the reality of the happiness and hope that people discover in resisting evil. In the church, the Spirit speaks most clearly in these negative contrast experiences, particularly as they are informed by the concrete hope for the reign of God that formed the core of Jesus' identity. Just as Jesus himself lived out the negative contrast experience in an eminent way in his own life, the church, living from his memory, reenacts in the power of God's Spirit that same negative contrast experience and that same hope.

For all of these reasons, Schillebeeckx's later theology does not locate authority in any one person, office, or role in the church; the whole church stands under the authority of these experiences. But since the whole church is also the potential *subject* of these experiences, the purpose of the specific ministries within the church, both magisterial and theological, is to aid in creating a Christian community where these experiences can speak most clearly. Schillebeeckx thinks that this situation will occur when all the different elements in the church's life—local communities, theologians, magisterium—can both speak and be heard; that is, when they preserve the appropriate nonantithetical and dialectical relationships that connect them all. This situation of tension and balance (reminiscent of Schillebeeckx's experience with Cardinal Alfrink's leadership in the Dutch Church) means that authority in the church is both under the authority of the Spirit and exercised only in relationships. When these dialectical interrelationships lead to experiences with this "critical, cognitive and productive" power, then the members of that interrelationship may truly be said to have authority. Formal church authority, as expressed in official declarations or canon law, would then for Schillebeeckx only indicate the *potential* for the actual exercise of authority; for example, papal authority does not exist simply because it has been dogmatically or canonically defined. These definitions show only the pope's role in making possible the experiences that should have *de facto* authority over the church's life.

Schillebeeckx's Call for Democracy in the Church

If Schillebeeckx thinks of the ideal relationship between theologians and the magisterium as a dialectical tension, then an actual breakdown of this relationship between them indicates a grave problem with one or both parties. Although he agrees that theologians could be the cause of this disruption,[18] his writings more clearly indicate that the reactionary and maximalizing tendency of the contemporary magisterium's claims for its own authority is the real problem now. His response to the Vatican's investigations of his work, his critique of *Veritatis Splendor* (which has essentially the same restrictive view of dissent as *Donum Veritatis*), and his spirited defense of the rights of critical communities are all examples of this viewpoint. Furthermore, the synthetic "theology of dissent" I have presented, if it is an accurate extension of Schille-beeckx's thought, is itself a thoroughgoing criticism of the current theology of church authority espoused by the magisterium and Curia. In this sense Schille-beeckx's own thought already provides an answer to these questions: Beyond even the theological dissent necessary for the church's "ideal" life, is a more radical "dissent" allowable in the face of magisterial attempts to collapse the dialectic of community, theologians, and magisterium into a monologue? Can theological dissent be not only an expression of an alternative possibility for Christian experience which differs from received expressions but also a criticism of the imbalances in church life which prohibit really authoritative experiences from coming to expression? Schillebeeckx implies that this must be possible; indeed, taken as whole, his thought is an example of this more radical form of dissent. The very concept of theologians and magisterium existing in a dialectically informing relationship within all the paradigms described above is itself a challenge to the current ideology of authority regnant in the magisterium. However, for Schillebeeckx this radical dissent and critique of the magisterium does not imply its rejection; he would perhaps argue that the most radical thing that theologians can do in the current situation is to attempt to create the ideal situation in the real life of the church: *to act as if the magisterium were the critical and dialectical partner of theologians and not their absolutely authoritative master.*

The theologian's dissent should be linked with the dissent of the community in another dialectical relationship. It would then hold that this radical theological dissent should find its source and disclosive test in a church community which enacts the ideal situation in its own life: *in a community which acts as if the authority of the Spirit really did act through the constant interplay of all the elements of the church's life.*

As I see it, this is the grounding for Schillebeeckx's call for the introduction of democratic rule in the church through its ministers, an argument that he makes most completely in *Church: The Human Story of God.*[19] Because the whole church is subject to the Word of God, authority in the church should come from a mutual dialogue of "speaking and letting oneself be told." In this way the Holy Spirit, who is the ultimate source of authority in the church, can work through all the members of the church and not just through the hierarchical magisterium. Without relying directly on contemporary "secular" models of democracy, Schillebeeckx can argue that the theology of the Holy Spirit just described provides intrinsic reasons for the exercising of democratic authority in the church. Since all members of the church can be instruments of the Spirit, and since the Spirit's authority calls the church to imitate the "vulnerable rule of God" made flesh in Jesus, there is no room for "master-slave" relationships within the church. Schillebeeckx argues that the current monarchical model of church governance cannot give real institutional form to this theology; a democratic form is a better, even if imperfect, model for creating a church in which the Spirit's impulse can be expressed by all Christians. Only if the church creates the "institutional space" for this web of dialectical and mutually informing relationships can the authority of the Spirit and the authority of human experience (which ultimately cannot be set against each other) truly be effective for the sake of both church and world.

Conclusion

For the purpose of this work these ideas must remain provocative suggestions for future exploration. Equally tentative must be the critical questions that would need to be addressed by anyone wishing to build further on the ecclesiological implications of Schillebeeckx's work.

For example, at a fundamental level, does the occasional ambiguity in Schillebeeckx's thought about the relationship of "experience" and "interpretation" pose problems for any ecclesiology that one might construct on the basis of his thought?[20] That is, as Caputo suggested, does Schillebeeckx's appeal to a "basic" experience of Jesus or to the three "limit concepts" of the Christian narrative betray a hidden reliance on his first epistemological circle (with its perspectivalist grasp on objective truth) that is unwarranted by his turns to hermeneutics and critical theory in his later thought? Doesn't the general thrust of his thought argue that the objectively real is only experienced in the interpretative act or in the moment of resistance, and thus can never be separated out and captured by language? If so, then do such appeals to "basic experience" or "limit concepts" have only tentative and probative value? Does then the very concept of "objectivity" become harder to affirm itself?

If this is so, then how great indeed is the "break" that Schillebeeckx proposes for the Catholic Church? For example, given Schillebeeckx's discussion of apostolicity with regard to the roles of theologians and magisterium in the church, what concrete form of the church would give these relationships adequate expression? Because he conceives this relationship (and indeed all relationships among elements in the church) as both necessary and irreducibly mutual, with no element possessing an absolute claim to authority, would such a church concretely no longer necessarily have any real hierarchical relationships? Would Schillebeeckx's democratized church, only hinted at in his writings, need to take shape in a radically decentralized polity? How would the classic Roman Catholic understanding of the "notes" of the (one, holy, catholic, apostolic) church look in such a community? Across such a seemingly wide "break," would such a community be recognizable as classically Catholic? Indeed, to put it frankly, would it matter if it weren't?

Critically following these lines of thought and responding to these questions is a task for Schillebeeckx and his many theological followers. For the present, however, Schillebeeckx's theology does direct the theologian and the community to bring about this ideal vision of the church in practice, even if this vision only lives on in critical communities amid a tide of institutional restorationism. The prospect seems dim that his vision will become an institutional reality for the whole Catholic Church anytime soon. Yet Schillebeeckx, having lived through the seemingly impossible change in direction brought about by the council, is still optimistic.

> This spiritual presence of Jesus in believers has consequences for Christian life. Just as positive anticipations of the resurrection and thus of the superior power of the grace of God could be seen in Jesus' life (and must be seen, if resurrection faith is not to become an ideology), so the same holds true for Christians. Within the defencelessness of our own lives we must be able to *experience* the superior power of God; otherwise we accept it with a faith that is presented as purely authoritarian.
>
> Anyone who begins to look for this element of present experience must, I think, first be well aware of the difference between our time-bound existence and God's eternity. As human beings, we know that silence is an element in any dialogue, of any talking. Now how is that to be understood in a dialogue between humans and God? What is a human life of at most between seventy and ninety years to the eternal God? A fraction in his divine life; a sigh, a moment in which we can say barely a few words to the listening God. Therefore God is silent in our earthly life. God listens to what we have to say to him. God can answer only when our fleeting life on earth is ended. Should the living God not be extremely interested in us all our lives, listen silently to our life story until we have expressed everything and each person has communicated his or her own life to God? Do we not all dislike being constantly interrupted before we have

finished? Nor does God interrupt us, but for him the whole of our life, however important, is just a breath, and God also takes it seriously; that is why he is silent; he is listening to our life story. Precisely because he is greater than our human heart, he never speaks as a tangible human voice in our innermost being but only as a "divine silence," a silence that only after our death takes on a distinctive voice and face that we can recognize. As long as the Eternal One is still listening to our life story of fifty or even a hundred years, the eternal God indeed seems to us to be powerless and defenceless. In this there is both a desperate trial for our historical existence and at the same time an experience full of hope and expectation.[21]

Living out this ideal vision of the church may bring about suffering for those who do so and no immediate positive effect. Yet Schillebeeckx is confident that as long as Christians remember that this vision of the church is really a vision for all humanity, whose future rests in God's ever-greater promise, then there is no need for despair and much reason to have hope.

Notes

Introduction

Unless otherwise indicated, emphasis in quotations is always in the original.

1. For a more complete listing of theologians whose works have been recently investigated or censured by the Congregation for the Doctrine of the Faith, see Patrick Granfield, *The Limits of the Papacy: Authority and Autonomy in the Church* (New York: Crossroad, 1987), 7–17. Even more recently two other theologians, Tissa Balasuriya and Paul Collins, have come under official censure or investigation by the Congregation. For information on Balasuriya's excommunication (and later reinstatement), see "Sri Lankan Priest Expelled," *Christian Century* 114 (January 29, 1997): 92–93, and "Chronology of Balasuriya's Troubles," *National Catholic Reporter*, January 20, 1998. For the particular work of Balasuriya's which drew the Congregation's censure, see his *Mary and Human Liberation: The Debate* (Harrisburg, Pa.: Trinity, 1997). For information on Paul Collins, see "Collins's Views on Papacy Face Heresy Investigation," *National Catholic Reporter*, February 20, 1998. This investigation has been particularly prompted by Collins's work, *Papal Power: A Proposal for Change in Catholicism's Third Millennium* (London: HarperCollins, 1997).

2. Congregation for the Doctrine of the Faith, "Oath of Fidelity: The New Profession of Faith and Oath of Fidelity (March 1, 1989)," *The Pope Speaks: The Church Documents Bimonthly* 34, 2 (July–August 1989): 170.

3. Ibid., 171. "With Christian obedience I shall associate myself with what is expressed by the holy shepherds as authentic doctors and teachers of the faith or established by them as the Church's rulers."

4. Congregation for the Doctrine of the Faith, "The Ecclesial Vocation of the Theologian," *The Pope Speaks: The Church Documents Bimonthly* 35, 6 (November–December 1990): 388–403. This document describes theological research in the following way: "In theology this freedom of inquiry is the hallmark of a rational discipline whose object is given by Revelation, handed on and interpreted in the Church under the authority of the Magisterium, and received by faith. These givens have the force of principles. To eliminate them would mean to cease doing theology" (p. 394).

Because of this definition of theology, "The willingness to submit loyally to the teaching of the Magisterium on matters per se not irreformable must be the rule" (p. 396). Privately, the theologian may have difficulties accepting the teaching of the magisterium, but this is ultimately "a call to suffer for the truth, in silence and in prayer, but with the certainty that if the truth really is at stake it will ultimately prevail" (p. 398). Dissent, which is "public opposition to the Magisterium of the Church" (p. 398), has no authentic justification. Neither the freedom of the act of faith nor the rights of conscience can legitimate dissent, because both of these presume "faith in the word of God, whose riches he [the theologian] must explore, but also love for the Church, from whom he receives his mission and respect for her divinely assisted Magisterium" (p. 401). See John P. Boyle, *Church Teaching Authority: Historical and Theological Studies* (Notre Dame, Ind.: University of Notre Dame Press, 1995), 142–60, for a more complete analysis of the Instruction.

    5. See Pope John Paul II, "Apostolic Constitution on Catholic Universities *Ex Corde Ecclesiae*," August 15, 1990, *Acta Apostolicae Sedis* 82 (1990): 1475–1509. English translation: *Origins* 20, 17 (October 4, 1990): 266–76.

    6. See National Conference of Catholic Bishops, "*Ex Corde Ecclesiae*: An Application to the United States," *Origins* 26, 24 (November 8, 1996): 381–84; "U.S. Implementation of *Ex Corde Ecclesiae*: New Draft Text," Origins 29, 16 (September 30, 1999): 245–54.

    7. See, for example, the case of the twenty-one professors at the Catholic University of America who issued a statement (along with sixty-six colleagues at other colleges and universities) on July 30, 1968, saying that "spouses may reasonably decide according to their conscience that artificial contraception in some circumstances is permissible and indeed necessary to preserve and foster the value and sacredness of marriage." Their conflict with the chancellor and board of trustees of the university over the possibility and appropriateness of public theological dissent is described in John F. Hunt and Terrence R. Connelly with Charles E. Curran, Robert E. Hunt, and Robert K. Webb, *The Responsibility of Dissent: The Church and Academic Freedom* (New York: Sheed and Ward, 1969).

    8. Congregation for the Doctrine of the Faith, "Reply to the 'Dubium,'" *The Pope Speaks: The Church Documents Bimonthly* 41, 3 (May–June 1996): 145. "*Dubium:* Whether the teaching that the Church has no authority whatsoever to confer priestly ordination on women, which is presented in the apostolic letter *Ordinatio Sacerdotalis* to be held definitively, is to be understood as belonging to the deposit of the faith. *Responsum:* In the affirmative. This teaching requires definitive assent, since, founded on the written Word of God and from the beginning constantly preserved and applied in the tradition of the Church, it has been set forth infallibly by the ordinary and universal magisterium. Thus, in the present circumstances, the Roman Pontiff, exercising his proper office of confirming the brethren (cf. Lk 22:32), has handed on this same teaching by a formal declaration, explicitly stating what is to be held always, everywhere,

and by all, as belonging to the deposit of faith." For diverse reactions to the CDF's statement, see, for example, Avery Dulles, "Pastoral Response to the Teaching on Women's Ordination," *Origins* 26, 11 (August 29, 1996): 177–80, and Hermann Josef Pottmeyer, "Refining the Question of Women's Ordination," *America* 175, 12 (October 26, 1996): 16–18.

9. See, for example, Charles Curran, *Faithful Dissent* (Kansas City: Sheed and Ward, 1986), 50–65. This distinction, argued for on the basis of a long tradition within the Catholic Church, was also employed by the eighty-seven original signatories of the Catholic University of America statement in 1968, among them Curran himself.

10. See Hans Küng, *Infallible? An Inquiry* (Garden City, N.Y.: Doubleday, 1971).

11. See, for example, Robert Barclay, *An Apology for the True Christian Divinity* (Philadelphia: Friends' Book Association, n.d.). The second of Barclay's *Theses Theologicae* reads: "Concerning Immediate Revelation. Seeing 'no man knoweth the Father but the Son and he to whom the Son revealeth him'; and seeing the revelation of the Son is in and by the Spirit; therefore the testimony of the Spirit is that alone by which the true knowledge of God hath been, is, and can only be revealed" (p. 13).

12. See the *First Dogmatic Constitution on the Church of Christ* from the First Vatican Council (1869–70) in *Decrees of the Ecumenical Councils*, vol. 2, *Trent to Vatican II*, ed. Norman P. Tanner (Washington, D.C.: Sheed & Ward and Georgetown University Press, 1990), 811–16. For further background on the theology and ecclesiology of this period, see Gerald A. McCool, *Catholic Theology in the Nineteenth Century: The Quest for a Unitary Method* (New York: Seabury/Crossroad, 1977), and T. M. Schoof, *A Survey of Catholic Theology, 1800–1970*, trans. by N. D. Smith (Glen Rock, N.J.: Paulist Newman, 1970).

13. See the *Dogmatic Constitution on the Church of Christ* of the First Vatican Council (1869–70), chap. 3, "On the power and character of the primacy of the Roman pontiff." "And so, supported by the clear witness of holy scripture, and adhering to the manifest and explicit decrees both of our predecessors the Roman pontiffs and of general councils, we promulgate anew the definition of the ecumenical council of Florence, which must be believed by all faithful Christians, namely, that the apostolic see and the Roman pontiff hold a world-wide primacy, and that the Roman pontiff is the successor of blessed Peter, the prince of the apostles, true vicar of Christ, head of the whole church and father and teacher of all Christian people. To him, in blessed Peter, full power has been given by our Lord Jesus Christ to tend, rule and govern the universal church" (p. 813).

14. See the decrees *Haec Sancta Synodus* (Session 5, April 6, 1415) and *Frequens* (Session 39, October 9, 1417) from the Council of Constance in *Decrees of the Ecumenical Councils*, vol. 1, *Nicaea I to Lateran V*, ed. by Norman P. Tanner (Washington, D.C.: Sheed & Ward and Georgetown University Press, 1990), 405–51.

15. See, for example, C. Gilbert Romero, *Hispanic Devotional Piety: Tracing the Biblical Roots* (Maryknoll, N.Y.: Orbis, 1991).

16. Edward Schillebeeckx, *Interim Report on the Books* Jesus *and* Christ, trans. by John Bowden (New York: Crossroad, 1980), 3–4.

17. Edward Schillebeeckx, *Theologisch Geloofsverstaan Anno 1983* (Baarn, Netherlands: H. Nelissen, 1983), 20. Schillebeeckx develops this idea further in "Breuken in christelijke dogma's," in *Breuklijnen; Grenservaringen en zoektoechten*, ed. E. Schillebeeckx, Bas van Iersel, Ad Willems, and Herman Wegman (Baarn, Netherlands: H. Nelissen, 1994), 15–49.

one   Human Experience, Knowledge, and Action

1. For details of these questionnaires, Schillebeeckx's responses, and the "conversation" in Rome, see *The Schillebeeckx Case: Official Exchange of Letters and Documents in the Investigation of Fr. Edward Schillebeeckx by the Sacred Congregation for the Doctrine of the Faith, 1976–1980*, edited with introduction and notes by Ted Schoof, trans. Matthew J. O'Connell (New York: Paulist, 1984).

2. Ibid., 117.

3. Ibid., 112.

4. Edward Schillebeeckx, *I Am a Happy Theologian: Conversations with Francesco Strazzari*, trans. John Bowden (New York: Crossroad, 1994), 36. This exchange does not appear in the official documentation of the "Conversation," although Schillebeeckx does cite the maxim from St. Thomas in his April 13, 1977, written response to the Congregation's first questionnaire. See Schoof, *The Schillebeeckx Case*, 55.

5. Robert Schreiter, "Edward Schillebeeckx: An Orientation to His Thought," in *The Schillebeeckx Reader*, ed. Robert Schreiter (New York: Crossroad, 1987), 10.

6. Ibid., 8–9.

7. I owe the particular phrasing "nonantithetical" to a conversation with Professor Robert Schreiter.

8. For a general history of Catholic theology in this period, see Schoof, *A Survey of Catholic Theology, 1800–1970*. For Leo XIII's encyclical *Aeterni Patris*, see *The Papal Encyclicals 1878–1903*, ed. Claudia Carlen (Raleigh: McGrath, 1981), 17–27. For Pius X's encyclical *Pascendi Dominici Gregis*, see *The Papal Encyclicals, 1903–1939*, ed. Claudia Carlen (Raleigh: McGrath, 1981), 71–98.

9. Philip Kennedy, "Continuity Underlying Discontinuity: Schillebeeckx's Philosophical Background," *New Blackfriars* 70 (1989): 266–67. For further information on De Petter and Schillebeeckx's philosophical training with him, see Philip Kennedy, *Deus Humanissimus: The Knowability of God in the Theology of Edward Schillebeeckx* (Fribourg: University Press, 1993), 41–44, 91–99. For a general overview of De Petter's thought, see C. E. M. Struyker Boudier, *Wijsgerig leven in Nederland en België 1880–1980, Deel II: De Dominicanen* (Nijmegen: Katholiek Studiecentrum; Baarn: Ambo, 1986), 78–90, with a bibliography on 299–301.

10. Ibid., 267.

11. Ibid.

12. Ibid.

13. Ibid., 267–68.

14. Edward Schillebeeckx, *God Is New Each Moment: Edward Schillebeeckx in Conversation with Huub Oosterhuis and Piet Hoogeven*, trans. David Smith (New York: Seabury, 1983), 13.

15. Kennedy, "Continuity Underlying Discontinuity," 268; see also, idem, *Deus Humanissimus*, 44–45. According to the *Encyclopedia of Catholicism*, ed. Richard P. McBrien (San Francisco: HarperSanFrancisco, 1995), s.v. "Chenu, M.-D.," by Walter Principe, Chenu's work in historical theology posed a threat to the speculative Thomist theologians of the day. "At that time, in part from fear of Modernism, historical studies in theology were viewed with suspicion, especially by the speculatively oriented Thomists who dominated the field and whose antihistorical fixations Chenu criticized. They influenced the Vatican to place the unpublished work on the Index of Forbidden Books (1942), and Chenu was deposed as rector of Le Saulchoir."

16. Kennedy, "Continuity Underlying Discontinuity," 268–69.

17. See Mary Ann Fatula, "Dogmatic Pluralism and the Noetic Dimension of Unity of Faith," *Thomist* 48 (1984): 419–32, for this terminology.

18. Since Schillebeeckx is particularly concerned to demonstrate how human beings have knowledge of God beyond their human conceptions, the "object" of human knowledge in these discussions is usually the Divine Being. However, following the Thomistic tradition, Schillebeeckx will maintain here that human knowledge always comes through the created world and the senses. Hence his epistemological discussion, although framed in terms of knowledge of God, depends on the human subject's noetic and ontological connection to the surrounding world as well. Knowledge of God does differ from "mundane" knowledge insofar as God's grace is needed to create the *lumen fidei* in the believer's mind, but otherwise the relationship of subject, "object," and concept will remain the same.

19. The main sources for his perspectivalist epistemology are "The Concept of Truth" (1962); "The Non-Conceptual Intellectual Element in the Act of Faith: A Reaction" (1963); and "The Non-Conceptual Intellectual Dimension of Our Knowledge of God According to Aquinas" (1952), all of which are contained in *Revelation and Theology*, vol. 2 (Theological Soundings 1/2), trans. N. D. Smith (London: Sheed and Ward; New York: Herder and Herder, 1968). Other sources include "Life in God and Life in the World," in *God and Man*, trans. Edward Fitzgerald and Peter Tomlinson (New York: Sheed and Ward, 1969); and the article "Geloofswarheid," in *Theologisch Woordenboek*, 2 (Roermond/Maaseik: J. J. Romen en Zonen, 1957). For another exposition of Schillebeeckx's perspectivalist epistemology, see Kennedy, *Deus Humanissimus*, 79–142.

20. Schillebeeckx, "The Non-Conceptual Intellectual Dimension of Our Knowledge of God," in *Revelation and Theology*, 2:162.

21. Ibid., 2:166–67.

22. Schillebeeckx, "The Concept of Truth," in *Revelation and Theology*, 2:7.

23. Ibid.

24. Ibid.

25. Schillebeeckx, "The Non-Conceptual Intellectual Dimension of Our Knowledge of God," in *Revelation and Theology*, 2:169–70.

26. Ibid., 171.

27. Ibid., 175.

28. Ibid., 176.

29. Ibid., 177.

30. Schillebeeckx, "The Concept of Truth," in *Revelation and Theology*, 2:8.

31. Ibid., 2:8–9.

32. Ibid., 2:25–26.

33. See Schillebeeckx, in *Theologisch Woordenboek*, 1, s.v. "Dogma," and "Dogmaontwikkeling"; also in *Theologisch Woordenboek*, 2, s.v. "Geloofsgeheim" and "Geloofswarheid." The article "Dogmaontwikkeling" appears as "The Development of the Apostolic Faith into the Dogma of the Church," in *Revelation and Theology*, 1:63–92.

34. Edward Schillebeeckx, "The New Trends in Present-Day Dogmatic Theology," in *Revelation and Theology*, 2:114.

35. See, among many examples, Edward Schillebeeckx, "Revelation, Scripture, Tradition and Teaching Authority," in *Revelation and Theology*, 1:3–26; "Salvation History as the Basis of Theology: *Theologia* or *Oikonomia*?" in *Revelation and Theology*, 2:79–105; and in *Theologisch Woordenboek*, 2, s.v. "Geschiedenis."

36. Philip Kennedy has argued that the nucleus of Schillebeeckx's theology is the idea of creation. According to Kennedy, the central problem of Schillebeeckx's work is the relationship of the universal and the particular, "the quandary of explaining how that which is absolute, called God, or Allah, in the context of religion, can be recognized and contacted in that which is limited, localized, historical and particular" (*Schillebeeckx*, p. 4). Schillebeeckx's answer to this problem is his doctrine of creation which is, briefly stated: creation is the continuing act of the infinite and transcendent God who establishes and preserves creatures in their finitude and is salvifically present and immanent to creatures precisely through their finitude. Creation, for Schillebeeckx, hence is primarily a doctrine of saving relationship. Kennedy then concludes that on the basis of this doctrine of creation, Schillebeeckx sees all of reality as relational; in fact, he possesses an "ontology of relation" which "involves an indivisible relation between God and everything that is finite" (p. 89). I would agree that indeed creation is one key to Schillebeeckx's thought but would differ from Kennedy by saying that even his doctrine of creation depends on the phenomenological Thomist formation he received from De Petter. In other words, Schillebeeckx sees creation as an irreducible saving relationship between God and the world because of his perspecti-

valist epistemology and ontology, not vice versa. The formal understanding of reality as mutually relational is prior to his explicit doctrine of creation. Recall also that recognizing creation as a doctrine of salvation depends on another mutually informing relationship to salvation experienced in Christ. Kennedy, I think, is correct about the fundamental question in Schillebeeckx's thought; however, he overemphasizes one doctrine as the key to the problem, when even Schillebeeckx's presentation of these doctrines is governed by the nonantithetical and dialectical relationships I have described. See Philip Kennedy, *Schillebeeckx*, Outstanding Christian Thinkers Series (Collegeville, Minn.: Liturgical Press, 1993); also, idem, *Deus Humanissimus*, 103–6, 231–32. For Schillebeeckx's doctrine of creation, see *Interim Report on the Books Jesus and Christ*, 105–24; and *God Among Us: The Gospel Proclaimed*, trans. John Bowden (New York: Crossroad, 1980), 91–102.

37. See, for example, his response to Bishop John A. T. Robinson's *Honest to God*, "Life in God and Life in the World," in *God and Man*. The two articles combined here were originally published in 1963 and 1964 in *Tijdschrift voor Theologie*.

38. Edward Schillebeeckx, *Jesus: An Experiment in Christology*, trans. by Hubert Hoskins (New York: Seabury [Crossroad], 1979), 618.

39. Ibid.

40. Ibid., 618–19.

41. For examples of his views on this relationship before and during the time of the council, see Edward Schillebeeckx, *World and Church*, trans. N. D. Smith (New York: Sheed and Ward, 1971).

42. See "The Pastoral Constitution on the Church in the Modern World," *Gaudium et Spes*, pars. 1–10, 40–45, 62; "Decree on the Training of Priests," *Optatam Totius*, pars. 13–18; "Decree on Ecumenism," *Unitatis Redintegratio*, pars. 9–12. These can be found in Austin Flannery, ed., *Vatican Council II: The Conciliar and Post-Conciliar Documents* (Boston: St. Paul Books and Media, 1992).

43. Kennedy, "Continuity Underlying Discontinuity," 272.

44. Ibid., 273. Kennedy argues that four factors influenced Schillebeeckx's epistemological change: His courses on hermeneutics and his eventual turn to the critical theory of Adorno and Habermas; his 1967 North American tour and his encounter with the theology of secularization there; the new Dutch Christology of 1966, written with A. Hulsbosch, which emphasized the humanity of Jesus; and the "Lessing problem" mentioned above. See idem, *Deus Humanissimus*, 143–217, for a more complete overview of these and other philosophical factors which led Schillebeeckx to change his epistemological framework. Kennedy argues that the combination of all these factors caused Schillebeeckx to abandon the perspectivalist viewpoint of his early period and to embrace negative contrast experiences as his basic epistemological model. In other words, using my terminology, Kennedy sees Schillebeeckx moving from the first to the third epistemological circles by way of these various transitional influences. In Kennedy's viewpoint there is no real distinct second epistemological circle because the

hermeneutics of the humanities provide only one element in Schillebeeckx's developing thought. I am arguing here that although Schillebeeckx does not remain long with a "purely" hermeneutical viewpoint, he nevertheless uses hermeneutics as an encompassing framework for understanding human knowledge and language long after he embraces critical theory as the basis for what I am calling his third epistemological circle.

45. Kennedy lists eighteen intellectual sources for the post–Vatican II thought of Schillebeeckx and names the four most important as hermeneutics, biblical studies, philosophy of language, and critical theory. See Kennedy, *Schillebeeckx*, 36–37.

46. Kennedy, "Continuity Underlying Discontinuity," 265.

47. Edward Schillebeeckx, "Erfahrung und Glaube," in *Christlicher Glaube in moderner Gesellschaft*, vol. 25 (Freiburg: Herder, 1982), 73–116; unpublished translation by Robert J. Schreiter, 3. See also, idem, *Christ: The Experience of Jesus as Lord*, trans. John Bowden (New York: Crossroad, 1980), 30–40, 50–55; *Church: The Human Story of God*, trans. John Bowden (New York: Crossroad, 1992), 15–20; "Towards a Catholic Use of Hermeneutics," in *God the Future of Man*, trans. N. D. Smith (New York: Sheed and Ward, 1968), 20–35; *Interim Report on the Books* Jesus *and* Christ, 13–19; *Ministry: Leadership in the Community of Jesus Christ*, trans. John Bowden (New York: Crossroad, 1981), 100–101; *Theologisch Geloofsverstaan anno 1983; The Understanding of Faith*, trans. N. D. Smith (New York: Seabury, 1974), 20–44, for similar presentations and elaborations on this basic hermeneutical structure.

48. Schillebeeckx, *Christ: The Experience of Jesus as Lord*, 53.

49. Schillebeeckx, *Interim Report on the Books* Jesus *and* Christ, 13. Schillebeeckx here refers the reader to *Jesus: An Experiment in Christology*. In *Interim Report, Jesus* and *Christ* are referred to as I and II, respectively.

50. Schillebeeckx, *Interim Report*, 13.

51. Ibid., 13–14.

52. Ibid., 13.

53. These distinctions do not resolve all of the ambiguities in Schillebeeckx's terminology regarding the relationship of experience and interpretation. Although he usually states that there is no uninterpreted experience or a "kernel" of pure experience separated from interpretation, occasionally his usage implies otherwise. For example, almost immediately following the passages just quoted, Schillebeeckx goes on to say, "In the New Testament we are confronted with a basic experience which binds all these writings together and therefore resulted in a canonical 'New Testament': Jesus, experienced as the decisive and definitive saving event; salvation from God, Israel's age-old dream" (*Interim Report*, 14–15). What is this "basic experience"? Does this refer to the inner, self-interpretative elements in certain experiences, as he described them above? If so, how can these be distinguished and named separately from the "external" interpretative elements? Schillebeeckx himself says that this cannot be done. Ultimately the ambiguity comes from two meanings which Schille-

beeckx attaches to the word "experience": first (and usually), "experience" means "an interpretative *encounter* with the objective world," but at times it means "a certain *reality of the objective world* encountered under different interpretative elements." His usage of "basic experience" above falls, I think, into this second category. Since his phenomenological and existentialist formation allowed him to see the objective world and the subjective knower in an irreducible dialectical relationship, after his hermeneutical turn he uses "experience" to cover both poles of the dialectic. This, however, results in the ambiguity seen above. For other discussions of this complex relationship, see Louis Dupré, "Experience and Interpretation: A Philosophical Reflection on Schillebeeckx's *Jesus* and *Christ,*" *Theological Studies* 43 (March 1982): 30–51; Gabriel J. Fackre, "Bones Strong and Weak in the Skeletal Structure of Schillebeeckx's Christology," *Journal of Ecumenical Studies* 21 (spring 1984): 248–77; Edward L. Krasevac, "Revelation and Experience: An Analysis of the Theology of George Tyrell, Karl Rahner, Edward Schillebeeckx, and Thomas Aquinas" (Ph.D. diss., Graduate Theological Union, 1986); Marcus Lefébure, "Schillebeeckx's Anatomy of Experience," *New Blackfriars* 64 (1983): 270–86; chapters by William L. Portier and Mary Catherine Hilkert in *The Praxis of Christian Experience: An Introduction to the Theology of Edward Schillebeeckx,* ed. Robert J. Schreiter and Mary Catherine Hilkert (San Francisco: Harper & Row, 1989).

54. Schillebeeckx, "Towards a Catholic Use of Hermeneutics," in *God The Future of Man,* 7–8.

55. Schillebeeckx, *The Understanding of Faith,* 38.

56. Ibid., 38–39.

57. Ibid., 39.

58. Schillebeeckx, "Towards a Catholic Use of Hermeneutics," in *God the Future of Man,* 8–9, 26–35, 39–40.

59. Ibid., 27–28.

60. In *Interim Report,* Schillebeeckx makes reference to "K. Popper, T. S. Kuhn, I. Lakatos, Feyerabend and the Erlangen School" as sources for the growing recognition of the "certain primacy" of the "theory or model over experience" (p. 17). He also makes reference to the literature listed in *Christ: The Experience of Jesus as Lord,* 853f, n.1.

61. Schillebeeckx, *Interim Report,* 6, 18–19.

62. Ibid., 18.

63. Ibid., 17–18.

64. See John D. Caputo, "Radical Hermeneutics and Religious Truth: The Case of Sheehan and Schillebeeckx," in *Phenomenology of the Truth Proper to Religion,* ed. Daniel Guerrière (Albany: State University of New York Press, 1990), 146–72. In analyzing the two *Jesus* books, Caputo argues that Schillebeeckx has not appreciated the radical implications of the turn to hermeneutics. Instead of recognizing that a consistent application of hermeneutics would submerge all human knowledge in the flux of history and language, Schillebeeckx, according to Caputo, "bails out" of this flux and

bases his faith "in a rock solid metaphysics—of morals" (p. 165). That is, Schillebeeckx's use of hermeneutics is based on a prior, unshakable (and to Caputo hermeneutically unwarranted) faith in the love of God for humanity and the ethical direction of history. Without going into Caputo's Levinasian analysis of the resurrection narratives and his asking whether radical hermeneutics must force one to ask the question of the "innocence" and "meaninglessness" of history (pp. 170–71), I would note that Caputo forcefully raises the question about the possibility of the experience of the objectively real in Schillebeeckx's hermeneutical thought. In this second circle Schillebeeckx will continue to assume that there is an *interpretandum* outside purely human subjectivity, or even intersubjectivity, but, as I will show, he quickly realizes that the hermeneutics of the humanities is not a sufficient basis alone for preserving this relationship of the subject and object.

65. Schillebeeckx, "Towards a Catholic Use of Hermeneutics," in *God the Future of Man*, 9.

66. Ibid., 32, 33.

67. Ibid., 39.

68. See Edward Schillebeeckx, *Dialectische Hermeneutiek: Deel I, Algemene Hermeneutiek*, student notes for "College Hermeneutiek," 1978–79, Catholic University of Nijmegen, 4–5. For further information on the development of Schillebeeckx's thought on hermeneutics, especially with regard to his teaching at the Catholic University of Nijmegen, see Ted M. Schoof, "E. Schillebeeckx: 25 years at Nijmegen," *Theology Digest* 38 (1991): 31–44. On p. 37 Schoof gives an outline of the lectures on hermeneutics cited above.

69. See Schillebeeckx, *Jesus: An Experiment in Christology*, 379–97, for a more extensive discussion of the resurrection stories.

70. Ibid., 392.

71. Ibid., 576–79.

72. Ibid., 577.

73. Ibid.

74. Ibid., 577–78.

75. Ibid., 578.

76. Schillebeeckx uses this view of history in the context of a discussion of Christological doctrine, particularly that of Chalcedon. The distinctions described above allow him to argue for both the permanent significance of Chalcedon and also the need to reinterpret the doctrine in a new phase of history. This analysis may also serve as the underpinning for what Schillebeeckx calls the "criterion of the proportional norm" or the "analogy of faith" when he talks about the perduring element in Christian faith and a standard for the measurement of orthodoxy. For discussion of these criteria, see *The Understanding of Faith*, 58–63; *Theologisch Geloofsverstaan anno 1983*, 12–16; *Church, The Human Story of God*, 40–45. I will present a more complete analysis of this criterion in chapter 5. Schillebeeckx briefly discusses this relationship

between conjunctural history and paradigms in "The Role of History in What Is Called the New Paradigm," in *Paradigm Change in Theology*, ed. Hans Küng and David Tracy (New York: Crossroad, 1989); reprinted in Edward Schillebeeckx, *The Language of Faith: Essays on Jesus, Theology and the Church* (Maryknoll: Orbis; London: SCM, 1995), 239–42. For a comparison of Schillebeeckx's discussion of history with that of Lonergan's, see Bernard J. McGinn, "Critical History and Contemporary Catholic Theology," *Criterion* 20 (Winter 1981): 18–25.

77. Schillebeeckx, "Towards a Catholic Use of Hermeneutics," in *God the Future of Man*, 36.

78. Schillebeeckx, "Epilogue: The New Image of God, Secularization and Man's Future on Earth," in *God the Future of Man*, 184.

79. John A. Coleman, *The Evolution of Dutch Catholicism, 1958–1974* (Berkeley and Los Angeles: University of California Press, 1978), 159–80. Using Durkheim's concept of "collective effervescence," Coleman describes the period of 1965–70 in the Dutch Church as one of the "creation of new institutional forms." This period is marked by a "revolutionary tempo of change," "psycho-social collective élan," "euphoric rhetoric with few parallels in Dutch national life," "residue of slogans," and "overdetermination of the use of slogans." Phrases drawn from the council and conciliar style theology such as "people of God," "collegiality," "church on the move," and "searching church" became sacral symbols of a new way of Dutch Catholic life and thus bore significance far beyond their original meaning. Coleman sees the Dutch Pastoral Council as a prime example of this collective effervescence (pp. 156–58).

80. Coleman describes several of these groups in his work, such as *Confrontatie*, a right-wing group which forged a coalition "with crucial decision-makers within the international church in Rome" and which tended to "view the church as a purified orthodox sect maintaining its membership by creating an intentional community of like-minded true believers" (pp. 235–37). On the left is *Septuagint* which began as a progressive group within the church whose program included "the erection of local, 'critical' congregations which would act as watchdogs against totalitarian abuses in church and society" (p. 240). As Coleman describes it, Septuagint became increasingly radical and diffuse so that after 1970 it was hardly different than any other leftist-secular party (p. 245). I will return to this topic below in chapter 5 in my analysis of Schillebeeckx's understanding of critical communities in the church.

81. William L. Portier, "Edward Schillebeeckx as Critical Theorist: The Impact of Neo-Marxist Social Thought on His Recent Theology," *Thomist* 48 (1984): 350. Coleman notes that before *Septuagint* dissolved its ties with the Catholic Church in the Netherlands, Schillebeeckx participated in some of its programs. He does not indicate whether Schillebeeckx was an actual member of the group. Given his other writings on the subject (see below), it is likely that he remained in the capacity of "sympathetic critic." See Coleman, *The Evolution of Dutch Catholicism, 1958–1974*, 246.

82. Portier, "Edward Schillebeeckx as Critical Theorist," 350.

83. See Karl Derksen, "Theologie-praxis-content," in *Meedenken met Edward Schillebeeckx: bij zijn afscheid als hooglerar te Nijmegen*, ed. Hermann Häring, Ted Schoof, and Ad Willems (Baarn, Netherlands: H. Nelissen, 1983), 115–29, for a description of the origins of this group of theologians and his later attempts to develop political theology in Europe.

84. Frans van den Oudenrijn and Marcel Xhaufflaire, eds., "Théologie de la christianisation du monde: théologie du sécularisation du monde," in *Les deux visages de la théologie de la sécularisation: analyse critique de la théologie de la sécularisation* (Paris: Casterman, 1970), 27.

85. Ibid., 42. "*[L]es temps modernes, en tant qu'ils réalisent la 'sécularisation du monde' et l' 'historisation de l'existence humaine' sont de fait et de droit la conséquence historique de la foi chrétienne*" (emphasis text's).

86. Ibid., 50.

87. Ibid., 59.

88. Ibid., 69. "Ce qu'on pourrait appeler la *théologie dialectique de la société* et la *théologie politique* essayent de 'corriger' la théologie de la sécularisation, mais (précisément comme 'théologie'!) semblent en farder les structures fondamentales. La 'correction' vise le personnalisme ou l'anthropocentrique propres aux théologiens de la sécularisation. Pour cela, elles se laissent inspirer par une *théorie de l'histoire* se ressourçant dans la problématique de l'*Aufklärung*, telle qu'elle est thématisée et prolongée par Hegel ou par la gauche hégélienne et E. Bloch. Il semble que E. Schillebeeckxs [*sic*] lui aussi se rapproche de cette nouvelle forme théologique de pensée."

89. Ibid., 74–75. "[L]es porteurs de fait de la 'critique liberatrice' de la société et e la 'médiation négative' ont-ils quelconque *raison*, théorique et surtout pratique, de s' 'identifier' (fût-ce partiellement-cf. 3, p.20) avec les institutions ecclésiales?"

90. Kennedy, "Continuity Underlying Discontinuity," 270–71; see idem, *Deus Humanissimus*, 233–48, for a more complete history of Schillebeeckx's engagement with critical theory. Schillebeeckx's most detailed discussions of critical theory are "Critical Theories and Christian Political Commitment," in *Political Community and Christian Community*, ed. Alois Müller and Norbert Greinacher, *Concilium* 84 (1973): 48–61; and *The Understanding of Faith*, 102–55. Commentaries on Schillebeeckx's use of critical theory include: Portier, "Edward Schillebeeckx as Critical Theorist; idem, "Schillebeeckx's Dialogue with Critical Theory," *Ecumenist* 21 (1983): 20–27; Kennedy, "Continuity Underlying Discontinuity," 264–77; idem, *Schillebeeckx*, 48–51; James A. Wiseman, "Schillebeeckx and the Ecclesial Function of Critical Negativity," *Thomist* 35 (1971): 207–46. Sources for critical theory itself are numerous; of interest for Schillebeeckx's work are: Theodor W. Adorno, *Negative Dialectics*, trans. E. B. Ashton (pseud.) (New York: Seabury, 1973); Theodor W. Adorno and Max Horkheimer, *Dialectic of Enlightenment*, trans. John Cumming (New York: Seabury, 1972); Jürgen Habermas, *Knowledge and Human Interests*, trans. Jeremy J. Shapiro (Boston: Beacon, 1971); idem, *Theory and Practice*, trans. John Viertel (Boston: Beacon, 1973); Max

Horkheimer, *Critical Theory: Selected Essays*, trans. Matthew J. O'Connell and others (New York: Herder and Herder, 1972); idem, *Die Sehnsucht nach dem ganz Anderen* (Gespräch mit Helmut Gumnior), in *Gesammelte Schriften, Band 7: Vorträge und Aufzeichnungen, 1949–1973*, ed. Gunzelin Schmid Noerr (Frankfurt am Main: Fischer Taschenbuch, 1985), 385–404.

91. Schillebeeckx, *Theologisch Geloofsverstaan anno 1983*, 18. "[H]et ontmaskeren van de naïve voorstelling dat *zijn* en *taal* (= denken en spreken), ondanks alle, klassiek reeds erkende, begrippelijke onadequaatheid, elkaar naar hun inhoud steeds zouden dekken."

92. See Schillebeeckx, *The Understanding of Faith*, 66–70, for his discussion on the weaknesses of a purely hermeneutical approach to theology. These remarks also hold for the more general epistemological discussion here. The overall purpose of his college lectures on hermeneutics in 1978–79 was to demonstrate the subjectivist and psychologizing weaknesses of classical hermeneutical thought and to argue that one should develop a critical hermeneutics in a dialogue both with critical theory and the philosophy of science. See Schillebeeckx, *Dialectische Hermeneutiek*.

93. Ibid., 66. The ideas in this quotation are frequently repeated in this section of the text.

94. Ibid., 59.

95. Schillebeeckx, "Erfahrung und Glaube," 18.

96. Schillebeeckx, *The Understanding of Faith*, 60.

97. Schillebeeckx, *Ministry: Leadership in the Community of Jesus Christ*, 101. Similarly, he states in "Erfahrung und Glaube" that "Theoretical ideologies have their adherents who carry out a faithful and thoroughgoing praxis as well. But this coherent praxis in no way determines the truth value of the respective theory" (pp. 17–18). In other words, the coherency and consistency of praxis with theory is not a sufficient ground for demonstrating the truth of either.

98. Kennedy calls this relationship in Schillebeeckx's thought "highly paradoxical." See his "Continuity Underlying Discontinuity," 270; see also, idem, *Deus Humanissimus*, 274–83, for a more extended discussion of the philosophical background of the term *praxis* and its usage in relation to theory in Schillebeeckx's thought.

99. Edward Schillebeeckx, foreword to Tadahiko Iwashima, *Menschheitsgeschichte und Heilserfahrung: Die Theologie von Edward Schillebeeckx als methodisch reflektierte Soteriologie* (Düsseldorf: Patmos, 1982), 17–18. "Wir erfahren außerdem nie eine befreiende Wahrheit in einer authentischen Praxis, ohne zugleich die Erschließung dessen wahrzunehmen, was hier und jetzt als wahr erkannt wird. Das sinn-erschließende 'Disclosure'-Modell der Wahrheit läßt sich nicht von dem 'unsinn- erklärenden' transformativen Modell der Wahrheit trennen. Jede Praxis, die menschen-knechtend wirksam ist, wird zwar a-priori als Wahrheitsanwärterin ausgeschlossen; aber anderseits ist sogar 'effektive,' das heißt tatsächlich befreiende

Praxis deshalb noch keine 'Wahrheitsnorm.' Wenn befreiende Praxis keinen Sinn und keine Wahrheit erschließt, besteht die Gefahr, daß es um eine inhaltlose Emanzipation geht, die, als halbierte Emanzipation, auf die Dauer selbst wieder menschen-knechtend wirksam wird."

100. William L. Portier, while describing the key ideas of critical theory and their influence on Schillebeeckx's theology, writes, "This is the 'critical negativity' which passionately refuses to recognize the identity of reason and reality in contemporary society. For fear that they would only reflect present contradictions, critical negativity likewise refuses to propose positive alternatives. Instead it maintains hope in what Horkheimer called 'the longing for the totally other' and engages in the kind of critical imaginings and rememberings that we find in Marcuse's *Eros and Civilization*." See "Edward Schillebeeckx as Critical Theorist," 347. James A. Wiseman writes in his article "Schillebeeckx and the Ecclesial Function of Critical Negativity": "Schillebeeckx acknowledges his dependence on T. W. Adorno's philosophical treatise, *Negative Dialektik*, for the term 'critical negativity' but adds that in a different perspective—and one that seems closer to Schillebeeckx's own—the expression had already been indirectly suggested to him by Paul Ricoeur, among others, especially by that French philosopher's article, 'Tâches de l'éducateur politique'" (p. 220). For works of Adorno and Horkheimer, see n. 90 above. For Ricoeur's article, see *Esprit* 33 (July–August 1965): 78–93.

101. Schillebeeckx, "Erfahrung und Glaube," 9.

102. Schillebeeckx, *The Understanding of Faith*, 91–92.

103. Ibid., 128. "Negative dialectics of critical theory are only meaningful insofar as they really presuppose and imply the possibility of a hermeneutics which make meaning possible." As William L. Portier puts it, "Ideology critique has become ideology. This is and will remain his basic difficulty with critical theory, including that of Habermas." In the place of a purely negative critical stance over against society, Portier argues that Schillebeeckx sees the need for a "conscious, positive," if critical relationship to the past, and particularly to the narratives of human suffering. See his "Schillebeeckx's Dialogue with Critical Theory," 23–24.

104. Schillebeeckx, *Jesus: An Experiment in Christology*, 621.

105. Schillebeeckx, "Erfahrung und Glaube," 8. I will argue in chapter 5 that this is also the language that Schillebeeckx will use to redefine the concept of "authority."

106. According to Professor Robert Schreiter (personal communication), Schillebeeckx had already developed an interest in exploring narrative categories of thought; Crites's article provided him with a particularly useful framework for directing these explorations. According to Crites's analysis, human consciousness itself, with its capacities for memory, present awareness, and future expectation, has a narrative structure to it. This narrative structure of consciousness therefore mediates between the mundane narratives of everyday life and the "sacred" stories which in a never fully expressible way shape the former. Compare this with Schillebeeckx's discussion of the

"structural," "conjunctural," and "ephemeral" levels of history. See Steven Crites, "The Narrative Quality of Experience," *Journal of the American Academy of Religion* 39, 3 (September 1971): 291–311. For a recent critique of the usage of Crites's article by theologians, see Daniel Beaumont, "The Modality of Narrative: A Critique of Some Recent Views of Narrative in Theology," *Journal of the American Academy of Religion* 65, 1 (Spring 1997): 125–39.

107. Schillebeeckx, "Erfahrung und Glaube," 9.

108. Schillebeeckx, *Christ: The Experience of Jesus as Lord*, 820. Speaking specifically here of the actualizing role of the Christian community, Schillebeeckx says: "From a social and historical point of view, the revolutionary critical epistemological value of the *memoria passionis Christi*, which presents a challenge to the world and society, does not lie directly in the past history of suffering (though that is where it has its origin) or in the kerygma or dogma, those so-called 'dangerous memorial formulas' which describe his suffering; rather it is communicated by the *living Christian community*, that is, by the contemporary church itself, *in so far as* it is an active *memoria passionis* of the risen Lord." Compare this language with the work of Johann Baptist Metz in his *Faith in History and Society: Toward a Practical Fundamental Theology* (New York: Crossroad, 1980).

109. Schillebeeckx, *The Understanding of Faith*, 91–95.

110. See, for example, his *Interim Report* and *Theologisch Geloofsverstaan anno 1983*. In the former, the discussion of the relationship between experience and interpretation (pp. 11–19) is largely done without reference to praxis; in the latter, praxis is indeed mentioned frequently, but how it is integrated with his complex discussion of the proportional relationship between understanding of faith and specific sociocultural situation (pp. 7–16) is not clear. Schillebeeckx speaks about the role of praxis later in the *Interim Report* (e.g., pp. 60–63), and the discussion of the "proportional norm" of Christian faith is set in a broader context both there and in *Church: The Human Story of God* (pp. 40–45), which includes a discussion of praxis. Nevertheless the questions remain: Does all significant knowledge come though negative contrast experiences, in their passive and active aspects? Can human beings interpretatively experience truth without a particular course of praxis? Schillebeeckx, I think, would affirm the need for the relationship between theory and praxis in discovering truth, the irreducible bond between "meaning-disclosing" and "meaninglessness-explaining transformative" models of truth. What may be necessary, however, is a more concise explanation of this relationship. How does praxis disclose truth, which theory nevertheless must test? What is the ontological basis of the fragmentary experience of the *humanum*, which seems to be the linchpin of this epistemological structure? See Portier, "Edward Schillebeeckx as Critical Theorist," 362, for the author's comments on Schillebeeckx's need to develop a "negative, realist metaphysics" to underpin his epistemology. See also Kennedy, *Deus Humanissimus*, 19–23, 363–64, for his central thesis that a "relational ontology" underlies all of Schillebeeckx's epistemological (and hence theological) claims.

111. Schillebeeckx, "Erfahrung und Glaube," 11.

112. Ibid., 11–12.

113. Ibid., 6–8. See also Schillebeeckx, *Church: The Human Story of God*, 16–20.

two   Salvation and Revelation in the Context of Human Experience

1. See Schoof, "E. Schillebeeckx: 25 years at Nijmegen," *Theology Digest* 37 (1990): 315; 38 (1991): 40, for an analysis, respectively, of Schillebeeckx's "synthetic" method of teaching and writing, and his "almost physical aversion to any trace of dualism."

2. Schillebeeckx, *I Am a Happy Theologian*, 47.

3. Kennedy, *Schillebeeckx*, 9–10.

4. Ibid., 82. According to Kennedy, besides the two works mentioned above, other full presentations of Schillebeeckx's doctrine of creation occur in *Interim Report*, 105–24, and *God among Us*, 91–102.

5. Thomas Aquinas, *Summa Theologiae*, Ia, 40–44. Kennedy argues that Schillebeeckx's views of creation are an extension of Ia, 1, 7, ad 2. See Kennedy, *Schillebeeckx*, 93.

6. Schillebeeckx, *Interim Report*, 113.

7. Ibid., 115.

8. Ibid., 115–16.

9. For Tadahiko Iwashima the real center of Schillebeeckx's theology lies in his understanding of salvation. See his *Menschheitsgeschichte und Heilserfahrung*, particularly 39–41 and 306–407. As Iwashima concludes: "*Theology for Schillebeeckx is therefore speaking about God as reflection on human salvation from the God of Jesus Christ*" (p. 401). He also recognizes, however, that Schillebeeckx's focus on salvation also depends on a fundamental understanding of the God-world relationship expressed in creation (p. 98).

10. See, for example, Schillebeeckx, in *Theologisch Woordenboek*, 2, s.v. "Geloofsgeheim," cols. 1750–52. "For precisely this reason God is called a mystery, not because He is in Himself the unknowable Truth: He becomes mystery because He reveals Himself to us as the reality of salvation. In other words, in the appearance of Christ God becomes for us a mystery, that is, a reality of salvation which is revealed *in a veiled way* to us in our earthly, visible realities and conceptual words" (col. 1751).

11. Schillebeeckx, "Revelation, Scripture, Tradition and Teaching Authority," in *Revelation and Theology*, 1.19. See also "Revelation-in-Reality and Revelation-in-Word" in the same volume, pp. 36–62.

12. Schillebeeckx, "Revelation, Scripture, Tradition and Teaching Authority," 5.

13. Schillebeeckx, in *Theologisch Woordenboek*, 3 (Roermond/Maaseik: J. J. Romen en Zonen, 1959), s.v. "Schrift, H.," cols. 4294–96. See also "Revelation, Scripture, Tradition and Teaching Authority," 5–6.

14. Mary Catherine Hilkert, "Hermeneutics of History in the Theology of Edward Schillebeeckx," *Thomist* 51 (1987): 136–37.

15. Schillebeeckx, "Revelation, Scripture, Tradition and Teaching Authority," 10.

16. Ibid., 10–11. See also Schillebeeckx, "Revelation-in-Reality and Revelation-in-Word," 40–45.

17. Schillebeeckx, "Revelation, Scripture, Tradition and Teaching Authority," 21–25.

18. See also Hilkert, "Hermeneutics of History," 136. "From his earliest writings Schillebeeckx has emphasized that the mystery of revelation requires a necessary mediation and interpretation, but that no conceptual expression of the mystery can ever exhaust or adequately name the salvific encounter. In his earliest writings Schillebeeckx grounded this claim in a metaphysical-epistemological explanation of the relationship between concept and the reality intended. Arguing that a non-conceptual but objective dynamism allows the human mind to transcend conceptual knowledge and approach reality, Schillebeeckx maintained that while the concept has a definite reference to reality, reality is never grasped or possessed by the concept."

19. Edward Schillebeeckx, *De sacramentele heilseconomie: Theologische bezinning op St. Thomas' sacramentenleer in het licht van de traditie en van de hedendaagse sacramentsproblematiek*, vol. 1 (Antwerpen: 't Groeit; Bilthoven: H. Nelissen, 1952). "The sacramental economy of salvation: Theological reflection on St. Thomas's teaching on the sacraments in the light of the tradition and the current sacramental problematic." For more information on this thesis, see Kennedy, *Schillebeeckx*, 60–61.

20. Edward Schillebeeckx, *Christ the Sacrament of the Encounter with God*, trans. Paul Barrett (New York: Sheed and Ward, 1963).

21. Ibid., 43–44.

22. Ibid., 7–13.

23. Schillebeeckx, *Church: The Human Story of God*, 6–9. "The religious significance of a worldly process presupposes a human significance: in other words, salvation history is a happening which liberates men and women. Revelation presupposes a process meaningful to men and women, an event which already has relevance for them and liberates them, without direct reference to God, *etsi Deus non daretur*. What is decisive is the good action which brings liberation, without which religious nomenclature becomes thin, a meaningless facade and a redundant superstructure. No one can stand above the parties in the struggle for good and against evil, any more than God can reveal his own being in just any arbitrary human event. Only in a secular history in which men and women are liberated for true humanity can God reveal his own being. There are also many histories of suffering and disaster in secular history; God cannot reveal himself in them except . . . as a veto or as judgment" (p. 7).

24. Edward Schillebeeckx, "Supernaturalism, Unchristian and Christian Expectations of the Future," in *World and Church*, 167. See also, idem, in *Theologisch Woordenboek*, 1, s.v. "Eschatologisch." This short article is less about eschatology than about the use of the term "eschatological" to characterize different schools of thought in contemporary Protestant and Catholic theology. Nevertheless, it does demonstrate the growing importance in preconciliar Catholic theology of linking the previously isolated "doctrine of the last things" with the actual life of grace experienced in the world. See also Schoof, "E. Schillebeeckx: 25 years at Nijmegen," 318–20, for details on Schillebeeckx's preconciliar development of courses on eschatology in relation to Christology. Schillebeeckx will continue to develop such courses after the council, which will provide a starting point for the research leading to his Christological trilogy (p. 328).

25. Schillebeeckx, "Epilogue: The New Image of God, Secularization and Man's Future on Earth," in *God the Future of Man*, 167–207. "In such a cultural framework, the God of those who believe in him will obviously reveal himself as the 'One who is to come,' the God who is *our* future. This, of course, brings about a radical change—the God whom we formerly, in the light of an earlier view of man and the world, called the 'wholly Other' now manifests himself as the 'wholly New,' the One who is *our future*, who creates the future of mankind anew." See also, idem, "Some Thoughts on the Interpretation of Eschatology," *Concilium* 5, 1 (1969); reprint in *The Language of Faith: Essays on Jesus, Theology and the Church* (Maryknoll: Orbis; London: SCM, 1995), 46–49.

26. See Edward Schillebeeckx, *For the Sake of the Gospel*, trans. John Bowden (New York: Crossroad, 1990), 171–72, where he speaks about the necessity of preserving all three elements (*anamnesis* of the past, action in the present, and hope or vision of the future) in order to avoid a reduction to a "pure traditionalism" of the past, a "pure opportunism" of the present, or a "pure futurism."

27. Schillebeeckx, "Some Thoughts on the Interpretation of Eschatology," 44–45. See also Schillebeeckx, *The Understanding of Faith*, 3–4.

28. Schillebeeckx, "Some Thoughts on the Interpretation of Eschatology," 47.

29. Ibid., 47–49. See also Schillebeeckx, *Christ: The Experience of Jesus as Lord*, 808, on God's dialectical relationship to all of history, past, present, and future.

30. Ibid., 49.

31. Schillebeeckx, *Church: The Human Story of God*, 246.

32. Ibid., 133–34. See also Edward Schillebeeckx, "Jeruzalem of Benares? Nicaragua of de Berg Athos?" *Kultuurleven* 50 (1983): 331–47; excerpted in *The Schillebeeckx Reader*, ed. by Robert J. Schreiter (New York: Crossroad, 1987), 258. Here Schillebeeckx speaks only of the first three metaphors and leaves out the *parousia* of Jesus. See also, idem, "Erfahrung und Glaube," 73–116; and the unpublished translation by Robert J. Schreiter, 12–13, where he speaks of only two "master symbols": the kingdom of God and the resurrection of the body.

33. Compare, for example, Iwashima, *Menschheitsgeschichte und Heilserfahrung,* 307. "*The chief result is the statement, that Christian salvation stands in a dialectical relationship with inner-worldly salvation*" (emphasis Iwashima's).

34. Quoted by Schillebeeckx in *Christ: The Experience of Jesus as Lord,* 790. The citation from Irenaeus comes from *Adversus Haereses,* bk. 4, chap. 20.

35. Ibid., 838. Further on, he summarizes his view of salvation in more technical language. "Putting it in more scholarly terms (but in that case we are saying everything and yet nothing); belief in salvation from God in Jesus Christ is a conviction, freely accepted (though through the medium of Christian churches, and therefore derived from real life)—*in* the conditions of our transitoriness—of our 'exaltation' above this finitude, thanks to the absolute freedom and generosity of the merciful presence of the God who takes our part, which we may experience *in* faith in our impenetrable finitude, though there what we experience corporeally is more his absence. This is the source of availability to all men, or as I would venture to repeat (even in regard of our own failure) above all for 'the least of my own'" (pp. 838–39).

36. Schillebeeckx, *Christ: The Experience of Jesus as Lord,* 837. See also *Church: The Human Story of God,* 245. The original Dutch title of the latter work also sums up this viewpoint well, *Mensen als verhaal van God,* "Human Beings as the Story of God." The English language publisher, perhaps looking for some symmetry with the *Jesus* and *Christ* books, to which this last work was to be the ecclesiological third part, began the title with "Church" and hence possibly misrepresented the focus of the work. In the introduction Schillebeeckx describes how his purpose in writing this work changed during the decade before its eventual publication because of the polarized situation in the Catholic Church, which required not a focus on secondary ecclesiological issues but a restatement of the fundamental theology which must underlie and judge any ecclesiology (pp. xiii–xvi).

37. Schillebeeckx, "Erfahrung und Glaube," 1. See also, idem, *Interim Report,* 11. "God's revelation is the opposite of our achievements or plans, but this contrast in no way excludes the fact that revelation also includes human plans and experiences and thus in no way suggests that revelation should fall outside our experience." See also, idem, *Christ: The Experience of Jesus as Lord,* 45–49, and *Church: The Human Story of God,* 22–23.

38. See Lefébure, "Schillebeeckx's Anatomy of Experience," 276–78, for a schematic presentation of the relationship of experience and revelation in Schillebeeckx's thought.

39. Schillebeeckx, "Erfahrung und Glaube," 1.

40. Edward Schillebeeckx, *On Christian Faith: The Spiritual, Ethical and Political Dimensions,* trans. John Bowden (New York: Crossroad, 1987), 4–6. This is a particularly eloquent passage on the need to see God as the "luxury" and "gift" for human lives. See also, idem, *Church: The Human Story of God,* 99–100.

41. Schillebeeckx, *Church, The Human Story of God,* 100.

42. Edward Schillebeeckx, "Christian Identity and Human Integrity," in *Is Being Human a Criterion of Being Christian?* ed. Jean-Pierre Jossua and Claude Geffré, *Concilium* 155 (1982); reprinted in Schillebeeckx, *The Language of Faith,* 185–87; idem, "The Crisis in the Language of Faith as a Hermeneutical Problem," in *The Crisis in the Language of Faith,* ed. Johann Baptist Metz and Jean-Pierre Jossua, *Concilium* 9, 5 (May 1973); reprinted in *The Language of Faith,* 87–89. These passages, and others like them, rest on the assumption, common in Schillebeeckx's thought, that reality is ultimately one despite the different and partial interpretative approaches which human beings take toward that one reality. However, on occasion, he introduces some confusion by also saying that, because of the irreducibly interpretative nature of experience, there is no neutral world "out there" free from interpretation. As a consequence, believers and nonbelievers can live in very different "worlds." Schillebeeckx here seemingly does not use the term "world" to refer only to a different psychological or hermeneutical framework for seeing that one reality (as in his language games approach), but invests the term with a quasi-ontological status. See *Christ: The Experience of Jesus as Lord,* 52. This ambiguity in his thought can be traced back to a more fundamental ambiguity (see chap. 1, n. 53): "experience" sometimes refers to a "interpretative *encounter* with reality" and sometimes to "the *reality* encountered through different interpretative frameworks." The latter coincides with the idea that believers and nonbelievers can use different "language games" to interpret the world, whereas the former seems to imply more readily that believers and nonbelievers really live in different "worlds" since they have such different interpretative encounters with reality. Ultimately these ambiguities derive from Schillebeeckx's insistence that knowledge is a nonantithetical and dialectical relationship between subjective knower and objective reality in which *both* are active shapers of knowledge. His writing at times leans more toward the activity of one pole or the other, resulting in these ambiguities, but in the final analysis he holds to the irreducible nature of the dialectical relationship.

43. Schillebeeckx, "The Crisis in the Language of Faith as a Hermeneutical Problem," 89.

44. See Schillebeeckx, *Christ: The Experience of Jesus as Lord,* 810–17, for extended analysis of the concept of the "mediated immediacy" of God's presence.

45. Schillebeeckx, *Jesus: An Experiment in Christology,* 634–35.

46. Schillebeeckx, "Erfahrung und Glaube," 2.

47. Ibid.

48. Schillebeeckx, *Church: The Human Story of God,* 6.

49. Although Schillebeeckx, in his later theology, eschews the term "apologetic" in favor of a discussion of the reasonableness or plausibility of Christian belief today, nevertheless his defense of the plausibility of belief occasionally opens up into critical questioning aimed at his atheist or humanist counterparts about the possibility for truly meaningful action on the behalf of humanity in a world with no belief in God. In *Church: The Human Story of God,* for example, he discusses the challenge of the

ethical dimension of human life, particularly the concrete demand of the other for ethical concern, as "'a privileged place' in which there can be a meaningful experience of God" (p. 92). Ultimately this ethical demand opens up an "aporia" if "human beings are the only and ultimate source of ethics," because "there is no guarantee whatsoever that evil will not have the last word" (p. 94). Using the stark example of the soldier who refuses to shoot an innocent hostage, knowing full well that he will be shot also and that his refusal will prove ineffective, Schillebeeckx asks the humanist, who also would support the soldier's gratuitous act, what are the grounds for his or her hope that such acts will ultimately prove meaningful. Why have "faith in human beings despite everything"? (p. 95). He argues that both the humanist and the religious response are autonomous ethical responses which trust in justice's superiority over injustice and evil. Yet he also states that 'the humanist does not know in the end whether reality itself will prove our ethical conviction of standing on the side of justice to be right!' The humanist can offer hope for the future, but "forgets the many sacrifices that have been made and the countless victims who still fall" (p. 96). The believer in God trusts even this absurdity to the "pure positivity of God" who gives hope to victims "who outside the religious perspective [are] written off for good" (p. 97). While still greatly respecting the humanist response even to such ethical challenges, Schillebeeckx seems to argue here that religious belief is not only plausible but is a ground for hope and concrete action which ultimately the humanist perspective does not have. In order for the fragmentary experiences of human salvation to be meaningful in the long run, the language of revelation may be necessary.

50. Schillebeeckx, "Erfahrung und Glaube," 2.

51. See Schillebeeckx, *Interim Report*, 25. "The names which the New Testament gives to Jesus (to be compared with the way in which in later tradition Christians continually give Jesus 'new names') provide us with a hermeneutical principle: on the one hand, the context of the explicit names which we give to Jesus on the basis of a particular experience of salvation with him, lies in the world of our specific, everyday experiences, i.e., in our everyday experiences in dealings with our fellow-men within a changing and changed culture in which we live. However, on the other hand the relevant key words which we introduce from our everyday life and experience of the world, and which we then 'project' on to Jesus (e.g., Jesus 'the liberator'), are also subject to criticism in terms of who Jesus really was."

52. Schillebeeckx, *Interim Report*, 126–28. "As a result, 'christology'—the second article of belief: salvation from God in Jesus—can only be understood as a specific way of making belief in creation more precise. It makes belief in creation more precise, gives it specific content, in terms of our human history and the historical appearance in it of Jesus of Nazareth. In that case, in Christian terms belief in creation is that to those who are non-divine or vulnerable, God's nature is liberating love in Jesus the Christ" (p. 127).

53. See Schillebeeckx, *Jesus: An Experiment in Christology*, 626–74, for an extended discussion of this terminology as a contemporary way of rendering the ancient

dogmas of Nicaea and Chalcedon understandable within the categories of contemporary thought and practice. See also, idem, "The 'God of Jesus' and the 'Jesus of God'," in *Jesus Christ and Human Freedom*, ed. Edward Schillebeeckx and Bas van Iersel, *Concilium* 10, 3 (1974): 110–15; reprinted in Schillebeeckx, *The Language of Faith*, 106–7.

54.   See, for example, Schillebeeckx, *For the Sake of the Gospel*, 70–75; idem, *The Church with a Human Face: A New and Expanded Theology of Ministry*, trans. John Bowden (New York: Crossroad, 1987), 34–39; idem, *Church: The Human Story of God*, 146–58, 216–21.

55.   Schillebeeckx, *Theologisch Geloofsverstaan anno 1983*, 12–14.

56.   My expression "limit concept" suffers from a certain ambiguity that, however, captures the dual nature of the function which these concepts play in Schillebeeckx's theology. On the one hand, these concepts, seen in the light of the positive content of faith which they express, are *limiting*, that is, they limit the range of possible authentic Christian interpretations and exclude other interpretations as being fundamentally outside of or even against any Christian meaning. For example, it would not be possible, according to Schillebeeckx, for a Christian authentically to speak of a God who tortures humankind for any reason or who is not transcendent to the finitude and failure of human life. These ideas contradict the limit concept of God's pure positivity and salvific will for humanity. On the other hand, these same *limiting* concepts are also *limited*; they themselves can only point to the realities they intend, not capture them (see n. 57). Again his formation in perspectivalist epistemology shows forth most clearly here. Otherwise it is difficult to see how a *limited* concept can also act as a *limiting* one. Only if objective reality (in this case the transcendent reality of God) directs the active knowledge of the subject toward truth can these *limited* concepts also exclude other possible interpretations. For a different usage and understanding of the term "limit language," see David Tracy, *Blessed Rage for Order: The New Pluralism in Theology* (Minneapolis: Winston/Seabury, 1975), 92–118.

57.   This paragraph summarizes ideas that can be found in various places in Schillebeeckx's work. See, for example, "The 'God of Jesus' and the 'Jesus of God.'" "Christian Identity and Human Integrity," *On Christian Faith: The Spiritual, Ethical and Political Dimensions*, or *Church: The Human Story of God* for relatively brief works which give a good overview of these three limit concepts. Even the expressions "God as pure positivity," "Jesus as the definitive revelation of God's cause as the human cause" or "the *humanum* as human wholeness both in actuality and anticipation" (to truncate the above paragraph even further) are themselves only approximations suited for contemporary language. If the realities behind these concepts are the "non-negotiable" center of Schillebeeckx's theology, their verbal expression nevertheless remains perspectival, bound to time and tradition and requiring constant actualization in praxis. It must be admitted, however, that at this point Schillebeeckx is most tempted to simply identify his limit language with the realities named by it. I would argue that this is so because his perspectivalist epistemology still is in play here an provides a

framework for understanding the latter two circles and not, as usual, vice versa. Although Schillebeeckx will consistently talk about the "narrative-practical nature of Christian faith and theology," this narrative, *as Schillebeeckx's theology construes it*, must fall within the conceptual framework of the limit concepts I described above. These in turn can only function as limit concepts if this perspectivalist epistemology is assumed. Here hermeneutics, narrative, and even critical theory and praxis are normed by his earlier framework even if they, in his truly dialectical fashion, also modify it.

58. Schillebeeckx, *Jesus: An Experiment in Christology*, 17–40, esp. 33, although here he does not use the adjective *historicus*. He also uses this terminology in *Interim Report*, 27–35, when answering the criticism that he has succumbed to a "neo-liberal" attempt to historically demonstrate that Jesus is the Christ. Here he also describes how his intent in *Jesus* was rather to follow the disciples' "*itinerarium mentis*" as they followed Jesus from the Jordan through his death and resurrection. Elsewhere, he describes this Christological methodology as a *manuductio* approach, that is, an attempt neither to proceed from the assumption of Christ's divinity nor to prove it, but simply "to lead by the hand" the contemporary reader on that same *itinerarium mentis* which the disciples followed two thousand years previously. See Schoof, *The Schillebeeckx Case*, 47–52, 121–23.

59. Schillebeeckx, *Jesus: An Experiment in Christology*, 36–40, 62–76. As Kennedy notes, Schillebeeckx's nearly decade-long exploration of contemporary biblical scholarship is one of the most profound influences on his later thought. See Kennedy, *Schillebeeckx*, 106–8.

60. Schillebeeckx, *Jesus: An Experiment in Christology*, 56–62. After rejecting a series of possible "unitive factors" which bind the various New Testament theologies together, Schillebeeckx writes: "As so far all these sallies have proved to be unsatisfactory, what in the way of a constant unitive factor is left? I would say (and this is really something): the Christian movement itself. In other words a Christian oneness of experience which does indeed take its unity from its pointing to the one figure of Jesus, while none the less being pluriform in its verbal expression or articulation" (p. 56). Further along, he elaborates: "Thus the Jesus event lies at the source of the 'local congregation' experience to which we have historical access; and it governs that communal experience. To put it another way: the constant factor is the changing life of the 'assembly of God' or 'assembly (congregation) of Christ', the community-fashioning experience evoked by the impress Jesus makes and, in the Spirit, goes on making upon his followers, people who have experienced final salvation in Jesus of Nazareth. Priority must be conceded to the actual offer that is Jesus; but this is embedded, vested in the assent of faith on the part of the Christian community we experience as being amidst us in our history" (p. 57).

61. Ibid., 256–71.

62. Ibid., 267.

63. Ibid. See also Schillebeeckx, "The 'God of Jesus' and the 'Jesus of God,'" 100–102.

64. Schillebeeckx, *Jesus: An Experiment in Christology*, 658. "In his humanity Jesus is so intimately 'of the Father' that by virtue of this very intimacy he is 'Son of God.' This implies that the centre of Jesus' being-as-man was vested not in himself but in God the Father—something borne out also by the historical evidence about Jesus; the centre, support, *hypostasis*, in the sense of what confers steadfastness, was his relationship to the Father with whose cause he identified himself. As this human being Jesus is constitutively 'allo-centric'; orientated upon the Father and on the 'salvation coming from God' for men; hence the profile and the face that he alone presents. This is what identifies Jesus of Nazareth. His autonomy as Jesus of Nazareth is his constitutive total relation to the One whom he calls 'Father,' the God whose special concern is with humanity. This is his *Abba* experience, soul, source and ground of his going out and his coming in, his living and dying."

65. Ibid., 666–67. "We said earlier on that Jesus' unique turning to the Father in absolute priority is 'preceded' and supported by the absolute turning of the Father to Jesus: and that this self-communication of the Father is precisely what early Christian tradition calls 'the Word.' Deeper than the *Abba* experience, therefore, and its ground, is the Word of God, the self-communication of the Father. This signifies some such thing as a 'hypostatic identification' without *anhypostasis:* this man, Jesus, within the human confines of a (psychologically and ontologically) personal-cum-human mode of being, is identically the Son, that is, the 'Second Person' of the Trinitarian plenitude of divine unity, 'the Second Person' coming to human self-consciousness and shared humanity in Jesus."

66. Ibid., 669.

67. Schillebeeckx, *Church: The Human Story of God*, 111–12.

68. Ibid., 114. See also, idem, *Church with a Human Face*, 18–23, for another short summary of the central elements in Jesus' career.

69. Schillebeeckx, *Church: The Human Story of God*, 116.

70. Ibid., 117.

71. Schillebeeckx, *Jesus: An Experiment in Christology*, 200.

72. Ibid., 203.

73. Ibid., 211.

74. Ibid., 218.

75. Schillebeeckx, *Church: The Human Story of God*, 120.

76. Schillebeeckx, *Jesus: An Experiment in Christology*, 315. See pp. 294–319 for a more complete discussion of the historical circumstances surrounding Jesus' death.

77. Ibid., 317.

78. Ibid., 320–97, for Schillebeeckx's complete discussion of the resurrection. At the heart of this discussion lie two assertions: first, that the resurrection experience was a communal (ecclesial) disclosure experience of the real significance of the entire life of Jesus and, second, that this disclosure experience had its origin in the crucified, yet living Jesus himself. With regard to the former, he writes: "These disciples did of

course come to realize—in a process of repentance and conversion which it is no longer possible to reconstruct on a historical basis—something about their experience of disclosure that had taken them by storm: their 'recognition' and 'acknowledgement' of Jesus in the totality of his life. This is what I call the 'Easter experience,' which could be expressed in a variety of ways: the crucified One is the coming Judge (a *maranatha* Christology); the crucified One as miracle-worker is actively present in his disciples; the crucified One has risen. And then we may indeed say: at that juncture there dawns the experience of their really seeing Jesus at last—the basis of what is being made explicit in the Easter appearances: Jesus 'makes himself seen' (*ôphthè*); not until after his death does he become 'epiphanous', that is, transparent; it is through faith that we grasp who he is" (p. 387). On the second point, he writes: "The objective, sovereignly free initiative of Jesus that led them on to a Christological faith—as initiative independent of any belief on the part of Peter and his companions—is a gracious act of Christ, which as regards their 'enlightenment' is of course revelation—not a construct of men's minds, but revelation within a disclosure experience, in this case given verbal embodiment later on in the 'appearances' model" (p. 390). Simply put, "after his death, Jesus himself stands at the source of what we are calling the 'Easter experience' of the disciples; at all events what we meet with here is an experience of grace. But *qua* human experience it is self-cognizant and spontaneously allied with a particular expression of itself" (p. 392).

three   *The Church in Schillebeeckx's Theology*

1. Schillebeeckx, *Jesus: An Experiment in Christology*, 56–57. See also, idem, *On Christian Faith*, 27–28, for this assertion about the relationship between the church's life and Jesus' presence. "Through and in this Christian belief in the resurrection of Jesus the crucified but risen Jesus remains at work in our history. Jesus' own resurrection, his sending of the Spirit, the coming into being of the Christian 'community of God' as the church of Christ which lives from the Spirit and the New Testament witness about all this, and thus also faith in the resurrection define each other reciprocally, though they cannot be identified with each other. One can say that the 'church of Christ' which came into being on the basis of the resurrection of Jesus is the deepest significance of 'the appearances of Jesus': in the church community 'assembled' in faith there appears, is present, the crucified, but risen Jesus."

2. See chap. 2, n. 53, for references to this frequently used sentence.

3. Kennedy, *Schillebeeckx*, 21–23. The research Schillebeeckx began in Paris eventually became his dissertation, the first part of which was published under the title *De sacramentele heilseconomie*. See chap. 2, n. 19, for more information on this thesis.

4. Schillebeeckx, *Christ the Sacrament of the Encounter with God*, 7–46. See also, idem, in *Theologisch Woordenboek*, 3, s.v. "Sacrament," cols. 4200–4202. The idea of the church as sacrament is not original to Schillebeeckx. De Lubac had used this metaphor as early as 1938 in his *Catholicism: A Study of Dogma in Relation to the Corporate Destiny of Mankind*, trans. Lancelot C. Sheppard (New York: Sheed and Ward, 1958), 29.

5. Schillebeeckx, *Christ the Sacrament of the Encounter with God*, 15.

6. Ibid.

7. Ibid., 40–45. "From this account of the sacraments as the earthly pro-longation of Christ's glorified bodiliness, it follows immediately that the church's sacraments are not things but encounters of men on earth with the glorified man Jesus by way of a visible form. On the plane of history they are the visible and tangible em-bodiment of the heavenly saving action of Christ. They are this saving action itself in its availability to us; a personal act of the Lord in earthly visibility and open availa-bility. Here the first and most fundamental definition of sacramentality is made evident. In an earthly embodiment which we can see and touch, the heavenly Christ sacramentalizes both his continual intercession for us and his active gift of grace. Therefore the sacraments are the visible realization on earth of Christ's mystery of saving worship" (pp. 44–45).

8. Ibid., 47–48.

9. See Pius XII, *Mystici Corporis*, in *The Papal Encyclicals, 1939–1958*, ed. Clau-dia Carlen (Raleigh, N.C.: McGrath, 1981).

10. Schillebeeckx, *Christ the Sacrament of the Encounter with God*, 48. See also, idem, "The New Trends in Dogmatic Theology," in *Revelation and Theology*, 2:133–35.

11. Schillebeeckx, *Christ the Sacrament of the Encounter with God*, 48–49. "We remarked that this visibility of grace defines the whole Church; not the hierarchical Church only, but also the community of the faithful. The whole Church, the people of God led by a priestly hierarchy, is 'the sign raised up among the nations.' The activity, as much of the faithful as of their leaders, is thus an ecclesial activity. This means that not only the hierarchy but also the believing people belong essentially to the primor-dial sacrament which is the earthly expression of this reality. As the sacramental Christ, the Church too is mystically both Head and members. When the twofold func-tion of Christ becomes visible in the sign of the Christian community, it produces the distinction between hierarchy and faithful—a distinction of office and those who hold them. Even though the hierarchy, on the one hand, are themselves part of the believ-ing church, and the faithful, on the other hand, share in the lordship of Christ and to some extent give it visibility, the sacramental functions of hierarchy and faithful differ within the Church and show the distinction."

12. Schillebeeckx, "Revelation-in-Reality and Revelation-in-Word," in *Revela-tion and Theology*, 1:46.

13. Schillebeeckx, "Revelation, Scripture, Tradition and Teaching Authority," in *Revelation and Theology*, 1:15–20.

14. Edward Schillebeeckx, "The Ecclesial Life of Religious Man," in *World and Church*, 151. See also, idem, *Christ the Sacrament of the Encounter with God*, 203–5.

15. Schillebeeckx, *Christ the Sacrament of the Encounter with God*, 54–82.

16. Schillebeeckx, "Religion and the World: Renewing the Face of the Earth," in *World and Church*, 1–18. This chapter was originally a separate article published in 1951. Schillebeeckx writes: "The kingdom of God comes about in human history itself. In being in the world, in which man humanises himself by spiritualising the material world which he recasts for his own use—in this being in the world, a deeper mystery is also accomplished. It acquires its ultimate meaning of a reality which is richer in meaning—being in Christ. Being in the world naturally demands, of itself, humanism. That is to say, as an evolving being that comes into spiritual possession of himself and fully realises himself in all his dimensions in extending the world, man has the task in this world of humanising himself by humanising the world. Being in Christ— christianity—does not contradict this evolution and task. Being a christian is not one of the many ways of being in the world. It is rather a dimension of depth which includes all the superficial dimensions of being in the world and not something added to them. A deeper life in God, in *Christ*, causes the whole of our being man to enter a new mystery. Being in the world is not the kingdom of God, but it is a part of it. Included in this way in the mystery, setting in order and humanising life in this world becomes a hidden beginning of the eschatological redemption, which is also a redemption of the material, humanised world. The temporal task of regulating life on this earth is thus, via man's moral and religious life, drawn into the eternal framework beyond the limits of the purely temporal" (p. 10).

17. See Kennedy, *Schillebeeckx*, 22, for a further description of this term, its relationship to the French "worker-priest" movement, and its influence on Schillebeeckx's intellectual development.

18. Schillebeeckx, *For the Sake of the Gospel*, 136–37. See also, idem, *Church: The Human Story of God*, 198–207. For the idea that a break with previous tradition can mark a return to the fundamental orientation of the Gospels, see, idem, "Breuken in christelijke dogma's," 15–49.

19. Schillebeeckx, *For the Sake of the Gospel*, 137–39.

20. Schillebeeckx, *Church: The Human Story of God*, xix. See also, idem, *I Am a Happy Theologian*, 74, and, idem, *On Christian Faith*, 31.

21. For complete texts of these documents, see Flannery, *Vatican Council II: The Conciliar and Post-Conciliar Documents*.

22. Edward Schillebeeckx, *The Real Achievement of Vatican II*, trans. H. J. J. Vaughan (New York: Herder and Herder, 1967), 29–32.

23. Ibid., 15–19, 30–32. The first pages cited, taken from a chapter originally written in 1965 as a commentary on the third session of the council, discuss *Lumen Gentium*'s definitive statement on collegiality, its relationship with the *nota praevia* appended to the constitution by the Theological Commission, and the prospects for

future collegial government in the church. At this time Schillebeeckx is optimistic that the "static" or "ontological" collegiality declared by the council will actually come about in the historical life of the church. He anticipates further "dogmatic development" with this doctrine and speculates on "papal collegiality" in the practice of the church after the council.

24. Ibid., 30–31. For an extended analysis of *Lumen Gentium*'s discussion of the reformability of the church, including the relationship between the Catholic Church and the body of Christ and the church's indefectibility, see Edward Schillebeeckx, "The Reformation of the Church," in *The Mission of the Church*, trans. N. D. Smith (London: Sheed and Ward; New York: Herder and Herder, 1973), 1–19. For an extended analysis of *Lumen Gentium*'s discussion of the role of the laity in the church, see, idem, "The Typological Definition of the Christian Layman According to Vatican II," in *The Mission of the Church*, 90–116.

25. *Lumen Gentium*, par. 1, in Flannery, *Vatican Council II: The Conciliar and Post-Conciliar Documents*, 350.

26. Schillebeeckx, *The Real Achievement of Vatican II*, 32.

27. Ibid., 49. He goes on to say: "The idea of 'Christian secularism' was finally accepted; so, therefore, was the autonomy of secularism on its own ground; as well as the fact that on every Christian rests the duty as a Christian to exert himself for the regulation of secular life as part of his religious practice, so that there is no breach between his life and his religion."

28. Ibid., 49–51. For an extended analysis of the theological anthropology and relationship with the world discussed in *Gaudium et Spes*, see Schillebeeckx, "Christian Faith and Man's Expectation for the Future on Earth," in *The Mission of the Church*, 51–89.

29. Schillebeeckx, *The Real Achievement of Vatican II*, 56.

30. Ibid., 58–66. Schillebeeckx writes: "Vatican II's conclusions on religion are, therefore, subtly drawn: while recognising the core of authentic religiousness in all religions, the council maintains the absolute uniqueness of Christ's church, in accordance with the biblical description of this church mystery as 'people of God, body of the Lord and temple of the Holy Spirit.' This unique biblical church mystery is to be found in the Roman Catholic Church, though veiled and ever open to further clarification" (p. 65).

31. Ibid., 56–57.

32. Ibid., 70–71. "Again these two views [on the meaning of 'world' in relationship to the church] converged in the main intention of this pastoral constitution: the church, i.e., God's people led by its pastors united in council, tries to express in a few fundamental themes her thoughts about the phenomenon of man as a being who, through his own embodiment, realizes himself in company with his fellow men in this world, and yet at the same time is personally addressed in the community of his fellow believers by the living God, the bearer of history, who is therefore in his Son made

man the alpha and the omega of man's stirring history. This formulation summarises not only the material content of the constitution but also its deeper meaning."

33. Ibid., 72–73.

34. Edward Schillebeeckx, "The Church and Mankind," in *The Church and Mankind, Concilium* 1 (1965): 69–100; reprinted in *The Language of Faith*, 1–24. For similar presentations on this theme from this time, see, idem, "The Church, Sacrament of the World," in *The Mission of the Church*, 43–50; idem, "Church and World," in *World and Church*, 96–114.

35. Schillebeeckx, "The Church and Mankind," 3.

36. Ibid., 5.

37. Ibid., 10. "Word-revelation, of which the church is the herald, only unfolds the implications of that absolute and gratuitous presence which, as revelation-reality, is already present in the lives of men, even prior to their encounter with the phenomenon 'Church.' Moreover, the free acceptance of the mystery's absolute and gratuitous presence is the very substance of what we call theologal or God-related faith. To believe is to have confidence in this mystery thus present; it means trusting in him in spite of everything and under all circumstances. That affirmation strikes me as of the utmost importance because what is implied is that the acceptance of real human existence, concretely taken with all its responsibilities, is in truth an act of God-centered faith: for Christ has shown us, by living it, that human existence taken concretely— not in the abstract—was for him, precisely in his human condition steeped as it was in the mystery, the objective expression of his communion with the Father in the *dynamis* of the Holy Spirit and for the benefit of his fellowmen."

38. Ibid., 11.

39. Ibid., 11–12.

40. Ibid., 16.

41. Edward Schillebeeckx, "The Church as a Sacrament of Dialogue," in *God the Future of Man*, 119–40.

42. Ibid., 123.

43. Ibid., 124–29.

44. See Schillebeeckx, *Church: The Human Story of God*, xiii–xvi.

45. See chap. 2, n. 4.

46. Schillebeeckx, *Jesus: An Experiment in Christology*, 47–48. See also, idem, *I Am a Happy Theologian*, 73. "In other words, the church is a movement of eschatological liberation with the aim of bringing together all men and women in a single unity, in a single peace, peace among them, peace among the peoples, peace with the environment. Ecclesiology therefore derives from this eschatological message of Jesus."

47. Schillebeeckx, *On Christian Faith*, 41.

48. According to surveys done in the 1980s, the Dutch population has become one of the most secularized in Europe. Some 47 percent of Dutch young people (18–24) professed no religious affiliation at all, according to a 1981–82 survey, and by

1984, some 31.3 percent of the whole population professed no religious affiliation. Mass attendance has fallen off from 64.4 percent in 1967 to 17.5 percent in 1986. For more information on these figures and other measures of the secularization of the Dutch people, see Karel Dobbelaere, "Secularization, Pillarization, Religious Involvement and Religious Change in the Low Countries," in *World Catholicism in Transition*, ed. Thomas M. Gannon (New York: Macmillan, 1988), 80–115; see also, Jan Kerkhofs, "Western Europe," in *Modern Catholicism: Vatican II and After*, ed. Adrian Hastings (London: SPCK; New York: Oxford University Press, 1991), 357–64.

49. Schillebeeckx, *Church: The Human Story of God*, 62. One should note that Schillebeeckx here is speaking more generally about "religions as the concrete context of talk about God." Although the general paradigm and examples he uses for describing religion fit better the Western religions of Judaism, Christianity, and Islam than Eastern religions, he seemingly intends to include all major religious traditions in this discussion. Hence his language about how religious communities are the chief locus of the naming of God in the modern world should not be taken as a call for a renewed "ecclesiocentrism." To be sure, within the Western, particularly European and North American, situation of rapid secularization, the Christian churches are certainly the dominant institution dedicated to this preservation of the naming of God, and therefore Schillebeeckx will be primarily concerned with their role in relationship to the world. However, this naming of God on the part of the church is always also a call to a particular praxis of service to the *humanum*, in which all should participate. Cf. idem, *On Christian Faith*, 43.

50. Schillebeeckx discusses this dialectic of the mystical and political at several places in his work, most notably in *Christ: The Experience of Jesus as Lord*, 804–21; "Jeruzalem of Benares? Nicaragua of de Berg Athos?" 331–47, excerpted in *The Schillebeeckx Reader*, 257–59; 272–74; and *On Christian Faith*, 65–83.

51. Schillebeeckx, *On Christian Faith*, 71–72. See also, Kennedy, *Deus Humanissimus*, 249–60, 366–67, for more background on the development of "mysticism" as an epistemological and theological category in Schillebeeckx's thought.

52. Schillebeeckx, "Jeruzalem of Benares? Nicaragua of de Berg Athos?" 274.

53. Ibid., 272–73. "With the Jewish and Christian tradition of faith as a compass or divining rod, as it were, we can check out whether our profane history squares with salvation history as God intends it. And precisely in this contrast experience lies the possibility of a new experience of Transcendence. There are two facets to such an experience: (a) on the one hand, a person, especially someone poor and oppressed, and someone who has declared him- or herself in solidarity with these experiences that God is *absent* in many human relationships of property and power in the world. Thus they experience alienation, the distance between God, the reign of God and our society. (b) On the other hand, the believer experiences precisely in political love and resistance against injustice an intense contact with God, the *presence* of the liberating God of Jesus. In modern times authentic faith seems to be able to be nourished in and

by a praxis of liberation. In that grows a realization that God reveals himself as the deepest mystery, the heart and soul of human liberation."

54. Ibid., 273.

55. Schillebeeckx is working on a new book on the sacraments, tentatively titled *Onderbroeken Verhaal—Verzet, Engagement, Viering: Sacramenten als Metaforische Vieringen* ("Interrupted Story—Resistance, Engagement, Celebration: Sacraments as Metaphorical Celebrations"). For more information about this work and his new viewpoint on the sacraments, see Schillebeeckx, "Verzet, Engagement en Viering," *Nieuwsbrief, Stichting Edward Schillebeeckx* 5 (October 1992): 1–3, and, idem, *Theologisch testament: Notarieel nog niet verleden* (Baarn, Netherlands: H. Nelissen, 1994), 185–89.

56. Schillebeeckx, *Christ: The Experience of Jesus as Lord*, 836.

57. Ibid.

58. Schillebeeckx, *Theologisch testament*, 190.

59. Ibid., 188–89.

60. Schillebeeckx, *Jesus: An Experiment in Christology*, 593–94. Schillebeeckx argues that even the early Christian community, although relatively powerless to effect political change in the Roman Empire, nevertheless witnessed to this universal brotherhood through the attempt to create it on a small scale within the Christian community itself. See Schillebeeckx, *Christ: The Experience of Jesus as Lord*, 553–99.

61. Schillebeeckx, *Christ: The Experience of Jesus as Lord*, 776.

62. Ibid., 774–75.

63. Ibid., 777–79. "But the God of Christians is 'not a God of the dead, but of the living' (Matt. 22.32). In other words, this concept of God assigns positivity simply and solely to God. 'God is love' (I John 4.8, 16); by nature he promotes the good and opposes all evil. And in that case, for the believer who seeks to follow God, the only orientation for action can be to further the good and to oppose evil, injustice and suffering in all its forms. This concept of God, which is not given to us as the result of a universal concept of God as found in the history of religions, but appears from and in Jesus of Nazareth, communicates to the Christian a quite definite orientation for action within what I have called the seven anthropological constants" (pp. 778–79).

64. One notable exception would be his treatment of the subject in *Christ the Sacrament of the Encounter with God*, 13–39. In this section Schillebeeckx discusses Christ's nature as the primordial sacrament of God in context of the inner-Trinitarian life of the Father, Son, and Spirit which is then made manifest in Christ, who is both God's offer and the human response to it. This presentation, however, is not a separate treatise on the Trinity (like the scholastic manuals of the day) and therefore is not a speculative examination the doctrine. Schillebeeckx remains here within the salvation historical approach of his early theology, even if he assumes the traditional language about the inner-Trinitarian life.

65. Schillebeeckx, *I Am a Happy Theologian*, 50–51.

66. Ibid., 53.

67. Ibid., 52. See also his sermon "The Johannine Easter: The Feast of the Giving of the Spirit," in *For the Sake of the Gospel*, 70–75. Here Schillebeeckx again acknowledges that the Spirit is the ever-present God in relationship to us in a hidden and elusive way. After using a series of different names for the Spirit from the Scriptures and Christian history, Schillebeeckx writes: "How can I sum up this enthralling process? *God's Spirit is a spirit 'which makes all things new'*" (p. 73).

four *The Apostolicity of the Church in Schillebeeckx's Early Theology*

1. See *Lumen Gentium*, chap. 3, on the college of bishops and their relationship to the primacy of the pope, especially pars. 20–27. "The holy synod teaches, moreover, that the fullness of the sacrament of Orders is transferred by episcopal consecration, that fullness, namely, which both the liturgical tradition of the Church and in the language of the Fathers of the Church is called the high priesthood, the acme of the sacred ministry. Now, episcopal consecration confers, together with the office of sanctifying, the duty also of teaching and ruling, which, however, of their very nature can be exercised only in hierarchical communion with the head and members of the college" (par. 21). For Vatican II documents, see Flannery, *Vatican Council II: The Conciliar and Post-Conciliar Documents*.

2. See Schillebeeckx, *Christ the Sacrament of the Encounter with God*, 47–54.

3. Ibid., 48–49. Schillebeeckx adds: "How are we to understand this distinction in office? The sacramental manifestation of the Lord in his role as head of the People of God is realized formally and functionally in the apostolic office, the ecclesiastical hierarchy. In this respect the hierarchical Church is sovereign with regard to the community of the faithful. On the other hand, the whole community of the faithful, or the People of God, is the sacramental realization on earth of the Lord as representatively the People of God. In this aspect the faithful themselves are the Church. In its entirety—apostolic office and community of the faithful—the Church is the sacramental or mystical Christ" (p. 49).

4. Ibid., 168–69. "Thus for the baptized and confirmed the lay state gives ecclesial status, and therefore their Christian mission as laymen is truly an ecclesial commission. Baptism together with confirmation gives us the commission to lay activity in the Church, and this is a priestly activity. At the Lay Congress held in Rome in 1957 Pope Pius XII broke, very rightly, with the mystique of the canonical 'mandate' to lay activity in the Church, through which the dogmatic sense of the mandate given by baptism and confirmation had been entirely lost. There has now been a return to the realization that by the fact of a person's bearing a character he possesses a commission to the lay apostolate in the Church." See also an earlier (1952–53) article entitled "Priest and Layman in a Secular World," in *World and Church*, which discusses both the priestly apostolate (pp. 36–66) and the revival of the lay apostolate (pp. 66–76).

Many of Schillebeeckx's more popularly accessible writings during his early period deal with the development of lay spirituality.

5. Schillebeeckx, "Priest and Layman in a Secular World," in *World and Church*, 73.

6. It is interesting to note that a contemporary Dutch-English dictionary uses the single word "ambt" to translate both "office, place, post, function" and (ecclesial) "ministry." Perhaps because of this dual sense of the term, Schillebeeckx tends to avoid either an excessively juridical sense of church office (because he always sees it as a ministry to the whole church), while also avoiding an excessively "spontaneous" or purely "functionalist" view of the ministry (because he always sees it as an office established in the church by Christ in the Spirit). See *Cassell's English-Dutch, Dutch-English Dictionary*, (1981), s.v., "ambt."

7. Schillebeeckx, in *Theologisch Woordenboek*, 3, s.v. "Priesterschap," cols. 3981–84.

8. Ibid., col. 3982. See also, idem, "Het apostolisch ambt van de Kerkelijke hierarchie," *Studia Catholica* 32 (1957): 258–90.

9. Schillebeeckx, in *Theologisch Woordenboek*, 3, cols. 3983–84.

10. Schillebeeckx, *Christ the Sacrament of the Encounter with God*, 170.

11. See Schillebeeckx, in *Theologisch Woordenboek*, 1, s.v. "Depositum Fidei." "By this [the *depositum fidei*] is meant the whole reality of revelation: facts of salvation, dogmas, institutions, and so forth, which constitute the whole of revelation and which have been entrusted to the Church so that it might preserve and interpret them wholly and without adulteration throughout history, without adding any *new* truths to them."

12. Schillebeeckx, in *Theologisch Woordenboek*, 1, s.v. "Censuur."

13. Ibid., col. 754.

14. Schillebeeckx, in *Theologisch Woordenboek*, 1, s.v. "Dogma," col. 1078.

15. Ibid., col. 1078.

16. Ibid., col. 1080. "Our concepts of faith, it is true, can never adequately or fully comprehend and determine the mystery of faith; they always stand open to an internally sharper determination along the lines of the content which has already been formulated. But that does not mean these inadequate concepts of faith are *inadequately true* (see AAS XLII, 1950, 566). The inadequate concepts of faith possess true and objective truth value and thus can never become false (l.c., 572). A new, nuanced concept of faith includes therefore the measure of truth of a less variegated representation of faith, which continues as the truth *in* the refined, internally more delineated concepts of faith" (572).

17. See Schillebeeckx, in *Theologisch Woordenboek*, 2, s.v. "Geloofsgeheim." For his complete discussion of the development of doctrine, see the article "Dogmaontwikkeling" in *Theologisch Woordenboek*, 1, cols. 1087–1106. This article also appears as "The Development of the Apostolic Faith into the Dogma of the Church," in *Revelation and Theology*, 1:63–92.

18. Schillebeeckx, "The Development of the Apostolic Faith into the Dogma of the Church," in *Revelation and Theology*, 1:82–91.

19. Ibid., 89–91.

20. Schillebeeckx, in *Theologisch Woordenboek*, 1, s.v. "Censuur," col. 754.

21. Ibid.

22. Ibid.

23. Ibid.

24. Ibid.

25. Schillebeeckx, in *Theologisch Woordenboek*, 2, s.v. "Geloofsbepaling." See also, idem, in *Theologisch Woordenboek*, 1, s.v. "Ex cathedra," col. 1481, where Schillebeeckx distinguishes truths declared by the pope *ex cathedra* from other truths of an infallible but not dogmatic nature. "An 'ex cathedra' declaration therefore must not be confused with an infallible declaration of other truths which do not belong to the deposit of faith, but can connect with it practically or speculatively."

26. Schillebeeckx, in *Theologisch Woordenboek*, 1, s.v. "Censuur," col. 754.

27. See Schillebeeckx, "What Is Theology?" in *Revelation and Theology*, 1:150–55, for his more complete analysis of the idea of the "theological conclusion" in the light of his early theological framework.

28. Schillebeeckx, in *Theologisch Woordenboek*, 1, s.v. "Censuur," col. 754.

29. Schillebeeckx, in *Theologisch Woordenboek*, 1, s.v. "Ex cathedra."

30. Schillebeeckx, in *Theologisch Woordenboek*, 2, s.v. "Kerkvergadering," cols. 2773–76.

31. Ibid., col. 2775. See also Boyle, *Church Teaching Authority*, 10–42, for a discussion of the historical development of the doctrine of the infallible ordinary magisterium of the bishops.

32. See Schillebeeckx, in *Theologisch Woordenboek*, 1, s.v. "Ex cathedra," col. 1481, for the more specific conditions under which the pope can make an infallible declaration.

33. Schillebeeckx, in *Theologisch Woordenboek*, 3, s.v. "Theologie," cols. 4485–4542; reprinted as "What Is Theology?" in *Revelation and Theology*, 1:95–183.

34. Schillebeeckx, "What Is Theology?" 110.

35. Ibid., 103–8.

36. Ibid., 113. "To conclude, then: theology, although it proceeds from faith, although it constantly presupposes this faith and serves it, is formally a question of scientific activity and insight, of research and of methodical precision."

37. Ibid., 107–8.

38. Ibid., 117ff.

39. Ibid., 119.

40. Ibid., 119–25. Schillebeeckx notes that positive theology cannot simply be considered a "théologie du magistère" as if the magisterium itself were the source of all theologically relevant ideas. Schillebeeckx recognizes and accepts the role of the magisterium in passing judgment on theologians' ideas, but he also notes that the

magisterium's normative decisions are such that they presuppose research and never replace it (pp. 122–23).

41. Ibid., 140.

42. Ibid., 143ff.

43. Ibid., 157ff.

44. Ibid., 168ff.

45. Ibid., 170ff.

46. Ibid., 177.

47. Ibid., 178. "Theology is, then, in the service of the church as the *human* (and thus fallible) critical authority of the life of the church—of its preaching, its spiritual life, and so on—whereas the church's teaching office is the official critical authority (and thus, in certain circumstances, infallible) for the whole of the life of the church and for theology itself."

48. Ibid., 163.

49. Schillebeeckx, *God Is New Each Moment*, 82.

50. Schillebeeckx, in *Theologisch Woordenboek*, 2, s.v. "Ketterij." Schillebeeckx defines "heresy" here as "the direct denial of (or grave doubt in) a revealed truth which has been held up to be believed as such by the church through the power of its extraordinary or ordinary and universal teaching authority." In this strict sense, "heresy" does not apply to the denial of either "catholic truths," since they are not revealed, nor to revealed truths which have not been formally defined by the teaching authority of the church. Schillebeeckx notes that because heresies lead to sharper definitions of the truths of faith, they can themselves be stimulating factors in the development of doctrine. However, quoting Karl Adam, he also notes that at times antiheretical definitions can also lead to "a type of 'provisional shifting of power' in the church." This can force later theology into a one-sided perspective which may take centuries to restore to "the original unity-in-tension of the totality of dogma." He then refers more specifically to a "typical counter-Reformation theology" in which "some early Christian, patristic and high scholastic elements disappeared into the background." From his *ressourcement* perspective, this dogmatic one-sidedness needs to be overcome by a more historically grounded understanding of the development of dogma, including the role that heresies played in it.

51. Schillebeeckx, "The Reformation of the Church," in *The Mission of the Church*, 12.

52. Ibid., 15.

53. Ibid., 13.

five   *The Apostolicity of the Church in Schillebeeckx's Later Theology*

1. Schillebeeckx, *Church: The Human Story of God*, xiii–xiv.

2. Schillebeeckx, *For the Sake of the Gospel*, 137.

3. *Lumen Gentium,* chap. 2, pars. 9–13, in Flannery, *Vatican Council II: The Conciliar and Post-Conciliar Documents.*

4. Edward Schillebeeckx, "The Catholic Understanding of Office in the Church," *Theological Studies* 30, 4 (December 1969): 567.

5. Ibid., 568.

6. Ibid., 568–69.

7. Ibid., 569.

8. See, for example, *Lumen Gentium,* par. 21.

9. Schillebeeckx, "The Catholic Understanding of Office in the Church," 574.

10. Ibid., 575.

11. Schillebeeckx, *Ministry: Leadership in the Community of Jesus Christ,* 5–37; idem, *The Church with a Human Face,* 13–123. *Ministry* is a revised version of several articles that Schillebeeckx wrote mostly in the late 1970s. See his introduction for a complete list of these works (pp. v–vi).

12. See, for example, Pierre Grelot, *Eglise et ministères: Pour un dialogue critique avec Edward Schillebeeckx* (Paris: Editions du Cerf, 1983). For other works in response to the *Ministry* book, see, for example, Georges Chantraine, "Apostolicity According to Schillebeeckx," *Communio (US)* 12 (Summer 1985): 192–222; Walter Kaspar, "Ministry in the Church: Taking Issue with Edward Schillebeeckx," *Communio (US)* 10 (Summer 1983): 185–95; William Portier, "Ministry from Above, Ministry from Below: An Examination of the Ecclesial Basis of Ministry According to Edward Schillebeeckx," *Communio (US)* 12 (Summer 1985): 173–91.

13. Schillebeeckx, *The Church with a Human Face,* 116.

14. Ibid.

15. Ibid.

16. Ibid.

17. Ibid., 117.

18. Ibid., 122.

19. Ibid., 257–58. See also, Schillebeeckx, *Ministry: Leadership in the Community of Jesus Christ,* 134–42.

20. See Schillebeeckx, *Theologisch testament,* 78–79.

21. Schillebeeckx, *The Understanding of Faith,* 55–72.

22. Ibid., 58. "From the purely theoretical point of view, orthodoxy cannot be verified. A purely theoretical hermeneutics, even of the existentially theoretical kind, based on a study of the humanities, such as that of Gadamer, cannot solve the problem adequately."

23. Ibid., 60–61.

24. Ibid., 62.

25. Ibid. "At the level of theory, all that we have at our disposal, then, is a proportional norm—models of structuration of faith, of which scripture supplies the first and normative ones."

26. Schillebeeckx, *Theologisch Geloofsverstaan anno 1983*, 14–15.

27. Ibid., 15.

28. Ibid. Schillebeeckx uses nearly the same wording and the same schematic representation to describe this criterion in *Church: The Human Story of God*, 41–44.

29. Schillebeeckx, *Theologisch Geloofsverstaan anno 1983*, 15.

30. Schillebeeckx, *The Understanding of Faith*, 65.

31. Ibid.

32. Ibid., 66.

33. Ibid.

34. Ibid., 68.

35. See, for example, Schillebeeckx, *Ministry: Leadership in the Community of Jesus Christ*, 101.

36. Schillebeeckx, *The Understanding of Faith*, 70.

37. Ibid., 71.

38. Ibid.

39. Ibid., 71–72.

40. See, for example, Edward Schillebeeckx, "Magisterium and Ideology," in *Authority in the Church and the Schillebeeckx Case*, ed. Leonard Swidler and Piet Fransen (New York: Crossroad, 1982), 11–12. "Second, there are others who seem to hold the opinion that the only authority which exists is that accepted by the community. They are right in emphasizing that, without what patristic and medieval theologians called '*receptio*' by the community of faith, authority in the church is meaningless. Proponents of this position forget, however, that authority does not become illegitimate without reception. In other words, no matter how important reception is for 'empowering of an authority,' it is not the foundation of authority, but only a response to a claim of authority. The foundation of authority must come from elsewhere." See also, idem, *Church: The Human Story of God*, 215.

41. See Schillebeeckx, *Jesus: An Experiment in Christology*, 52–57, for the use of this terminology to describe the continuous factor in the interpretation of Jesus in the New Testament. Schillebeeckx names this factor as "the Christian movement itself" (p. 56).

42. Schillebeeckx, *Theologisch testament*, 73. See also Schillebeeckx, "Breuken in christelijke dogma's," 16–19, for a nearly identical discussion of the meaning of dogma. In this article Schillebeeckx uses the same definition of dogma cited above and adds: "Non-Catholic, Christian churches will rather speak of 'formulas of unity'" (p. 19).

43. Schillebeeckx, *Theologisch Geloofsverstaan anno 1983*, 20.

44. See chap. 1, pp. 37–40. In "Breuken in christelijke dogma's," Schillebeeckx makes the interesting suggestion that the difficulty now in the translation of the experience of faith into a new situation is caused by a shift in the structural level of history, that is, in the level even deeper than the conjunctural. He states that the history of Christianity up to now took place within three conjunctural phases of history (patris-

tic, medieval, and modern) which however all were manifestations of one deeper structural phase. The "post-modern paradigm" may not share in this deeper structural unity; hence the task of the reinterpretation and reactualization of dogma now becomes both more difficult, more potentially radical, and more necessary (pp. 27–30).

45. Schillebeeckx, "Breuken in christelijke dogma's," 30.

46. Ibid., 31–32.

47. Ibid., 33. "Our knowledge of the truth is always perspectival, that is to say, we catch sight of the truth from a defined point of entry. The truth recognized by us is, as it were, always filtered or broken, as through a prism."

48. Ibid., 34.

49. Ibid., 34–35. "This council did not have the least intention to define dogmatically, of all things, the existence of angels and devils. At that time no one disputed their existence! On the contrary. For some people there was, next to God as first principle of all goodness, also a spiritual, first principle of all evil. This council reacted against that. The actual intention of the council was to make a statement about the fundamental idea that everything which exists outside of God *is a creation of* God."

50. Ibid., 35. "If we place the term 'dogma' within the whole of the entire Christian tradition of the 'Catholica,' it becomes clear that we as believers cannot act as if belief in Jesus the Messiah and the belief in the Trinity implied therein (however that also will be further filled in) lie on the same level as agreement with structures of the church which have grown up historically: for example, 'seven sacraments, no more, no less,' as the Council of Trent says; or also an episcopal rather than a presbyterian church structure, and the place of the Petrine function therein; or everything which was said, following a church order which was indeed valid at the time (and which nevertheless grew up out of historically contingent situations), about the relationship of the laity to the clergy in the church, above all in connection with the administration of the sacraments."

51. Ibid., 35–36. Schillebeeckx mentions the theologian Jacques Pohier in this connection.

52. Ibid., 36.

53. Ibid., 37. "Personally I would thus dare say, that however true dogmas also may be within the historical context in which they were formulated, they can become fully irrelevant in another historical context. A dogmatic pronouncement only has truth-value within the asked question to which it intends to be the answer and within the language game in which those questions and answers come to speech. An answer given to an unasked question is always a stab in the air; it is neither *false nor true:* the old truth is now simply irrelevant. There is no communication!"

54. Ibid., 37.

55. Ibid. "Human growth in consciousness and knowledge, along with deeper human wisdom, after the course of time which creates new opportunities and also brings us into new crises, stands in need of getting a more clearly refined, more nu-

anced and more contemporarily satisfactory expression of the dogmas which have been handed down."

56. Ibid., 38.

57. Ibid.

58. Ibid.

59. Schillebeeckx, *The Understanding of Faith*, 17–19. "A confession of faith, expressing, at least in outline, at a certain period of history, the good news of the gospel, has primarily a doxological value; in other words, it is a confession praising God for everything he does for us in human history. If we take as our point of departure the idea of the first Vatican Council that the 'mutual connection between the mysteries' is a theological criterion on the basis of which it is necessary to judge truths which, compared with the essential message, have to be regarded as peripheral, then these truths which result from or are presupposed in the Christian message, must have the same doxological meaning, at least so long as they aim to be not merely logically consistent, but theologically relevant. A theological statement attempts to express the content of a definite act of trust in God" (pp. 17–18).

60. Schillebeeckx, "Towards a Catholic Use of Hermeneutics," in *God the Future of Man*, 36.

61. The clearest example of this principle at work in Schillebeeckx's thought is his treatment of the Chalcedonian dogma in his Christology. As he expresses several times in his work, his purpose with the Christological trilogy was not to simply assume Chalcedon, but to "lead people by the hand" (*manuductio*) through the process by which the Christian community came to develop its confession about Jesus. This exercise, however, does not simply stop at Chalcedon either but is intended to be a prolegomena for a Christology to be developed in reference to the contemporary situation. See Schillebeeckx, *Jesus: An Experiment in Christology*, 636–69, for his more complete discussion about the reinterpretation of that dogma. However, in response to the criticism that he intended to dispense with Chalcedon because of his methodological bracketing of its determinative status at the beginning of his work, he says: "Well, as far as I am concerned, Chalcedon is the norm that governs all of my theological studies; it is to this dogma that I wish to 'lead by the hand' *(manuducere)* the Christians of our day who have their fill of books about the 'death of God' and about Jesus being only a man, though a great prophet. If I regard Chalcedon as a dead letter, I would not have the courage or desire to write two books on Jesus which together come to over fourteen hundred pages." See Edward Schillebeeckx, "Replies of Edward Schillebeeckx, O.P. to Questionnaire No. 46/66 addressed to him by the Congregation for the Doctrine of the Faith," in Schoof, *The Schillebeeckx Case*, 65. In a similar way he addresses the question about the liturgical use of the classic creeds, even if contemporary congregations largely find their language irrelevant. "I think it is quite right to formulate modern creeds—if we Christians have any real self-respect, we are bound in the long run to do that. At the same time, however, I think the old creed ought to be

retained for all Christians, as a standard liturgical hymn, a kind of shared sign of recognition. It shouldn't be touched. It has, I know, become unintelligible, at least parts of it have, but it has a function in the liturgy as a sign of recognition. But it certainly requires explanation. The Our Father also gives rise to a great number of questions, but that doesn't mean the text ought to be changed." See Schillebeeckx, *God Is New Each Moment*, 43.

62. Schillebeeckx, "Magisterium and Ideology," 12. See also, idem, *Church: The Human Story of God*, 216.

63. Schillebeeckx, "Magisterium and Ideology," 12.

64. Edward Schillebeeckx, "Magisterium: An Interview with Edward Schillebeeckx," interview by Manuel Alcalá, trans. Anthony M. Buono, *America* 144, 12 (March 28, 1981): 255; reprint from *Ecclesia* (April 26, 1980). When asked about the roots of the differences between himself and the magisterium during the second "process" over Christology, Schillebeeckx responded: "To put it more clearly, it seems to me that emphasis is placed on the Bible as the remote rule of faith and the magisterium as the proximate rule of faith. This is an attitude that Vatican II has surpassed with its constitution Dei Verbum on divine revelation. On the other hand, emphasis was also placed on the absoluteness of some affirmations of the magisterium, prescinding from their historico-cultural conditionings." See also, idem, "Theologische overpeinzing achteraf," *Tijdschrift voor Theologie* 20, 3 (1980): 424–25; idem, *The Understanding of Faith*, 74, where Schillebeeckx simply says: "It is even possible to say that the church's teaching authority is not a criterion of orthodoxy since it is itself subject to the word of God."

65. Schillebeeckx, *The Understanding of Faith*, 73. Roman Sanchez Chamoso criticizes Schillebeeckx on this very point. In his doctoral dissertation he argues that one of the "contravalores" of Schillebeeckx's work is that he conceives of the magisterium as pastoral and not doctrinal, as one element in Catholic hermeneutics and not one of the criteria of such hermeneutics. In this vein Sanchez Chamoso accuses Schillebeeckx of not seeing the magisterium as having an interpretative function in the church and of doing little to establish a real dialogue with the magisterium. Although I would argue that Sanchez Chamoso's perspective bespeaks a conservative and excessive fear of Protestant influence on Catholic thought (which he associates with the "new hermeneutic" present in Schillebeeckx's work), I would agree that Schillebeeckx's epistemological shifts (along with his reading of Vatican II) move the magisterium from being an *interpreting source* of theology to it being a supervisor and court of last appeal over the plurality of Christian understandings of the faith. See Roman Sanchez Chamoso, *La teoria hermeneutica di E. Schillebeeckx: Principios y criterios para la actualización de la tradición cristiana* (Ph.D. diss., Universidad Pontificia de Salamanca, 1977), Salamanca, 1982, 352ff.

66. See Edward Schillebeeckx, "Is the Church Adrift?" in *The Mission of the Church*, 34–35, for an early expression of this principle. "The teaching office of the church can only, critically, authoritatively and selectively, bring forward what is al-

ready present and living in the tradition of faith of the whole church. Thus the teaching authority of the church in fact functions quite differently from how one might conclude that it would function according to the definition of faith as formulated in isolated precision at the first Vatican Council." This idea will remain constant in his thought through his most recent writings. See, for example, Schillebeeckx, *Theologisch testament*, 74–76. Note also that in both cases, Schillebeeckx argues that his conclusions about the magisterium flow from Vatican II's location of the teaching office more clearly within the entire body of the faithful.

67. See, for example, the carefully worded official *relatio* of Bishop Vinzenz Gasser on papal infallibility at the First Vatican Council, which describes both the powers and limits of the pope's authority. Vinzenz Gasser, *The Gift of Infallibility: The Official* Relatio *of Bishop Vincent Gasser at Vatican Council I,* translated, with commentary and a theological synthesis on infallibility by James T. O'Connor (Boston: Daughters of St. Paul, 1986), 40–55.

68. See the *First Dogmatic Constitution on the Church of Christ,* First Vatican Council (1869–70), in Tanner, *Decrees of the Ecumenical Councils,* 2:811–16, for the full text of the decrees on the primacy and infallibility of the pope. The Dogmatic Constitution on the Church (*Lumen Gentium*) of the Second Vatican Council (1962–65) reaffirms the teaching of Vatican I on papal infallibility (par. 25), while also affirming the infallibility of the whole episcopal college teaching together with the pope (par. 22) and the infallibility of the *sensus fidei* of the whole community of the church (par. 12). See Flannery, *Vatican Council II: The Conciliar and Post-Conciliar Documents* for a complete text of *Lumen Gentium.*

69. Edward Schillebeeckx, "The Problem of the Infallibility of the Church's Office: A Theological Reflection," in *Truth and Certainty,* ed. Edward Schillebeeckx and Bas Van Iersel, *Concilium* 83 (1973): 78–81.

70. Ibid., 80. "It is hardly possible to accept, from the ecclesiological point of view, that the Church, in its confession of baptism, can 'remain in the truth' if there is no promise that its teaching will not have similar lasting value. The Church's 'remaining in the truth' implies faithfulness in the teaching church." Hence, "[t]he same 'presence in veiled form' (*subsistere in*) of the biblical mystery in the Roman Catholic Church applies not only to the community of God as a whole, but also to the church's confession in the teaching of those holding office."

71. Schillebeeckx, *Theologisch testament,* 73. "For a solemn definition of dogma the teaching office always refers to the assistance of the Holy Spirit; and rightly so, as the Spirit is also active in the life and the beliefs of the people of God. But what is often not said with regard to this is that this assistance of the Spirit is not automatically or magically active, but proceeds through the free will, the understanding and the experience of the human office bearers." See also, idem, *Jesus: An Experiment in Christology,* 39.

72. Ibid. "The gift of the Spirit is therefore either positively mediated through the free co-operation of the office bearers with God's grace, or distorted in negative

ways through unfaithfulness, intrigue and manipulation, or then yet through non-culpable negligence, from which truth comes to appearance in mutilated formulas."

73. Schillebeeckx, "The Problem of the Infallibility of the Church's Office: A Theological Reflection," 81–87.

74. Ibid., 91.

75. Cf. Schillebeeckx, "Magisterium and Ideology," 13, where Schillebeeckx names the ways in which even an infallible statement is "relative to" a variety of different limiting conditions.

76. Ibid., 93.

77. Schillebeeckx, *Theologisch testament*, 78. "For is 'infallible' now really the most opportune word available for what is meant by the truth-quality of a dogma? That word calls up all sorts of inadequate associations. 'Inerrancy' (the term which Protestant Christians use above all for the Bible), *freedom from error*, would already be better. But why not just call a spade a spade? Why not just opt for the term 'true,' 'truth'? Dogmatic definitions of faith are simply 'true.' A dogma is a truth given in Jesus Christ. In the end one surely intends to say just that! A dogma is simply true, no more and no less. What can 'infallible' add to this . . . unless a heightened appearance of certainty?"

78. Ibid., 76–77. "Finally, the judgment that the definitions are irrevocable 'ex sese' does not mean in any sense, according to Vatican I, that they are that from the power of the papal office. 'Ex sese' refers to the definitions themselves: to expressions which are infallible in themselves, because the pope stands under the obligation to draw his dogmatic definitions from revelation and (if I may express myself so graphically) from the faith-arsenal or -potential of the whole church. He is himself normed" (p. 76).

79. Ibid., 78.

80. Schillebeeckx, *Theologisch Geloofsverstaan anno 1983*, 18–19.

81. Schillebeeckx, *Church: The Human Story of God*, 199.

82. Edward Schillebeeckx, "The Teaching Authority of All: A Reflection on the Structure of the New Testament," in *The Teaching Authority of Believers*, ed. Johann-Baptist Metz and Edward Schillebeeckx, *Concilium* 180 (1985); reprinted in *The Language of Faith*, 234–35. The phrase "stability of the exchange rate" perhaps refers to the idea of the proportional norm as a criterion of orthodoxy. The church in and through its leaders has the ability (in the Spirit) to maintain the same proportional relationship (or "exchange rate") between the understanding of faith and the socio-cultural situation across historical eras.

83. Schillebeeckx, *God Is New Each Moment*, 83–84.

84. Schillebeeckx, *The Understanding of Faith*, 74. See also, idem, "The Church as Sacrament of Dialogue," in *God the Future of Man*, 117–40.

85. Schillebeeckx, 'What Is Theology?" in *Revelation and Theology*, 1:110.

86. Schillebeeckx, *The Understanding of Faith*, xiii.

87. All of these terms receive a more complete exposition in *Theologisch Geloofsverstaan anno 1983*, 4–17. Schillebeeckx also deals more generally with the method of critical correlation between past and present in *Interim Report*, 50–63. See also, idem, "Theologische overpeinzing achteraf," 423–24. For other sources on the method of critical correlation, see Paul Tillich, *Systematic Theology*, vol. 1 (Chicago: University of Chicago, 1986), 3–68; David Tracy, *Blessed Rage for Order*, 32–63; idem, *The Analogical Imagination: Christian Theology and the Culture of Pluralism* (New York: Crossroad, 1989).

88. So, for example, William L. Portier, using David Tracy's distinction of the three "publics" of the theologian, can say: "His public is therefore much more the church than the academy. But it is the church conceived in a particular way, as a community of participating believers who are also part of society or the world—albeit a prophetic part—rather than ranged against society and the world in resignation and resentment." Portier argues that the situation in Dutch Catholicism after the council leads to this particular orientation of Schillebeeckx's thought. See Portier's chapter "Interpretation and Method," in *The Praxis of Christian Experience*, ed. Schreiter and Hilkert, 22.

89. Schillebeeckx, *Theologisch Geloofsverstaan anno 1983*, 1.

90. Schillebeeckx, "The Teaching Authority of All," 234.

91. Schillebeeckx, *Theologisch Geloofsverstaan anno 1983*, 20; idem, "Interdisciplinarity in Theology," *Theology Digest* 24 (1976): 137–42.

92. Schillebeeckx, "Interdisciplinarity in Theology," 142.

93. Schillebeeckx, "Magisterium and Ideology," 14–17.

94. Schillebeeckx, *Theologisch Geloofsverstaan anno 1983*, 5.

95. Ibid.

96. Schillebeeckx, *Theologisch Geloofsverstaan anno 1983*, 6.

97. Ibid.

98. Ibid., 10.

99. Ibid., 9.

100. Ibid., 10.

101. Ibid., 2.

102. Ibid., 12–13.

103. Ibid., 17.

104. Ibid. See chap. 1, n. 91, for the full quotation and translation.

105. Schillebeeckx, *God Is New Each Moment*, 82.

106. Schillebeeckx, *Ministry: Leadership in the Community of Jesus Christ*, 1–3; idem, *The Church with a Human Face*, 1–12, esp. 10.

107. Schillebeeckx, *Church: The Human Story of God*, xv.

108. Portier, "Edward Schillebeeckx as Critical Theorist, 357, n. 29. "From a comparison with John A. Coleman's *The Evolution of Dutch Catholicism, 1958–1974* (Berkeley: U. of California, 1978) it is clear that the 'critical communities' to which Oosterhuis and Schillebeeckx are referring derive from the Septuagint movement

which Coleman incorporates into his sociological analysis of Dutch Catholicism on pp. 239–247." Coleman notes that even before the council, the Dutch Church began cautious experimentation with new organizational forms and specialized liturgies for different needs for the Catholic population. These experiments often took place in the context of the campus parishes for students (pp. 132–33). After the council the new atmosphere in the Dutch Church created a variety of further experimental parishes or "critical communities," including some that had an open, ecumenical membership (pp. 220–21). However, in this generally progressive atmosphere of change, a variety of "contestation groups," on the right and left, arose within Dutch Catholicism either to resist change (e.g., the right-wing *Confrontatie* group) or to accelerate it (e.g., *Septuagint*). Septuagint began as a left-wing, progressive group within the church whose program included "the erection of local, 'critical' congregations which would act as watchdogs against totalitarian abuses in church and society" (p. 240). With the adherence of many of the progressive leaders of the Dutch Church (including leading liturgical lights like Huub Oosterhuis), Septuagint soon advocated unilateral action on behalf of married priests (i.e., without waiting on the rest of the church to follow). After the defeat of its immediate aims on the level of official policy of the national church, Septuagint began to take up a more radical viewpoint on the nature of a "critical community" and saw itself as "a free movement of Catholics, Protestants, and even non-believers who joined together to perform a critical, prophetic, even revolutionary role in society"—increasingly on the model of the New Left in late 1960s (pp. 242–43). They eventually came into conflict with the Dutch bishops over Oosterhuis's celebrating Mass as a married priest in 1970 at the Amsterdam Student Center and, as a result, were declared "outside the responsibility of the bishop." After 1970 the group's power waned as it became more amorphous and hardly distinguishable from a leftist-secular political party. Coleman evaluates the group in the following way: "In general, Septuagint dismisses the idea of structures for the church, appealing to models of the church as a non-institutionalized social movement. Priests are to be charismatic prophets who arise out of local charismatic critical communities" (p. 245). He adds: "Members of the group have contact with important middle-level decision makers and elites in Dutch Catholicism and have, on occasion, drawn prominent theologians such as Edward Schillebeeckx or F. Haarsma to participate in its programs" (p. 246). Yet, despite this connection with more mainstream Catholicism, the group's basic ecclesiology was not accepted. Decision makers at the center of Dutch Catholicism "do not share its view of the church as a loose social movement of charismatics drawn together around concrete leftist political programs" (p. 246). See Coleman, *The Evolution of Dutch Catholicism, 1958–1974*, for a more complete analysis of the transitions in Dutch Catholicism during this period. After the period analyzed in Coleman's work, critical communities in the Dutch Church continue to exist, although their focus turns more toward issues of internal church reform and resistance to what they see as the reactionary papacy of John Paul II. For more information on the history of these reform movements, see Eric Borgman, Bert van Dijk, and Theo Salemink, eds., *De Vernieuwingen in Katholiek Nederland: Van Vaticanum II tot Acht Mei Beweging* (Amersfoort/Louvain: De Horstink, 1988).

109.   Schillebeeckx, "Critical Theories and Christian Political Commitment," 54–55. Schillebeeckx points out that the development of critical communities within the church does not depend on knowledge of the "critical theory" of the Frankfurt School or any other critical theory. Rather a more general "spirit of sharp contestation" in society has led both to the development of critical theory and critical communities as well (pp. 53–54).

110.   Schillebeeckx, "Critical Theories and Christian Political Commitment," 58. "Within this remembrance of varied religious inspiration, Christians find, in the life praxis of Jesus, that is, in their remembrance of his life and of his death and resurrection, both the basis of the promise and the criticism which comes from this and at the same time an orientation for their action in making the world free. Jesus the Christ is, in other words, the norm for the Christian's emancipative interest. The Christian does not regard the perspective of the Kingdom of God, of the human freedom for which he is looking, as a utopia. For him, this is something that is already given—it has already been realized in a concrete historical form in the life praxis of Jesus, whose proclamation of the Kingdom of God is the thematization of this praxis. Habermas speaks of a purely theoretical anticipation of the ideal of a 'good life' lived in a community in which communication is free from coercion. The Christian, on the contrary, in his practical anticipation, follows Jesus in his activity in bringing about freedom. Jesus' motivation in this praxis of life led in the service of freedom [is] to be found in his relationship with God, his Father, who set him free to identify himself with all men." See also, idem, *Christ: The Experience of Jesus as Lord*, part 4, for an extended discourse on human utopian expectations, salvation from suffering, and the Christian understanding of both of these ideas.

111.   Schillebeeckx, "Critical Theories and Christian Political Commitment," 57. "It is possible for a critical community to be politically committed, but to fail to provide this distinctively Christian perspective and to celebrate the promise in the liturgical language which prayerfully expresses the transcendent element. Such a community might achieve very fruitful results, but it would not be acting as a Christian community. It would be in danger of becoming a purely political cell without evangelical inspiration—one of the very many useful and indeed necessary political pressure groups, but not an *ecclesia Christi*." Schillebeeckx perhaps is thinking here of the Septuagint movement which gradually became so diffuse that its specifically Christian orientation was lost.

112.   Schillebeeckx, "Critical Theories and Christian Political Commitment," 54. See also, idem, *The Understanding of Faith*, 137–38.

113.   See, for example, Edward Schillebeeckx, "Offices in the Church of the Poor," in *La Iglesia Popular: Between Fear and Hope*, ed. Leonardo Boff and Virgil Elizondo, *Concilium* 176 (1984): 98–107; reprinted in *The Language of Faith*, 211–24. For theological

discussions of base or critical communities in other contexts, see, for example, Leonardo Boff, *Church, Charism & Power: Liberation Theology and the Institutional Church*, trans. John W. Diercksmeier (New York: Crossroad, 1985); idem, *Ecclesiogenesis: The Base Communities Reinvent the Church*, trans. Robert R. Barr (Maryknoll, N.Y.: Orbis, 1986). For a feminist perspective on critical communities, see Rosemary Radford Ruether, *Women-Church: Theology and Practice of Feminist Liturgical Communities* (San Francisco: Harper & Row, 1988).

114. Schillebeeckx, *For the Sake of the Gospel*, 159. He later incorporates the substance of this address nearly verbatim into chapters 1 and 4 of *Church: The Human Story of God*, which indicates again the close link between the concrete situation in the Dutch Church and his theological work. In the address that he gave on May 8, 1985, to the gathering of the movement at 's Hertogenbosch, Schillebeeckx even more strongly argues for the ecclesial and Catholic nature of the critical communities (*For the Sake of the Gospel*, 160–64). Faced with the criticism of the movement by the Dutch episcopate and (implicitly) by the 1985 Special Synod of Bishops in Rome, he forcefully states, "we have an identity which cannot be taken from us by any fellow human being or fellow believer" (p. 160). More specifically, this means that the title "people of God" cannot be stripped from those who gather in Jesus' name and "in the name of many people who suffer in and over the church" (p. 161). Because "[w]e shall not even let our Second Vatican Council be taken away from us under the mist of flowery lip service to that council" (p. 161), the critical communities of Catholics have the right and obligation to pursue that council's mandate, which Schillebeeckx locates in the mystical and political action of believers within the eschatological proviso and hope for God's reign (pp. 162–64). From both of these addresses derive Schillebeeckx's language about the critical communities being expressions of the "other face" of the church, in distinction from the increasingly authoritarian and hierarchical pre–Vatican II mentality which characterizes the "official church."

115. Schillebeeckx, *For the Sake of the Gospel*, 172–73.

116. Schillebeeckx, *Ministry: Leadership in the Community of Jesus Christ*, 82–83. "The alternative practice of critical communities which are inspired by Jesus as the Christ is 1. possible from an apostolic and dogmatic point of view (I cannot pass judgment on all the details here). It is a legitimate way of living a Christian life, commensurate with the apostolicity of the church, which has been called into being by the needs of the time." "Furthermore, 2. given the present canonical church order, the alternative practice is not in any way *contra* (against) *ordinem;* it is *praeter ordinem*. In other words, it does not follow the letter of existing church order (it is *contra* this letter), but it is in accordance with what church order really set out to safeguard (in earlier situations)." Cf., idem, *The Church with a Human Face*, 254–58, where he does not make this claim explicitly but speaks about the "diagnostic and dynamic effect" and the "normative power" that such alternative practices have, al-

though these also must be set into a critical dialogue with the theological tradition. In another context, Schillebeeckx advocates for the recognition of developing ministries in the "church of the poor" through a new form of ordination. "I am personally in favour of a suitable form of ordination (a laying on of hands accompanied by a special *epiclesis* that is specific to office) for those who have in recent years emerged as 'animators' of the ecclesial communities of the poor." See his "Offices in the Church of the Poor," 224.

117. Edward Schillebeeckx, "The Christian Community and Its Office Bearers," in *The Right of a Community to a Priest, Concilium* 133 (New York: Seabury, 1980); reprinted in *The Language of Faith*, 160.

118. See Schillebeeckx, "The Teaching Authority of All," 225–36.

119. See, for example, Schillebeeckx, *Christ: The Experience of Jesus as Lord*. At the beginning of part 1, "The Authority of New Experiences and the Authority of the New Testament," he writes: "In this analysis I shall not be immediately concerned with experience in the more superficial sense of 'It says nothing to me,' 'It means something to me,' even if 'experience,' the phenomenon to be analysed, does have something to do with this. Nor am I so concerned with experience in the sense of a particular state, disposition and feeling, or of qualities of experience, although these emotional aspects are essential, above all in religious experiences. In the analysis the main emphasis will be on *the particular cognitive, critical and productive force of human experiences*. Under this aspect, above all, revelation has everything to do with 'experience'" (p. 29, my emphasis). A few pages later, at the beginning of the section on "The authority of experiences," he then links this "critical and productive force" with "authority" (p. 37). Near the end of the text, he then addresses more directly the "particular critical and productive epistemological force" (and therefore authority) of negative contrast experiences of human suffering (pp. 817–18). Similarly, in another place he writes: "If they are critically reflected on, human experiences have in fact authority and validity as revelations of reality or of that not conceived and not produced by human beings. They have a *cognitive, critical and productive, or liberating power* in the enduring speech of humanity for truth and goodness, for justice and human happiness." See, idem, "Erfahrung und Glaube," 73–116; unpublished translation by Robert J. Schreiter, 8 (my emphasis).

120. Schillebeeckx, *Church: The Human Story of God*, 216–28.

121. Ibid., 220–21.

six Symbols of the Church to Come

1. Christopher O'Donnell, *Ecclesia: A Theological Encyclopedia of the Church* (Collegeville, Minn.: Liturgical Press, 1996), s.v. "Dissent." "The question of dissent came up during Vatican II: four bishops cited the possibility of a learned person who

could not internally assent to non-infallible teaching. The Doctrinal Commission refused to deal with this in LG 25 but said: 'About this matter approved theological treatments are to be consulted (*probatae expositiones theologicae*).' At that time what was almost certainly meant were the manuals of theology being used in the theological schools. Some of these granted that internal assent can in exceptional circumstances be withheld, but they did not allow public dissociation from authoritative teaching of the Holy See." O'Donnell refers particularly to the authors listed in I. Salaverri's *De Ecclesia*, 719–20. For more on these "auctores probati," see Joseph Komonchak, "Ordinary Papal Magisterium and Religious Assent," in Charles E. Curran and Richard A. McCormick, eds., *The Magisterium and Morality*, Readings in Moral Theology, 3 (New York: Paulist, 1982), 70–78. Komonchak agrees that "the manuals are generally rather negative on the possibility of public dissent or disagreement" (p. 73), but they do teach both "the duty of internal religious assent to ordinary teaching and the possible legitimacy of dissent" (p. 77). Komonchak argues that this largely "internal" space for dissent provides the background for the postconciliar appeals by theologians to the tradition of recognizing the possibility of dissent from authoritative and non-infallible statements (ibid.).

    2. Pius IX, *Ineffabilis Deus* (December 8, 1854), in *Acta Pii IX*, vol. 1, sec. 1, 616. For histories of the development of the term "magisterium" and of the relationships between the teaching office of pastors and that of theologians, see Yves Congar, "A Semantic History of the Term 'Magisterium,'" and "A Brief History of the Forms of the Magisterium and Its Relations with Scholars," in *The Magisterium and Morality*, ed. Curran and McCormick, 297–313, 314–31.

    3. National Conference of Catholic Bishops, "Norms of Licit Theological Dissent," in *Dissent in the Church*, ed. Charles E. Curran and Richard A. McCormick, Readings in Moral Theology, 6 (New York: Paulist, 1988), 127–28. See also in the same volume the statement by the West German Bishops, "The Document of the German Bishops Addressed to All Members of the Church Who Are Commissioned to Preach the Faith" (pp. 129–32). The bishops concede that "in the exercise of its official function this teaching authority of the Church can, and on occasion actually does, fall into errors" (p. 129). This possibility of error does not extend to "those statements of doctrine which are proclaimed as propositions to be embraced with the absolute assent of faith, whether by a solemn definition on the part of the Pope, a general council, or by the exercise of the ordinary *magisterium*" (ibid.). Such a dogma does admit of "development in our understanding" so as to eliminate "any misinterpretations which may perhaps have been attached to it hitherto" (pp. 129–30), but this does not permit dissent from it. This dissent, which must be exercised with great caution, applies only to "nondefined statements of dogma" or "not *de fide* definitions" (p. 130). Compare these also with the 1975 statement of the International Theological Commission, written by Otto Semmelroth and Karl Lehmann, "The Ecclesiastical Magisterium and Theology," in *The Magisterium and Morality*, ed. Curran and McCormick, 151–70.

4. See Introduction, n. 4.

5. See, for example, Schillebeeckx, *I Am a Happy Theologian*, 32–40; idem, "Magisterium: An Interview with Edward Schillebeeckx"; idem, "Magisterium and Ideology"; idem, "Theologische overpeinzing achteraf"; see also his responses to the CDF in Schoof, *The Schillebeeckx Case*. Of course, this lack of usage of the term does not mean that Schillebeeckx never deals with the question of the relationship between theologians and the magisterium. Rather, it indicates that he approaches this question from a different perspective, which I will describe below.

6. Schillebeeckx, "Breuken in christelijke dogma's," 39–48.

7. Ibid., 39.

8. Ibid., 39–40. "Nevertheless it is a fact that with regard to non-*ex cathedra*-statements, since the non-acceptance of n. 14 of the encyclical *Humanae Vitae* about birth control by the great majority of Catholics, in official Vatican documents along with the so-called new World Catechism, one can perceive the origin of a maximalizing tendency to draw those non-infallible and therefore fallible magisterial statements as closely as possible into proximity with infallible definitions: they stand, so it is formulated, '*in the logic of*' (an expression personally used and preferred by the theologian J. Ratzinger) or '*as the extension of*' (an expression of the so-called universal World Catechism, n. 891) statements which lay a claim upon our obedience of faith" (p. 40). For the text of the encyclical, see John Paul II, *The Splendor of Truth (Veritatis Splendor)* (Boston: Pauline Books and Media, 1995).

9. Schillebeeckx, "Breuken in christelijke dogma's," 41. Schillebeeckx notes that this tradition of dissent extends from Paul's disagreement with Peter all the way down to the current Code of Canon Law, which declares, "'No doctrine is considered to be infallibly defined, unless that is manifestly established' (*C.I.C.*, can. 749, §3)" (p. 41).

10. Ibid., 43–44. "Here I am analyzing this encyclical only on one point, namely the papal demand that one must nevertheless accept this non-infallible doctrine purely and simply on papal authority and that no public criticism (even from experts) of this statement is permitted on penalty of professional prohibition, or even that Catholic institutions would have their 'Catholic' name taken from them (see n. 110–116). It is asked of expert moral theologians that they should provide the example 'in a loyal *internal* and *external* agreement with the teaching of the Magisterium in the domain of both dogma and morality' (n. 110). Moreover, it is also said that in case of 'dissent, one may not publicly express that disagreement with defined aspects of this encyclical through the social means of communication: that is contrary to the church's *communio* and to the proper understanding of the hierarchical constitution of the people of God' (n. 113). The encyclical points out 'the right of believers to receive Catholic doctrine in its purity and integrity.' With that last point I am in agreement: moral theologians may not conceal from believers what the church officially proclaims. But that in no way implies, ecclesiologically speaking, that therefore they must also conceal their potential criticism."

11. Ibid., 44. One can see how far Schillebeeckx has come from a Counter-Reformation mentality by comparing this statement with one of Ignatius of Loyola's "Rules for Thinking with the Church." "If we wish to be sure that we are right in all things, we should always be ready to accept this principle: I will believe that the white I see is black, if the hierarchical church so defines it." See Ignatius of Loyola, *The Spiritual Exercises of St. Ignatius*, trans. Anthony Mottola with an introduction by Robert W. Gleason (New York: Doubleday, 1989), 140–41.

12. Schillebeeckx, "Breuken in christelijke dogma's," 45–46. "Thus it is officially recognized that an unequivocal, uniform agreement is not demanded; there are gradations possible according to the gravity of the matter, the strength or weakness of the arguments advanced by the teaching office. Philips meant by 'obsequium' not submission (as some translate that word) but respect. 'Religious' respect means: not *only* on rational grounds" (p. 45).

13. Ibid., 45.

14. Ibid., 47–48.

15. Schillebeeckx, "Magisterium and Ideology," 5; idem, *Church: The Human Story of God*, 223–28; idem, "Theologische overpeinzing achteraf," 422.

16. Schillebeeckx, *The Understanding of Faith*, 142–43. "The theological process of making the apostolic faith present and actual in the world of today should not be a purely ideological process. There should, in other words, be a firm basis in history itself for the actualising interpretation of faith if this is to be at all credible. If this historical basis is overlooked, the process of making present will become purely speculative and theoretical and—as has so often happened—it will give the impression that all that theologians do is to make use afterwards of what has already been discovered and exploited. The precondition for a credible theological process of continuing and actualising the christian message is that faith can still survive once its ideological framework has been broken down. In other words, the point of departure is that christianity is able to transcend the ideological form in which it appears, and that it can affect this transcendence in history, by means of that process which takes place in history. No attempt should be made to devise a new theology without first creating the sociological and therefore ecclesiological conditions for that theology."

17. See, for example, his trenchant assessment of John Paul II's vision for the church. "The present Pope seems to be denying modernity with his project of the re-evangelization of Europe. The Pope says that there is a need to return to the old Europe of Cyril and Methodius and St. Benedict. For John Paul II, the return to the Catholicism of the first millennium is the great challenge. Then followed the centuries of schism, first with the East and then within Western Christianity. In the second millennium Europe declined, and with it the whole of Western culture. To re-evangelize Europe there is a need to overcome modernity and all the modern values and go back to the first millennium. To return to rural Christianity, the model of all Christianity. If that is so—I would add—there is also the need to have the courage to accept the the-

ology of ministry in the first millennium. But this Pope says nothing about that. Premodern, agricultural, uncritical Christianity is the model of Christianity in the Pope's thought: 'France, what have I done for your baptism?' That is the typical expression of this return. I criticize this return because the modern values of freedom of conscience, tolerance and religion are not in fact values of the first millennium." Schillebeeckx, *I Am a Happy Theologian*, 43.

18. Schillebeeckx, *The Understanding of Faith*, 74. "I think that it is inevitable that there will, in the future, be a tension and indeed a certain conflict between theological views and the views of the church's *magisterium*. This is bound to be a normal situation in the church, if the catholic church is not to become a mere ideology. (I do not wish to suggest here, of course, that theologians represent 'openness' in the church or that an inhibiting 'closedness' characterises the hierarchical leaders of the church. The very reverse is by no means impossible.)"

19. Schillebeeckx, *Church: The Human Story of God*, 214–28. See also Eugene C. Bianchi and Rosemary Radford Ruether, eds., *A Democratic Catholic Church: The Reconstruction of Roman Catholicism* (New York: Crossroad, 1993). For an actual proposal for a democratic constitution for the Catholic Church, see Leonard Swidler, *Toward a Catholic Constitution* (New York: Crossroad, 1996).

20. See chap. 1, nn. 53 and 64.

21. Ibid., 130–31.

Bibliography

Works by Edward Schillebeeckx

"Het apostolisch ambt van de kerkelijke hiërarchie." *Studia Catholica* 32 (1957): 258–90.

"Breuken in christelijke dogma's." In *Breuklijnen: Grenservaringen en zoektoechten,* ed. Edward Schillebeeckx, Bas van Iersel, Ad Willems, and Hermann Wegman, 15–49. Baarn, Netherlands: H. Nelissen, 1994.

"Can Christology Be an Experiment?" *Proceedings of the Catholic Theological Society of America* 35 (1980): 1–14.

"The Catholic Understanding of Office in the Church." *Theological Studies* 30, 4 (December 1969): 567–87.

Christ: The Experience of Jesus as Lord. Translated by John Bowden. New York: Crossroad, 1980.

Christ the Sacrament of the Encounter with God. Translated by Paul Barrett. New York: Sheed and Ward, 1963.

"The Christian Community and Its Office Bearers." In *The Right of a Community to a Priest. Concilium* 133: 95–133. New York: Seabury, 1980.

"Christian Identity and Human Integrity." In *Is Being Human a Criterion of Being Christian?* ed. Jean-Pierre Jossua and Claude Geffré. *Concilium* 155 (1982). Reprinted in *The Language of Faith: Essays on Jesus, Theology and the Church,* 185–98. Maryknoll, N.Y.: Orbis; London: SCM, 1995.

"The Church and Mankind." In *The Church and Mankind. Concilium* 1 (1965): 69–100. Reprinted in *The Language of Faith: Essays on Jesus, Theology and the Church,* 1–24. Maryknoll, N.Y.: Orbis; London: SCM, 1995.

Church: The Human Story of God. Translated by John Bowden. New York: Crossroad, 1990.

The Church with a Human Face: A New and Expanded Theology of Ministry. Translated by John Bowden. New York: Crossroad, 1987.

"The Crisis in the Language of Faith as a Hermeneutical Problem." In *The Crisis in the Language of Faith,* ed. Johann-Baptist Metz and Jean-Pierre Jossua. *Concilium* 9, 5 (May 1973). Reprinted in *The Language of Faith: Essays on Jesus, Theology and the Church,* 83–94. Maryknoll, N.Y.: Orbis; London: SCM, 1995.

"Critical Theories and Christian Political Commitment." In *Political Community and Christian Community,* ed. Alois Müller and Norbert Greinacher. *Concilium* 84 (1973): 48–61.

Dialectische Hermeneutiek: Deel I, Algemene Hermeneutiek. Student notes for "College Hermeneutiek," 1978–79. Catholic University of Nijmegen.

"Erfahrung und Glaube." In *Christlicher Glaube in moderner Gesellschaft,* vol. 25, 73–116. Freiburg: Herder, 1982. Unpublished translation by Robert J. Schreiter.

The Eucharist. Translated by N. D. Smith. New York: Sheed and Ward, 1968.

For the Sake of the Gospel. Translated by John Bowden. New York: Crossroad, 1990.

Foreword. Tadahiko Iwashima, *Menschheitsgeschichte und Heilserfahrung: Die Theologie von Edward Schillebeeckx als methodisch reflektierte Soteriologie,* Düsseldorf: Patmos, 1982.

God among Us: The Gospel Proclaimed. Translated by John Bowden. New York: Crossroad, 1980.

God and Man. Translated by Edward Fitzgerald and Peter Tomlinson. New York: Sheed and Ward, 1969.

God Is New Each Moment: Edward Schillebeeckx in Conversation with Huub Oosterhuis and Piet Hoogeven. Translated by David Smith. New York: Seabury, 1983.

"The 'God of Jesus' and the 'Jesus of God.'" In *Jesus Christ and Human Freedom,* ed. Edward Schillebeeckx and Bas van Iersel. *Concilium* 10, 3 (1974): 110–15. Reprinted in *The Language of Faith: Essays on Jesus, Theology and the Church,* 95–108. Maryknoll, N.Y.: Orbis; London: SCM, 1995.

God the Future of Man. Translated by N. D. Smith. New York: Sheed and Ward, 1968.

I Am a Happy Theologian: Conversations with Francesco Strazzari. Translated by John Bowden. New York: Crossroad, 1994.

"Interdisciplinarity in Theology." *Theology Digest* 24 (1976): 137–42.

Interim Report on the Books Jesus *and* Christ. Translated by John Bowden. New York: Crossroad, 1980.

"Jeruzalem of Benares? Nicaragua of de Berg Athos?" *Kultuurleven* 50 (1983): 331–47; Excerpted in *The Schillebeeckx Reader,* ed. Robert J. Schreiter, 257–59, 272–74. New York: Crossroad, 1987.

Jesus: An Experiment in Christology. Translated by Hubert Hoskins. New York: Seabury (Crossroad), 1979.

The Language of Faith: Essays on Jesus, Theology and the Church. Concilium Series. Maryknoll, N.Y.: Orbis; London: SCM. 1995.

"Magisterium: An Interview with Edward Schillebeeckx." Interview by Manuel Alcalà. Translated by Anthony M. Buono. *America* 144, 12 (March 28, 1981): 254–58. Reprint from *Ecclesia* (April 26, 1980).

"Magisterium and Ideology." In *Authority in the Church and the Schillebeeckx Case,* ed. Leonard Swidler and Piet Fransen, 5–17. New York: Crossroad, 1982.

Ministry: Leadership in the Community of Jesus Christ. Translated by John Bowden. New York: Crossroad, 1981.

The Mission of the Church. Translated by N. D. Smith. London: Sheed and Ward; New York: Herder and Herder, 1973.

"Offices in the Church of the Poor." In *La Iglesia Popular: Between Fear and Hope,* ed. Leonardo Boff and Virgil Elizondo. *Concilium* 176 (1984): 98–107. Reprinted in *The Language of Faith: Essays on Jesus, Theology and the Church,* 211–24. Maryknoll, N.Y.: Orbis; London: SCM, 1995.

On Christian Faith: The Spiritual, Ethical and Political Dimensions. Translated by John Bowden. New York: Crossroad, 1987.

"The Problem of the Infallibility of the Church's Office: A Theological Reflection." In *Truth and Certainty,* ed. Edward Schillebeeckx and Bas Van Iersel. *Concilium* 83 (1973): 77–94.

"Questions on Christian Salvation of and for Man." Originally published as "God, Society and Human Salvation" in *Toward Vatican III: The Work That Needs to Be Done,* ed. David Tracy, Hans Küng, and Johann B. Metz, 27–44. New York: Seabury and Concilium, 1978. Reprinted in *The Language of Faith: Essays on Jesus, Theology and the Church,* 109–26. Maryknoll: Orbis; London: SCM, 1995.

The Real Achievement of Vatican II. Translated by H. J. J. Vaughan. New York: Herder and Herder, 1967.

"The Religious and Human Ecumene." In *The Future of Liberation Theology: Essays in Honor of Gustavo Gutierrez.* Maryknoll, N.Y.: Orbis, 1989. Reprinted in *The Language of Faith: Essays on Jesus, Theology and the Church,* 249–64. Maryknoll, N.Y.: Orbis; London: SCM, 1995.

Revelation and Theology, vol. 1. (Theological Soundings 1/1) Translated by N. D. Smith. London: Sheed and Ward; New York: Herder and Herder, 1967.

Revelation and Theology, vol. 2. (Theological Soundings 1/2) Translated by N. D. Smith. London: Sheed and Ward; New York: Herder and Herder, 1968.

"The Role of History in What Is Called the New Paradigm." In *Paradigm Change in Theology,* ed. Hans Küng and David Tracy. New York: Crossroad, 1989. Reprinted in *The Language of Faith: Essays on Jesus, Theology and the Church,* 23–48. Maryknoll, N.Y.: Orbis; London: SCM, 1995.

De sacramentele heilseconomie: Theologische bezinning op St. Thomas' sacramentenleer in het licht van de traditie en van de hedendaagse sacramentsproblematiek, 1. Antwerpen: 't Groeit; Bilthoven: H. Nelissen, 1952.

"De sociale context van de verschuivingen in het kerkelijk ambt." *Tijdschrift voor Theologie* 22 (1982): 24–59.

The Schillebeeckx Reader. Edited by Robert J. Schreiter. New York: Crossroad, 1987.

"Some Thoughts on the Interpretation of Eschatology." *Concilium* 5, 1 (1969). Reprinted in *The Language of Faith: Essays on Jesus, Theology and the Church,* 43–53. Maryknoll, N.Y.: Orbis; London: SCM, 1995.

"The Teaching Authority of All: A Reflection on the Structure of the New Testament." In *The Teaching Authority of Believers,* ed. Johann-Baptist Metz and Edward Schillebeeckx. *Concilium* 180 (1985). Reprinted in *The Language of Faith: Essays on Jesus, Theology and the Church,* 225–36. Maryknoll, N.Y.: Orbis; London: SCM, 1995.

Theologisch Geloofsverstaan anno 1983. Baarn, Netherlands: H. Nelissen, 1983.

Theologisch testament: Notarieel nog niet verleden. Baarn, Netherlands: H. Nelissen, 1994.

In *Theologisch Woordenboek,* 1. Roermond/Maaseik: J. J. Romen en Zonen, 1952. S.v. "Censuur," "Depositum fidei," "Dogma," "Dogmaontwikkeling," "Eclectisme," "Eschatologisch," "Ex cathedra."

In *Theologisch Woordenboek,* 2. Roermond/Maaseik: J. J. Romen en Zonen, 1957. S.v. "Geloofsbepaling," "Geloofsgeheim," "Geloofswarheid," "Gescheidenis," "Handoplegging," "Kerkvergadering," "Kerygmatische Theologie," "Ketterij," "Merkteken."

In *Theologisch Woordenboek,* 3. Roermond/Maaseik: J. J. Romen en Zonen, 1959. S.v. "Mysterie," "Mysteriëncultus," "Nouvelle Théologie," "Obex," "Overlevering," "Priesterschap," "Reliquiënverering," "Sacrament," "Sacramentale," "Schat der Kerk," "Scheeben," "Schisma," "H. Schrift," "Simulatie," "Symbolum," "Theologie," "Verrijzenis," "Voorgeborchte," "Vormsel," "Wijding," "Zalving," "Zegening," "Zekerheid."

"Theologische overpeinzing achteraf." *Tijdschrift voor Theologie* 20, 3 (1980): 422–26.

The Understanding of Faith: Interpretation and Criticism. Translated by N. D. Smith. New York: Seabury, 1974.

"Verzet, Engagement en Viering." *Nieuwsbrief, Stichting Edward Schillebeeckx* 5 (October 1992): 1–3.

World and Church. Translated by N. D. Smith. New York: Sheed and Ward, 1971.

Secondary Works

Adorno, Theodor W. *Negative Dialectics.* Translated by E. B. Ashton (pseud.). New York: Seabury, 1973.

Adorno, Theodor W., and Max Horkheimer. *Dialectic of Enlightenment.* Translated by John Cumming. New York: Seabury, 1972.

Balasuriya, Tissa. *Mary and Human Liberation: The Debate.* Harrisburg, Pa.: Trinity, 1997.

Barclay, Robert. *An Apology for the True Christian Divinity.* Philadelphia: Friends' Book Association, n.d.

Beaumont, Daniel. "The Modality of Narrative: A Critique of Some Recent Views of Narrative in Theology." *Journal of the American Academy of Religion* 65, 1 (Spring 1997): 125–39.

Bianchi, Eugene C., and Rosemary Radford Ruether, eds. *A Democratic Catholic Church: The Reconstruction of Roman Catholicism.* New York: Crossroad, 1993.

Boff, Leonardo. *Church, Charism & Power: Liberation Theology and the Institutional Church.* Translated by John W. Diercksmeier. New York: Crossroad, 1985.

———. *Ecclesiogenesis: The Base Communities Reinvent the Church.* Translated by Robert R. Barr. Maryknoll, N.Y.: Orbis, 1986.

Borgman, Eric, Bert van Dijk and Theo Salemink, eds. *De Vernieuwingen in Katholiek Nederland: Van Vaticanum II tot Acht Mei Beweging.* Amersfoort/Louvain: De Horstink, 1988.

Boyle, John P. *Church Teaching Authority: Historical and Theological Studies.* Notre Dame, Ind.: University of Notre Dame Press, 1995.

Caputo, John D. "Radical Hermeneutics and Religious Truth: The Case of Sheehan and Schillebeeckx." In *Phenomenology of the Truth Proper to Religion,* ed. Daniel Guerrière, 146–72. Albany: State University of New York, 1990.

Carlen, Claudia, ed. *The Papal Encyclicals, 1878–1903.* Raleigh, N.C.: McGrath, 1981.

———. *The Papal Encyclicals, 1903–1939.* Raleigh, N.C.: McGrath, 1981.

Chantraine, Georges. "Apostolicity According to Schillebeeckx." *Communio (US)* 12 (Summer 1985): 192–222.

"Chronology of Balasuriya's Troubles." *National Catholic Reporter,* January 20, 1998.

Coleman, John A. *The Evolution of Dutch Catholicism, 1958–1974.* Berkeley and Los Angeles: University of California Press, 1978.

Collins, Paul. *Papal Power: A Proposal for Change in Catholicism's Third Millennium.* London: HarperCollins, 1997.

"Collins's Views on Papacy Face Heresy Investigation." *National Catholic Reporter,* February 20, 1998.

Congar, Yves. "A Brief History of the Forms of the Magisterium and Its Relations with Scholars." In *The Magisterium and Morality,* ed., Charles E. Curran and Richard A. McCormick, 314–31. Readings in Moral Theology, 3. New York: Paulist, 1982.

———. "A Semantic History of the Term 'Magisterium'." In *The Magisterium and Morality,* ed. Charles E. Curran and Richard A. McCormick, 297–313. Readings in Moral Theology, 3. New York: Paulist, 1982.

Congregation for the Doctrine of the Faith. "The Ecclesial Vocation of the Theologian." *The Pope Speaks: The Church Documents Bimonthly* 35, 6 (November–December 1990): 388–403.

———. "Oath of Fidelity: The New Profession of Faith and Oath of Fidelity (March 1, 1989)." *The Pope Speaks: The Church Documents Bimonthly* 34, 2 (July–August 1989): 170.

————. "Reply to the 'Dubium'." *The Pope Speaks: The Church Documents Bimonthly* 41, 3 (May–June 1996): 145.

Crites, Steven. "The Narrative Quality of Experience." *Journal of the American Academy of Religion* 39, 3 (September 1971): 291–311.

Curran, Charles E. *Faithful Dissent.* Kansas City: Sheed and Ward, 1986.

Curran, Charles E., and Richard A. McCormick, eds. *Dissent in the Church.* Readings in Moral Theology, 6. New York: Paulist, 1988.

————. *The Magisterium and Morality.* Readings in Moral Theology, 3. New York: Paulist, 1982.

Derksen, Karl. "Theologie-praxis-content." In *Meedenken met Edward Schillebeeckx: bij zijn afscheid als hooglerar te Nijmegen,* ed. Hermann Häring, Ted Schoof, and Ad Willems, 115–129. Baarn, Netherlands: H. Nelissen, 1983.

Dobbelaere, Karel. "Secularization, Pillarization, Religious Involvement and Religious Change in the Low Countries." In *World Catholicism in Transition,* ed. Thomas M. Gannon, 80–115. New York: Macmillan, 1988.

Dulles, Avery. *Models of Revelation.* Garden City, N.Y.: Doubleday, 1983.

————. *Models of the Church.* 2d ed. New York: Doubleday, 1987.

————. "Pastoral Response to the Teaching on Women's Ordination." *Origins* 26, 11 (August 29, 1996): 177–80.

Dupré, Louis. "Experience and Interpretation: A Philosophical Reflection on Schillebeeckx's *Jesus* and *Christ.*" *Theological Studies* 43 (March 1982): 30–51.

Fackre, Gabriel J. "Bones Strong and Weak in the Skeletal Structure of Schillebeeckx's Christology." *Journal of Ecumenical Studies* 21 (Spring 1984): 248–77.

Fatula, Mary Ann. "Dogmatic Pluralism and the Noetic Dimension of the Unity of Faith." *Thomist* 48 (1984): 409–32.

Flannery, Austin, ed. *Vatican Council II: The Conciliar and Post-Conciliar Documents.* Boston: St. Paul Books and Media, 1992.

Gadamer, Hans-Georg. *Truth and Method.* New York: Crossroad, 1982.

Galvin, John. Review of *Christ: The Christian Experience in the Modern World* and *Interim Report on the Books* Jesus *and* Christ, by Edward Schillebeeckx. In *Heythrop Journal* 23, 1 (January 1982): 78–82.

Gannon, Thomas M., ed. *World Catholicism in Transition.* New York: Macmillan, 1988.

Gasser, Vinzenz. *The Gift of Infallibility: The Official* Relatio *of Bishop Vincent Gasser at Vatican Council I.* Translated, with commentary and a theological synthesis on infallibility by James T. O'Connor. Boston: Daughters of St. Paul, 1986.

Granfield, Patrick. *The Limits of the Papacy: Authority and Autonomy in the Church.* New York: Crossroad, 1987.

Grelot, Pierre. *Eglise et ministères: Pour un dialogue critique avec Edward Schillebeeckx.* Paris: Editions du Cerf, 1983.

Groot, Jan C. "Holland and Rome." In *Those Dutch Catholics,* ed. Michel van der Plas and Henk Suér, 143–56. London: Geoffrey Chapman, 1967.

Habermas, Jürgen. *Knowledge and Human Interests*. Translated by Jeremy J. Shapiro. Boston: Beacon, 1971.

———. *Theory and Practice*. Translated by John Viertel. Boston: Beacon, 1973.

Häring, Hermann, Ted Schoof, and Ad Willems, eds. *Meedenken met Edward Schillebeeckx: bij zijn afscheid als hooglerar te Nijmegen*. Baarn, Netherlands: H. Nelissen, 1983.

Hastings, Adrian, ed. *Modern Catholicism: Vatican II and After*. London: SPCK; New York: Oxford University Press, 1991.

Hebblethwaite, Peter. *The New Inquisition? The Case of Edward Schillebeeckx and Hans Küng*. San Francisco: Harper and Row; London: SCM, 1980.

———. *The Runaway Church: Post-conciliar Growth or Decline*. Rev. ed. London: Collins, 1975.

———. "The Synod of Bishops." In *Modern Catholicism: Vatican II and After*, ed. Adrian Hastings, 200–209. London: SPCK; New York: Oxford University Press, 1991.

Hilkert, Mary Catherine. "Hermeneutics of History in the Theology of Edward Schillebeeckx." *Thomist* 51 (1987): 97–145.

Hill, William J. "Schillebeeckx's New Look at Secularity: A Note." *Thomist* 33 (1969): 162–70.

Horkheimer, Max. *Critical Theory: Selected Essays*. Translated by Matthew J. O'Connell and others. New York: Herder and Herder, 1972.

———. *Die Sehnsucht nach dem ganz Anderen* (Gespräch mit Helmut Gumnior). In *Gesammelte Schriften, Band 7: Vorträge und Aufzeichnungen, 1949–1973*, ed. Gunzelin Schmid Noerr, 385–404. Frankfurt am Main: Fischer Taschenbuch, 1985.

Hunt, John F., and Terrence R. Connelly, with Charles E. Curran, Robert E. Hunt, and Robert K. Webb. *The Responsibility of Dissent: The Church and Academic Freedom*. New York: Sheed and Ward, 1969.

Ignatius of Loyola. *The Spiritual Exercises of St. Ignatius*. Translated by Anthony Mottola with an introduction by Robert W. Gleason. New York: Doubleday, 1989.

International Theological Commission (Otto Semmelroth and Karl Lehmann). "The Ecclesiastical Magisterium and Theology." In *The Magisterium and Morality*, ed. Charles E. Curran and Richard A. McCormick, 151–70. Readings in Moral Theology, 3. New York: Paulist, 1982.

Iwashima, Tadahiko. *Menschheitsgeschichte und Heilserfahrung: Die Theologie von Edward Schillebeeckx als methodisch reflektierte Soteriologie*. Düsseldorf: Patmos, 1982.

Jacko, Dorothy A. "Schillebeeckx's Creation-based Theology as Basis for an Ecological Spirituality." In *An Ecology of the Spirit: Religious Reflection and Environmental Consciousness*, ed. Michael Barnes, 145–58. Annual Publication of the College Theology Society, 36 (1990). Lanham, Md.: University Press of America, 1994.

John Paul II. *The Splendor of Truth (Veritatis Splendor)*. Boston: Pauline Books and Media, 1995.

Kasper, Walter. "Ministry in the Church: Taking Issue with Edward Schillebeeckx." *Communio (US)* 10 (Summer 1983): 185–95.

Kennedy, Philip. "Continuity Underlying Discontinuity: Schillebeeckx's Philosophical Background." *New Blackfriars* 70 (1989): 264–77.

———. *Deus Humanissimus: The Knowability of God in the Theology of Edward Schille-beeckx.* Fribourg: University Press, 1993.

———. *Schillebeeckx.* Oustanding Christian Thinkers Series. Collegeville, Minn.: Liturgical Press, 1993.

Kerkhofs, Jan. "Western Europe." In *Modern Catholicism: Vatican II and After,* ed. Adrian Hastings, 357–64. London: SPCK; New York: Oxford University Press, 1991.

Komonchak, Joseph. "Ordinary Papal Magisterium and Religious Assent." In *Magisterium and Morality,* ed. Charles E. Curran and Richard A. McCormick, 70–78. Readings in Moral Theology, 3. New York: Paulist, 1982.

Krasevac, Edward L. "Revelation and Experience: An Analysis of the Theology of George Tyrell, Karl Rahner, Edward Schillebeeckx, and Thomas Aquinas." Ph.D. diss., Graduate Theological Union, 1986.

Küng, Hans. *Infallible? An Inquiry.* Translated by Edward Quinn. Garden City, N.Y.: Doubleday, 1971.

Laishley, F. J. "Unfinished Business: Ecclesial and Theological Pluralism." In *Modern Catholicism: Vatican II and After,* ed. Adrian Hastings, 221–25. London: SPCK; New York: Oxford University Press, 1991.

Lefébure, Marcus. "Schillebeeckx's Anatomy of Experience." *New Blackfriars* 64 (1983): 270–86.

Lernoux, Penny. *People of God: The Struggle for World Catholicism.* New York: Viking, 1989; reprint, New York: Penguin, 1990.

Lubac, Henri de. *Catholicism: A Study of Dogma in Relation to the Corporate Destiny of Mankind.* Translated by Lancelot C. Sheppard. New York: Sheed and Ward, 1958.

McBrien, Richard P., ed. *Encyclopedia of Catholicism.* San Francisco: HarperSanFrancisco, 1995. S.v. "Chenu, M.-D.," by Walter Principe.

McCool, Gerald A. *Catholic Theology in the Nineteenth Century: The Quest for a Unitary Method.* New York: Seabury/Crossroad, 1977.

McDade, John. "Catholic Theology in the Post-Conciliar Period." In *Modern Catholicism: Vatican II and After,* ed. Adrian Hastings, 422–33. London: SPCK; New York: Oxford University Press, 1991.

McGinn, Bernard J. "Critical History and Contemporary Catholic Theology." *Criterion* 20 (Winter 1981): 18–25.

Merleau-Ponty, Maurice. *Phenomenology of Perception.* Translated by Colin Smith. London: Routledge & Paul; New York: Humanities, 1962.

———. *Sense and Non-sense.* Translated with a preface by Hubert L. Dreyfus and Patricia Allen Dreyfus. Evanston, Ill.: Northwestern University Press, 1964.

Metz, Johann Baptist. *Faith in History and Society: Toward a Practical Fundamental Theology.* New York: Crossroad, 1980.

Mueller-Vollmer, Kurt, ed. *The Hermeneutics Reader: Texts of the German Tradition from the Enlightenment to the Present.* New York: Continuum, 1992.

National Conference of Catholic Bishops. "Norms of Licit Theological Dissent." In *Dissent in the Church,* ed. Charles E. Curran and Richard A. McCormick, 127–28. Readings in Moral Theology, 6. New York: Paulist, 1988.

O'Donnell, Christopher. *Ecclesia: A Theological Encyclopedia of the Church.* Collegeville, Minn.: Liturgical Press, 1996. S.v. "Dissent," "Ecclesiology," "Reception," "Theologians," "Theological Notes."

O'Donovan, Leo. "Salvation as the Center of Theology," review of *Christ: The Experience of Jesus as Lord,* by Edward Schillebeeckx. In *Interpretation: A Journal of Bible and Theology* 36, 2 (April 1982): 192–96.

Oudenrijn, Frans van den, and Marcel Xhaufflaire, eds. "Théologie de la christianisation du monde: théologie du sécularisation du monde." In *Les deux visages de la théologie de la sécularisation: analyse critique de la théologie de la sécularisation,* 11–83. Paris: Casterman, 1970.

Palmer, Richard E. *Hermeneutics: Interpretation Theory in Schleiermacher, Dilthey, Heidegger and Gadamer.* Evanston, Ill.: Northwestern University Press, 1969.

Pius IX. *Ineffabilis Deus* (December 8, 1854). In *Acta Pii IX,* vol. 1, sec. 1.

Plas, Michel van der. "Vatican II and the Dutch Catholics." In *Those Dutch Catholics,* ed. Michel van der Plas and Henk Suér, 45–62. London: Geoffrey Chapman, 1967.

Plas, Michel van der, and Henk Suér, eds. *Those Dutch Catholics.* London: Geoffrey Chapman, 1967.

Portier, William. "Edward Schillebeeckx as Critical Theorist: The Impact of Neo-Marxist Social Thought on His Recent Theology." *Thomist* 48 (1984): 341–67.

———. "Ministry from Above, Ministry from Below: An Examination of the Ecclesial Basis of Ministry According to Edward Schillebeeckx." *Communio (US)* 12 (Summer 1985): 173–91.

———. "Schillebeeckx's Dialogue with Critical Theory." *Ecumenist* 21 (1983): 20–27.

Pottmeyer, Hermann Josef. "Refining the Question About Women's Ordination." *America* 175, 12 (October 26, 1996): 16–18.

Ricoeur, Paul. "Tâches de l'éducateur politique." *Esprit* 33 (July–August 1965): 78–93.

Rikhof, Herwi. "Of Shadows and Substances: Analysis and Evaluation of the Documents in the Schillebeeckx Case." *Journal of Ecumenical Studies* 19 (Spring 1982): 244–67. Previously published in *Tijdschrift voor Theologie* 22, 4 (1982): 376–409.

Romero, C. Gilbert. *Hispanic Devotional Piety: Tracing the Biblical Roots.* Maryknoll, N.Y.: Orbis, 1991.

Ruether, Rosemary Radford. *Women-Church: Theology and Practice of Feminist Liturgical Communities.* San Francisco: Harper & Row, 1988.

Sanchez Chamoso, Roman. *La teoria hermeneutica di E. Schillebeeckx: Principios y criterios para la actualización de la tradición cristiana.* Ph.D. diss., Universidad Pontificia de Salamanca, 1977. Salamanca, 1982.

Schoof, Ted M. "E. Schillebeeckx: 25 years at Nijmegen." *Theology Digest* 37 (1990): 313–32; 38 (1991): 31–44.

———. "Masters in Israel: VIII. The Later Theology of Edward Schillebeeckx." *Clergy Review* 55, 12 (1970): 943–60.

———. *A Survey of Catholic Theology 1800–1970.* Translated by N. D. Smith. Glen Rock, N.J.: Paulist Newman, 1970.

Schoof, Ted M., ed. *The Schillebeeckx Case: Official Exchange of Letters and Documents in the Investigation of Fr. Edward Schillebeeckx by the Sacred Congregation for the Doctrine of the Faith, 1976–1980.* Translated by Matthew J. O'Connell. New York/Ramsey: Paulist, 1980.

Schreiter, Robert J. "Edward Schillebeeckx: An Orientation to His Thought." In *The Schillebeeckx Reader,* ed. Robert Schreiter, 1–24. New York: Crossroad, 1987.

Schreiter, Robert J., and Mary Catherine Hilkert, eds. *The Praxis of Christian Experience: An Introduction to the Theology of Edward Schillebeeckx.* San Francisco: Harper & Row, 1989.

"Sri Lankan Priest Expelled." *Christian Century* 114 (January 29, 1997): 92–93.

Struyker Boudier, C. E. M. *Wijsgerig leven in Nederland en België, 1880–1980, Deel II: De Dominicanen.* Nijmegen: Katholiek Studiecentrum; Baarn: Ambo, 1986.

Suér, Henk. "The Dutch Pastoral Council." In *Those Dutch Catholics,* ed. Michel van der Plas and Henk Suér, 127–42. London: Geoffrey Chapman, 1967.

Swidler, Leonard. *Toward a Catholic Constitution.* New York: Crossroad, 1996.

Swidler, Leonard, and Piet Fransen, eds. *Authority in the Church and the Schillebeeckx Case.* New York: Crossroad, 1982.

Tanner, Norman P., ed. *Decrees of the Ecumenical Councils.* Vol. 1, *Nicaea I to Lateran V.* Washington, D.C.: Sheed & Ward and Georgetown University Press, 1990.

———. *Decrees of the Ecumenical Councils.* Vol. 2, *Trent to Vatican II.* Washington, D.C.: Sheed & Ward and Georgetown University Press, 1990.

Thomas Aquinas. *An Aquinas Reader: Selections from the Writings of Thomas Aquinas.* Edited, with an introduction by Mary T. Clark. Garden City, N.Y.: Image Books, 1972.

———. *Summa Theologica.* 5 vols. Translated by Fathers of the English Dominican Province. Westminster, Md.: Christian Classics, 1981.

Tillich, Paul. *Systematic Theology,* vol. 1. Chicago: University of Chicago, 1986.

Tracy, David. *The Analogical Imagination: Christian Theology and the Culture of Pluralism.* New York: Crossroad, 1989.

———. *Blessed Rage for Order: The New Pluralism in Theology.* Minneapolis: Winston/Seabury, 1975.

Van Hees, Nico. "Everyone's Bishop." In *Those Dutch Catholics*, ed. Plas and Suér, 63–86. London: Geoffrey Chapman, 1967.

West German Bishops. "The Document of the German Bishops Addressed to All Members of the Church Who Are Commissioned to Preach the Faith." In *Dissent in the Church*, ed., Charles E. Curran and Richard A. McCormick, 129–32. Readings in Moral Theology, 6. New York: Paulist, 1988.

Wiseman, James A. "Schillebeeckx and the Ecclesial Function of Critical Negativity." *Thomist* 35 (1971): 207–46.

Xhaufflaire, Marcel. "La théologie après la théologie de la sécularisation." In *Les deux visages de la théologie: analyse critique de la théologie de la sécularisation*, ed. Frans van den Oudenrijn and Marcel Xhaufflaire, 87–105. Paris: Casterman, 1970.

Index

DANIEL SPEED THOMPSON
is assistant professor of theology and associate department chair at
Fordham University's Lincoln Center campus.